Managing Death

Managing Death

James M. Hoefler

WestviewPress

A Division of HarperCollins*Publishers*

Copyright © 1997 by Westview Press, A Division of HarperCollins Publishers, Inc.

Published in 1997 in the United States of America by Westview Press, 5500 Central Avenue, Boulder, Colorado 80301-2877, and in the United Kingdom by Westview Press, 12 Hid's Copse Road, Cumnor Hill, Oxford OX2 9JJ

Library of Congress Cataloging-in-Publication Data
Hoefler, James M.
  Managing death / James M. Hoefler.
    p. cm.
  Includes bibliographical references and index.
  ISBN 0-8133-2816-0 (hc)
  1. Right to die. 2. Terminal care—Moral and ethical aspects.
I. Title.
R726.H564 1997
179.7—dc21   97-2593
                                                                CIP

10   9   8   7   6   5   4   3   2   1

For Gram

Contents

List of Tables, Figures, and Boxes ix

Preface xi

Acknowledgments xiii

Introduction 1

1 The Case of Joey Fiori 7

Judge Sokolove Finds the Balance of Interests Tipping in
Sherman's Favor, 13
Sherman's Attorneys Plead Their Case Before the
Superior Court, 14
Judge Beck Puts the Ball Back in Sherman's Court, 15
Judge Wieand Emphasizes the "Best Interests" of the Patient, 16
Judge Popovich Emphasizes the Importance of the
Court's Role as Parens Patriae, 17
The Pennsylvania Attorney General's Prolife Approach, 18
The Prolife Argument of the Pennsylvania Catholic
Conference, 21
The Pennsylvania Medical Society Argues in Favor of
Allowing the Withdrawal of Treatment, 22
"Choice in Dying" Cites Trends in the States Favoring
the Right to Choose, 24
University Hospitals Cite Clinical Realities in Support of
the Right to Choose, 25
The Pennsylvania Supreme Court Leaves No Doubt:
"Sherman Was Right," 29
Summary, 30

2 The Emergence of Consensus 33

Building Blocks of Consensus, 39
Decision Making, 40
Forgoing Treatment Versus Suicide, 46
Withholding Versus Withdrawing Treatment, 50
Terminal Illness, 52

ANH and the Ordinary-Extraordinary Distinction, 55
Summary, 60

3   **A Broader Consensus**   62

Religion, 62
Catholic Teachings, 63
Other Religious Positions, 66
Public Opinion, 70
Physicians, 76
Cracks in the Consensus, 80
Summary, 88

4   **Beyond the PVS: Severe Dementia**   89

Pathogenesis of Severe Dementia, 90
Similarities Between PVS and Severe Dementia, 93
Differences Between PVS and Severe Dementia, 95
Resources, 100
State Court Cases Involving Severe Dementia and
   the Right to Die, 105
Summary, 110

5   **Artificial Nutrition and Hydration**   112

Methods of ANH, 113
The Dehydration Alternative, 117
Why Is Tube Feeding So Common? 123
Antibiotics: Another End-of-Life Dilemma, 128
Summary, 131

6   **Conclusion and Recommendations**   135

Standards of Care, 136
The Hospice Alternative, 140
Medical Futility, 143
Education, 149
The Slippery Slope, 154
Advance Directives, 160
Summary, 161

Notes   165
References   183
About the Book and Author   199
Index   201

Tables, Figures, and Boxes

Tables

1.1	PVS and Syndromes Often Confused with PVS	9
2.1	Medical Consensus Groups	35
2.2	Legal Consensus Groups	36
2.3	Ethics Consensus Groups	38
2.4	The "New Consensus"	60
3.1	Preferences for Withholding Treatment, by Demographic Group	71
3.2	Attitudes About Refusing Life-Sustaining Treatment for Oneself	72
3.3	Choices Regarding the Use of Life-Sustaining Treatments, If in a PVS	73
3.4	Attitudes About the Rights of Others to Refuse Life-Sustaining Treatment	74
3.5	Attitudes About Who Should Be Permitted to Make End-of-Life Decisions	75
3.6	Attitude Versus Behavior Regarding Advance Directives	83
3.7	Institutional Objections to Withholding or Withdrawing Treatment: Hospitals	86
3.8	Institutional Objections to Withholding or Withdrawing Treatment: Nursing Homes	87
4.1	Actual and Projected Growth of the Elderly and Demented Populations in the United States	92
4.2	Similarities Between PVS and Severe Dementia	94
4.3	Differences Between PVS and Severe Dementia	96
4.4	Choices Regarding the Use of Life-Sustaining Treatments	99
5.1	The Hydration of Political Hunger Strikers	119
6.1	Proposed "Standards of Care" Grid	137
6.2	Replacing the "Slippery Slope"	158

Figures

4.1   Elderly Support Ratio   103

Boxes

1.1   The Persistent Vegetative State (PVS)   8
1.2   The Plight of Nancy Jobes   31

3.1   The Hippocratic Oath   78

4.1   Saving Money Using Advance Directives   101

5.1   Dehydration and Physician-Assisted Suicide   123

6.1   Forgoing ANH—A Primer   162

Preface

Every year, thousands of caregivers, hundreds of thousands of patients, and millions of family members are forced to deal with questions about what life-sustaining medical procedures should be started, withheld, or withdrawn near the end of life. These decisions tend to be made in haste and late in the dying process, without the benefit of having full information on choices and alternatives. Often, patients suffer a good deal more than necessary at the end of life as a result, and family members are left with a haunting sense of guilt about the decisions they finally made: Did we stop the use of technology too soon? Or did we let things drag on too long?

Patients, those who care for them, and members of the medical care team should and frequently do collaborate on end-of-life treatment decisions. But too often, these decisions are shaped by a flawed understanding of what is appropriate in such circumstances. As a result, doing everything possible until the very end becomes the default rule—a rule that, when challenged, sometimes turns bedside discussions into courtroom deliberations.

There is widespread agreement among bioethicists, medical clinicians, legal experts, and religious leaders about what decision-making principles should apply as death approaches. This consensus holds that:

1. Patients should be able to make any decisions they choose about what medical technology they will accept or refuse (whether they are terminally ill or not);
2. If the patient is unable to make decisions for him- or herself, surrogates—family members or close friends—should be fully empowered to step in and make decisions based on what they think the patient would want or what they believe would be in the patient's best interests;
3. There should be no distinction between withholding and withdrawing treatment; it should be just as acceptable to stop treatment once started as it is not to start treatment in the first place;
4. Artificially provided nutrition and hydration—tube feeding—should be thought of as a medical procedure that patients or their surrogates can decide to accept or forgo like any other medical treatment.

More often than not, frontline clinicians and members of the lay public are utterly unaware of these consensus principles; consequently, they act the way they think they are supposed to act—but fighting death at every turn, until the bitter, inevitable end.

In this book, I attempt to shed new light on the issues surrounding the difficult decisions that must be made as death draws near. By presenting and clarifying the essential elements of the "consensus position," this volume will, I hope, help those confronting such decisions make truly informed choices—choices that take into account a broader range of options and reflect more humanity than is evident in the dying process most Americans suffer through today. The truth is that sometimes, perhaps often, the process of dying can be eased and even enhanced by a decision to shift from the medical technology of curing to the hands-on approach of caring. However, this truth cannot have much impact if the decisionmakers are unaware of it. Americans need to become empowered about death; we must know more about death if we are to make good decisions in the twilight of life. Most of us would prefer to die well, and it is hoped that *Managing Death* will help make that desire a reality.

James M. Hoefler

Acknowledgments

I am indebted to a number of people for their time, expertise, and encouragement as this book took shape. Let me begin by thanking Rosemarie Sherman, who was so kind and thoughtful in agreeing to share her story with me at a time in her life when she was still grieving deeply for her son. Thanks also to the many caregivers, administrators, judges, and lawyers who spoke with me about the subject of this book—those directly involved in Joey Fiori's case and others. All of you are busy people who took the time to share your thoughts and insights with me openly, and for that I am grateful. I promised you all that our talks would be confidential, so a heartfelt but generic "thank you" will have to suffice.

Special thanks are due to Dr. Greg Lewis and Professor Norman Cantor, both of whom provided me with thoughtful comments and guidance at important junctures along the way. Feedback from Alan Meisel and encouragement from Sherwin Nuland were also very much appreciated. Of course, I alone remain responsible for any errors in fact or judgment that remain in the final copy.

Special thanks are also due to Joan Sherman, who, for the second time, has worked her magic with one of my sometimes plodding and circuitous manuscripts. It is hard to imagine what my work might look like if Joan did not help shape the final product in a very thoughtful and often substantive way. As always, other members of the Westview Press team were most supportive as well, especially Jennifer Knerr and Leo Wiegman.

Back on the home front, Judy Welch is deserving of mention; her cheerful assistance in gathering research materials was most appreciated. Thanks, as always, are due Vickie Kuhn for providing staunch support and an expert eye in all the various facets of the book-writing process. I am also indebted to the rest of my Dickinson College colleagues who together make this school such a stimulating and supportive place to work and teach.

Finally, thanks to my girls—Susan, Jill, and Jenny—for all the love and support they shower me with daily. It is a love that, as much as anything I can think of, gives purpose and meaning to this earthly life.

J.M.H.

Introduction

The vast majority of Americans will die in hospitals or nursing homes, and most will pass through a state of incompetence before they die—a condition that will render them unable to make decisions about life-sustaining medical treatment. Some will be incompetent for only a few hours or days; others will spend their last months or years in a state ranging from profound confusion to complete unconsciousness. Inevitably, other individuals will be called on to make difficult decisions about prolonging the dying process and about the medical technology that will be used.

Making end-of-life decisions is a relatively recent phenomenon. In earlier times, life-sustaining treatment decisions never had to be made because medical treatment, such as it was, could do very little to prolong life when illness struck. Indeed, before the twentieth century, hospitals and doctors were just as likely to be responsible for precipitating one's demise as they were for prolonging one's life. In those days, infection was the primary cause of death, and pneumonia, influenza, and related disorders normally took their toll with some dispatch.

Today, instead of dying days or weeks after infection sets in, Americans typically die months or years after a chronic, degenerative illness is diagnosed. Thanks to modern medical technology, victims of some of the leading killers in the United States (e.g., heart disease, cancer, and stroke) may enjoy an extended period of time after illness is diagnosed, with symptoms managed so that a reasonable quality of life is maintained. Often, medical technology can stall or even reverse the disease process so that health is completely restored in a patient who would surely have died just a few decades ago.

As Mark Twain reminds us, however, there is nothing quite so sure in life as death and taxes. Though death can be forestalled, it always wins in the end, and therein lies the problem. Although medical technology often can provide patients with a good quality of life as they begin to die, it can also extend biological life even at the edge of death, when the quality of conscious life is quite low. The fact is that an aggressive use of antibiotics, tube

1

feeding, artificial respiration, and cardiopulmonary resuscitation can extend life long after the patient's conscious appreciation of it has ebbed. The situation can be summed up in a single question, one that never had to be asked in the past: At what point do we say enough is enough and allow the patient to slip from this world into the next?

The American Hospital Association estimates that as many as three out of four hospital deaths occur after decisions are made to forgo life-sustaining medical treatments that have the potential, by definition, to prolong the patients' lives. But though these decisions are made thousands of times each day across the nation, the individuals who are called on to make the decisions often find themselves facing life-and-death choices for the very first time. Physicians have more experience in these matters than members of the lay public, but they, too, often find themselves responding without a full understanding of all the considerations and options involved. As likely as not, the physicians who counsel the patient and family have received little if any training in such matters during a medical education that focused on sustaining life rather than managing death. Most professional associations—the American Medical Association, the American College of Physicians, and the American Nurses Association, for example—have issued statements of guiding principles that address end-of-life decision making. But for any number of reasons, knowledge of these guiding principles often does not reach the hospitals and nursing homes where rank-and-file caregivers practice.

Even if these guidelines were communicated more systematically, caregivers might continue to harbor concerns about legal liability, moral culpability, and ethical responsibility. Personal, ideological belief systems that contradict the positions of professional associations also may make it difficult for some caregivers to act according to standards and guidelines promulgated by others.

This book is written with both groups—family members and caregivers—in mind. Its purpose is to clarify the medical, legal, ethical, and clinical issues associated with end-of-life decision making on behalf of those who have become irreversibly incompetent before an inevitable (if not imminent) death.

The book opens with a discussion of the legal travails of Rosemarie Sherman, the mother of a man who had been persistently vegetative for nearly two decades. Throughout those years, Sherman had cared for her son, Joey Fiori, both at home and later in a nursing home, and she had long held out hope that Joey would regain consciousness. After seventeen years, however, she began to believe the doctors, all of whom agreed that her son's condition would never improve. Ultimately, Mrs. Sherman decided, as thousands of others do every day, that the family member she was responsible for would not want to continue existing in biological limbo, so she asked that life-sustaining medical procedures be withdrawn from her son.

But unlike thousands of other family members who are allowed to make such decisions quietly and privately at the patient's bedside, Sherman was forced to go to court for permission to withdraw treatment. Once there, she was opposed by the attorney general of Pennsylvania, whose legal team argued that she had no right to, as they put it, "starve" her son to death.

The case of Joey Fiori is not typical in a strict sense because it was heard before a state supreme court and because Fiori survived in a persistent vegetative state (PVS) for a much longer period of time than most severely demented patients. Fiori's case *is* typical, however, in the sense that there are approximately 25,000 PVS patients and hundreds of thousands of severely demented patients in the United States today whose conditions approach the "vegetative" category. Arguments made on both sides in the Fiori case are also entirely typical of arguments made regarding end-of-life decision making in cases that fit this general class of patients.

Chapter 2 covers the key points of consensus on end-of-life decision making, a consensus that has been evolving in the medical, legal, and ethics communities since the mid-1980s. Chapter 3 broadens the consensus debate to include the positions of mainstream religious groups in the United States, the opinions of the general public, and the role that clinical practitioners play regarding the provision of life-sustaining medical treatment for hopelessly ill patients. This consensus supports the right of a patient's surrogate to withhold or withdraw *any* life-sustaining medical treatment, including tube feeding, when the patient has irreversibly lost the capacity to understand or interact with his or her environment. Chapter 3 closes with a review of some of the sticking points of the consensus position, discussing various reasons why the position does not always inform the decision-making process that actually takes place at the bedside.

Chapter 4 broadens the discussion to address the plight of individuals who are severely demented. There are approximately 25,000 patients who would qualify as persistently vegetative in the United States today, but there are nearly 2 million patients who are severely demented. These individuals, typically victims of strokes or patients in the end stages of Alzheimer's, Pick's, or Parkinson's disease, are sustained at the end of life for weeks, months, or perhaps even years through the use of artificial nutrition and hydration (ANH) and the aggressive use of antibiotic therapy. Do the arguments regarding end-of-life decision making for persistently vegetative patients apply equally well to the millions who are suffering from advanced dementia? Chapter 4 attempts to answer this question.

This leads to a detailed discussion of artificial nutrition and hydration in Chapter 5. Advances in tube-feeding techniques, equipment, and solutions since the 1970s have made ANH one of the most common medical procedures employed today. Because the ability to swallow is either lost or seriously compromised in all persistently vegetative patients and most severely demented patients, the provision of ANH is often a requirement for sustaining life. Is artificial feeding a medical treatment like any other, or is feeding, even through tubes, a basic requirement of life that must always be provided? When ANH is withheld or withdrawn, is much suffering involved, and do patients really "starve" to death as a result?

These kinds of unanswered questions lead family members to worry that deciding to forgo food and fluids for another may cause pain or at least discomfort (even though it would not). They also worry that a decision to forgo food and fluids would fly in the face of standard medical practices and accepted ethical principles (even though it does not). No changes in the American psyche can take place overnight. But perhaps, if armed with knowledge about the reality of dehydration at the end of life as laid out in Chapter 5, Americans could think more clearly about the subject as we proceed toward the cultural change that can and must ultimately take place.

Chapter 6 summarizes some of the key findings of the first five chapters. Recommendations for improving a decision-making policy that has, to this point, lurched forward, sideward, and sometimes even backward are also proposed here. Every day, caregivers and family members find themselves grappling with end-of-life decisions that challenge us to rediscover the meaning of caring and the essence of humanity. It is hoped that Chapter 6 will lead us toward a more enlightened understanding in these areas.

The days of allowing nature to take its course because nothing more could be done for the patient are over. Now, there is almost always something that can be done to sustain—or at least attempt to sustain—life for the hopelessly ill. If the patient is competent, there is very little controversy about his or her options: An adult can accept or reject *any* medical treatment. The only real controversy arises with regard to patients who are not competent to make decisions for themselves. In such cases, the question facing caregivers and family members is: How far should we go to sustain the life of one who is hopelessly ill and irreversibly and severely demented (at best) before we choose to allow nature to take its course?

The question inevitably has a complex answer: It depends. Conclusions about forgoing life-sustaining treatment may depend on how severely demented and how hopelessly ill the patient is. They may depend on what the patient would have wanted, if able to decide. They may depend on the degree of bodily invasion and violation of dignity involved in continued treatment. And they may depend on how burdensome continued treatment would be to the patient, to the family, and to society as a whole.

Although life is indeed a sacred trust that we should not toy with lightly, the sanctity of life does not automatically trump all other interests and considerations when it comes to end-of-life decision making. The simplistic "never give up" answer to the life-sustaining treatment dilemmas may be suitable for some, but there must be room for other answers to the question in a pluralistic society that puts so much emphasis on individual rights and human dignity.

"It depends" is really the only route out of the thicket. But this, of course, only begs another question: "It depends on what?" It is hoped that the text that follows will help decisionmakers (caregivers, family members, and policymakers alike) find answers to this question, a question that promises to come into play when, with the "help" of medical technology, we are caught between two worlds—this one and the next—at the end of conscious life.

Chapter One

The Case of Joey Fiori

By all accounts, Daniel Joseph "Joey" Fiori was an intelligent and vigorous young man with a promising future. He played drums in his high school band in suburban Philadelphia and engaged in a variety of sports, including football at school and surfing at the beach where he spent much time during the summer as a teenager. After graduation, Joey was looking forward to furthering his education by studying nuclear physics, a goal that seemed well within his reach given his IQ of 147.

The Vietnam War intervened, however, and in 1968, rather than be drafted by the army, Joey enlisted in the navy. He served with distinction in Vietnam and was going home on leave in 1971 to marry his childhood sweetheart when tragedy struck. Just ten days before the wedding, Fiori was involved in a motorcycle accident that caused him severe brain damage (Hinds 1994).

Fiori was still severely impaired when he regained consciousness after more than a year in a coma. His vocabulary consisted of only two words—*itch* and *eye*—and his ability to interact with and understand his environment was extremely limited. He was also wheelchair-bound. Rosemarie Sherman, Joey's mother, took her son home and cared for him with the help of home health care aides.

Joey Fiori's medical problems were compounded in 1976 when he fell while attempting to get out of his wheelchair and walk. The fall caused a break in his leg that was serious enough to require a stay at the local veterans' hospital. While he was convalescing there, hospital personnel failed to provide the required antiseizure medication Fiori had taken for years. As a result, he suffered a grand mal seizure that left him in a persistent vegetative state (PVS) (see Box 1.1). Mrs. Sherman brought legal action against the hospital, and the Veterans Administration ultimately agreed to compensate her fully for the cost of her own health care (as the primary caregiver) and her son's health care for the duration of his life.

As with most patients in a PVS, the vegetative functions of Fiori's lower brain—where heartbeat, respiration, and body temperature are regulated—

BOX 1.1   The Persistent Vegetative State (PVS)

The Multi-Society Task Force on PVS was established in 1991 to address definitional and clinical aspects of the persistent vegetative state (PVS). The task force was created by drawing two physicians from each of five medical societies (the Child Neurological Society, the American Academy of Neurology, the American Neurological Association, the American Association of Neurological Surgeons, and the American Academy of Pediatrics). The group's findings were published as a two-part series in the *New England Journal of Medicine* (Multi-Society Task Force on PVS 1994a, 1994b).

According to the task force, the persistent vegetative state is a relatively new phenomenon, which was first identified by medical researchers in 1972 (Multi-Society Task Force on PVS 1994a: 1499). The task force went on to define the syndrome as "a clinical condition of complete unawareness of the self and environment" (Multi-Society Task Force on PVS 1994a: 1499).

Even though PVS patients may exhibit sleep-and-wake cycles, they show no evidence of response to or understanding of environmental stimuli. Patients in a PVS resulting from a loss of oxygen to the brain can reliably be considered permanently vegetative after three months; those in a PVS resulting from a blow to the head can reliably be considered permanently vegetative after one year (Multi-Society Task Force on PVS 1994b: 1575). Recoveries from a PVS after the designated time has elapsed are exceedingly rare, and they are inevitably associated with severe and permanent disability (e.g., blindness and paralysis). The life expectancy for patients in a PVS ranges from two to five years, though occasionally, patients can be sustained a good deal longer (Multi-Society Task Force on PVS 1994b: 1575). On average, the cost of caring for a patient in a PVS exceeds $250,000 the first year and runs approximately $150,000 a year thereafter (Multi-Society Task Force on PVS 1994b: 1576).

---

remained intact. Fiori also exhibited standard sleep-and-wake cycles, another common characteristic of PVS patients. But the thinking part of Fiori's brain—the harbor of memory, emotion, communication, and understanding—was entirely and irreversibly destroyed. His swallowing reflex was compromised as well, so Fiori received nutrition and fluids through a gastrostomy tube that was surgically implanted in his stomach. Fiori also had a tracheostomy tube that was hooked up to an oxygen mist machine several times a day in order to make breathing a bit easier for him (see Box 1.1).

After Fiori's condition stabilized, his mother took him home again, where she tended to him for the next fifteen years. Fiori needed to be rolled periodically (to prevent bedsores), cleaned (he was completely incontinent), and have his limbs stretched (to help forestall the muscle atrophy and limb contracture that result from complete inactivity), so private duty nurses were retained to help with these physically demanding tasks. Despite what the doctors were telling her about the permanence of her son's vegetative condition,

TABLE 1.1   PVS and Syndromes Often Confused with PVS

Persistent vegetative state (PVS)	A clinical condition of complete unawareness of the self and environment. Even though PVS patients may exhibit sleep-and-wake cycles, they show no evidence of response to or understanding of environmental stimuli.
Brain death	Brain death involves the irreversible loss of all brain functions, including vegetative functions. The body can only be maintained for short periods of time (hours or perhaps days) even with aggressive treatment. Brain-dead patients can be pronounced legally dead after two electroencephalograms taken twenty-four hours apart confirm the absence of all brain activity. Typically, vegetative functions are artificially maintained only long enough to harvest organs and tissues for transplantation.
Coma	Comas are unarousable, sleeplike conditions resulting from injury to the brain stem. A coma, the condition Joey Fiori was in immediately following his accident, may last for an extended period of time, but rarely are comas permanent; many comas last only a few hours, days, or weeks. Sometimes, a coma can evolve into the more permanent PVS.
Locked-in state	The locked-in state is sometimes referred to as the state of severe and permanent paralysis. Patients in a locked-in state suffer from a complete and irreversible loss of all motor functions, making it very difficult or impossible for them to acknowledge or communicate with others even though they maintain normal levels of consciousness. The end stage of amyotrophic lateral sclerosis (Lou Gehrig's disease) is a common cause of the locked-in state. Diagnostic tests (e.g., CT scans and MRIs) can reliably distinguish between the locked-in state and the PVS.

SOURCE: Information for this table is drawn primarily from Cranford 1991a: 14–16.

she held out hope that Joey would "snap out" of his vegetative state, just as he had awakened from his yearlong coma in 1972 (see Table 1.1).

In 1990, Sherman's health began to fail, making it impossible for her to continue caring for her son at home. So in 1991, she agreed to have Joey put in a suburban Philadelphia nursing home, where she continued to visit him daily or as often as her health would allow. During this time, Mrs. Sherman also helped do his laundry, coordinated nursing schedules, and held bedside prayer vigils with friends as she continued to hope for a miraculous recovery.

Then, on Valentine's Day 1992, Rosemarie Sherman had a revelation. She had taken a bouquet of flowers and two plastic hearts to her son's bedside, saying, "One heart is yours, Joey, and one heart is mine" (Morris 1994). At that moment, Mrs. Sherman became fully aware, for the first time, of the utter lack of understanding behind her son's blinking eyes. "'He didn't even know I was there. All these years I thought he knew I was there,' she said, her voice cracking. 'He didn't know'" (Morris 1994). It was on that day that Rosemarie Sherman accepted the fact that her son would never recover.

Sherman suffered a heart attack later that year, which increased her ever present concern that Joey would survive her and have no one to provide him with the kind of devoted, hands-on care and advocacy she had given him for over twenty years. Now, with her sharpened appreciation for the hopelessness of her son's predicament, Sherman began to see the futility in the ongoing processes of blood testing, poking, prodding, turning, cleaning, toileting, respirating, and medicating her son. "Is there no end to the insanity?" she remembered wondering (quote is from a personal interview).

The only reasonable course of action, she concluded, was to ask that her son's feeding tube be withdrawn. "My Joey's between two worlds," she explained at the time. "I want my son to die with dignity. . . . If he could speak, there is no way he would want to live this way" (Hinds 1994).

Joey's siblings were reluctant to go along with this decision at first. But in a family meeting, their mother asked each of them in turn, "What would *you* want done if it were *you* in the situation that Joey is in?" (quote is from a personal interview). To a person, they all said that they would want life-sustaining treatment removed. "So that," said Sherman, "is what I will do for Joey." Mrs. Sherman conferred further with several priests and doctors familiar with the case and was reassured that withdrawal of feeding was an appropriate course of action in the situation.

The nursing home disagreed, however, and suggested that Sherman obtain a court order approving the removal of the feeding tube. As one administrator affiliated with the nursing home explained, forgoing feeding would constitute a "hospice response" to Fiori's situation, and that was problematic for two reasons. First, technically speaking, Fiori was not terminally ill (which is a standard prerequisite for receiving hospice care); all his caregivers agreed that he could live, with continued life-sustaining medical treatment and good nursing care, for many more years. Second, even if Fiori were terminally ill, the nursing home did not have a hospice program in place: "Withdrawing feeding . . . that's just not something we do," explained the administrator (quote is from a personal interview). Even if the court approved Mrs. Sherman's request, this same administrator speculated, the institution's directors would likely ask that Fiori be transferred to another facility rather than have the nursing home become involved in the withholding of feeding.[1]

Sherman decided to fight the institution's decision, and the first stop in the legal battle over her son's life and death was the Orphans' Court of Bucks

County (Pennsylvania). A motion was filed in May 1992, and a hearing was held before Judge Leonard B. Sokolove in September of that year. Sherman was opposed in court by the office of the Pennsylvania state attorney general (AG). Two physicians, one of whom was secured by the attorney general's office, provided concurring testimony that although Fiori was in a persistent vegetative state and would not improve, he could survive for ten to twenty more years with good nursing care (Eastburn and Schaeffer 1994: 5). For her part, Mrs. Sherman testified that "I knew my son better than anyone knew him . . . he liked living . . . he would not want to live this way." She closed with the passionate request that her son be afforded the opportunity to "rest in peace and be with God" (Eastburn and Schaeffer 1994: 6).

Although not contesting either the medical diagnosis or the prognosis, the lawyers from the attorney general's office argued that judges are better and more impartially positioned than family members to make end-of-life decisions and that no decisions about terminating life-sustaining medical treatment should be made without clear and convincing evidence that forgoing treatment is what the patient would want. Louis J. Rovelli, the executive deputy attorney general, later opined that "we are talking about starving a person to death, in layman's terms" (Morris 1994). He subsequently argued that there is no reason to treat patients in a persistent vegetative state that way, for they "may be healthy, physically . . . or as healthy as one could be in a coma" and "they are provided for financially and feeling no pain" (Galewitz 1995).

In February 1993, Judge Sokolove granted Sherman's petition, but the attorney general's office filed an appeal with the state's superior court, which shortly thereafter agreed to hear the case. In a 2-to-1 decision issued in November 1993, a panel of three superior court judges reversed Judge Sokolove's trial court ruling and accepted the attorney general's position that clear and convincing evidence of a patient's wishes must be presented before life-sustaining medical treatments are either withheld or withdrawn. Failing the presentation of such evidence (and none existed in Joey Fiori's case), the panel argued that the courts should rule in favor of preserving life.

The majority opinion of the three-judge panel was not well crafted, however. In fact, the decision was so unclear and left so many questions unresolved that both Sherman *and* the attorney general's office filed applications for the case to be reheard en banc (before a panel of nine superior court judges). The superior court voted to accept the case for rehearing, the court's three-judge panel decision was withdrawn, and a panel of nine superior court judges was selected to rehear the case. At about this time, as stories of the decision began to appear in the local papers, right-to-life protagonists began making disturbing calls to Mrs. Sherman. "Is 'Danny' there? Can I speak with him? Is Danny hungry?" the callers asked. Mrs. Sherman was forced to have her telephone number changed. (Obviously, the callers were not familiar enough with the family or the case to know that Daniel Fiori went by the nickname "Joey.")

The dissenting judge in the 2-to-1 panel decision, Phyllis W. Beck, found herself part of a 6-to-3 majority after the nine judges reheard the case. Subsequently, Beck was assigned the task of authoring the superior court's opinion, which affirmed Judge Sokolove's original trial court ruling and was issued in January 1995.

Once again, the attorney general's office appealed the ruling, this time to Pennsylvania's highest court, the state's supreme court. The Pennsylvania Supreme Court agreed to hear the case, but before arguments could be heard, Fiori contracted pneumonia, his ninth episode since 1976. Each time previously, antibiotics were given as a matter of course and the infection was resolved. This time, however, at Rosemarie Sherman's request, antibiotics were not administered. The pneumonia was allowed to take its natural and ultimately fatal course, claiming the life of Daniel Joseph Fiori on February 6, 1995. Fiori was forty-four and had been in a persistent vegetative state for nearly two decades. At the time of his death, his health care bill was approximately $165,000 a year. And since 1976, more than $3 million had been spent caring for this now middle-aged man.

The legal battle did not end there, however, for the attorney general's office argued that a case like this one would probably arise again. Because there was no definitive case law on the books (aside from the January ruling of the superior court), the AG's office pressed the supreme court to continue with the case and issue a ruling, even though that decision would be moot with regard to Joey Fiori. The supreme court agreed and proceeded to schedule hearings.

Meanwhile, with her son dead and with limited resources at her disposal, Rosemarie Sherman agreed to grant the Pennsylvania Medical Society (PMS) the right to continue arguing the case on her behalf. The PMS had already filed an amicus curiae (friend-of-the-court) brief in support of Sherman's position before the superior court, so the group was familiar with the case and its potential implications. As one lawyer close to the case explained, "If you do not get involved in these kinds of landmark cases, you let others make the law for you" (quote is from a personal interview). Seeing that an important question was at stake and appreciating the fact that law was about to be made, the PMS stepped quickly into the breach and took on the role of lead counsel in support of Sherman's petition.

The supreme court heard oral arguments from the PMS (Hoffman 1995) and the attorney general's office (Unger and Knorr 1995) in April 1995. In addition to the oral and written briefs supplied by these organizations, a friend-of-the-court brief in support of the AG's position was provided by the Pennsylvania Catholic Conference (Connell and Quinlan 1995). Two other amicus briefs were supplied in support of the position advanced by Sherman and the PMS: one from a New York–based right-to-die organization called Choice in Dying (CID) (Kavolius and Fade 1995) and a second brief jointly issued by the University of Pittsburgh Center for Medical Ethics and the University of Pennsylvania Medical Center (Meisel and Adler 1995). A review of these five briefs, together with Rosemarie Sherman's brief before the superior court (Eastburn and Schaeffer 1994), the opinions rendered by the trial court judge (Sokolove 1993) and three superior court judges from the en banc decision (Beck 1995; Wieand 1995; Popovich 1995),[2] and the final decision of the Pennsylvania Supreme Court (Cappy 1996), provides an excellent opportunity to assay the arguments on each side of the two important and closely related questions in this case: Who can make end-of-life decisions for another? And on what basis should those decisions be made?

Judge Sokolove Finds the Balance of Interests Tipping in Sherman's Favor

The first ruling in this case was issued on February 3, 1993, by Leonard B. Sokolove, judge of the Orphans' Court Division of the Bucks County Court of Common Pleas, located in Doylestown, Pennsylvania. Sokolove began his analysis by reviewing the state's interest in preserving life, an interest that is traditionally expressed as four separate but related interests: (1) the prevention of suicide, (2) the protection of innocent third parties, (3) the preservation of the integrity of the medical profession, and (4) the preservation of life. Sokolove argued that the first three goals did not apply in Joey Fiori's case.

Sokolove reasoned that because Fiori was unaware of his circumstances, the proposed action—the withdrawal of feeding—could not be considered a suicide. Sokolove also dismissed the second state interest: There were no innocent third parties to be adversely affected because the mother was bringing the action and Fiori had no spouse or children depending on him. With regard to the third interest, Judge Sokolove contended that the medical profession would not be adversely affected since every representative of the profession involved in the case supported the petitioner's request (Sokolove 1993: 4).

Finally, with regard to the sweeping "preservation of life" role the state assumes for itself, Judge Sokolove made three points. First, he cited the only other decision in a case of this type in Pennsylvania—*Ragona*, another trial court case without the force of precedent. In that case, it was argued that "the Commonwealth's interest [in preserving life] weakens and the individual's right grows as the prognosis dims and the intrusiveness of the treatment increases" (cited in Sokolove 1993: 5). Second, Sokolove determined that the plaintiff was acting in good faith in conjunction with sound medical advice. And third, he argued that the rationale for withdrawing life-sustaining medical treatment could be at least partially built on the foundation of public opinion, for "an overwhelming majority of society would, in similar circumstances, exercise such a choice in the same way for themselves or for those closest to them" (Sokolove 1993: 6, citations omitted). Sokolove bolstered this last point by referring to an influential and well-regarded federal report that endorsed the process of determining what decision was in the best interest of the patient via objective, societally shared criteria (see President's Commission 1993: 134–135).

Summing up, Judge Sokolove argued that "the medical evidence is convincing that Daniel Joseph Fiori's life is without content, let alone any quality. . . . The petition of Rosemarie Sherman [is] granted, and the [nursing home is] authorized to discontinue artificial feeding and all other means of life-sustaining procedures" (Sokolove 1993: 8–9).

Sherman's Attorneys Plead Their Case Before the Superior Court

After winning at the trial court level and seeing the original ruling overturned by a 2-to-1 panel decision in the superior court, the attorneys representing Mrs. Sherman—William Eastburn and John Schaeffer—found themselves arguing before an en banc session of the superior court. In their presentation, the attorneys reiterated what they perceived to be the relevant facts of the relationship between Sherman and her son. They pointed out that Sherman had been Fiori's mother for forty-four years and had lived with or cared for him for all but two of those years (the years Fiori spent in the navy). She had cared for her vegetative son in her home for thirteen years and had visited him several times a day (and participated in his care) at the nursing home thereafter. She had made all decisions regarding his welfare for twenty-two years and had been the legally appointed guardian of her son for the last twelve years of his life. "Who, more than Rosemarie Sherman, was better equipped to make medical treatment decisions for Joey Fiori?" they asked (Eastburn and Schaeffer 1994: 22).

To bolster the argument that family members should be allowed to make end-of-life decisions for their loved ones without court involvement, Sherman's attorneys cited the Connecticut Superior Court decision in the case of Sandra Foody. That court ruled that if a patient was permanently and irreversibly incapacitated and if concerned family members were present to act in good faith, those family members could make any treatment decision that the patient could have made for him- or herself, if competent:

> The courts have recognized the rights of a guardian of the person to *vicariously* assert the right of an incompetent or unconscious ward to accept or deny medical care. To deny this exercise because the patient is unconscious or incompetent

would be to deny the right. It is incumbent upon the state to afford an incompetent the same panoply of rights and choices it recognizes in competent persons (Eastburn and Schaeffer 1994: 17–18, emphasis added, citations omitted).

Sherman's attorneys criticized the attorney general's suggestion that clear and convincing evidence should be required before waiving life-sustaining medical treatment. Requiring that standard of proof, they argued, would eliminate any balancing of governmental and individual interests for patients who did not have the forethought to issue explicit instructions about treatment decisions they themselves would make at the end of conscious life. The attorneys contended that such a ruling would allow the government to prevail—despite the family's and the patient's physical and emotional ordeal, despite the hopeless prognosis, and despite the absence of any quality of life or hope of improvement in the patient's condition. "The Commonwealth's proposed standard would, quite simply, abrogate Mr. Fiori's constitutional rights to refuse treatment, a right which should only be abridged upon a showing of compelling state interest. No such interest exists in this case," Sherman's attorneys concluded (Eastburn and Schaeffer 1994: 20–21).

Judge Beck Puts the Ball Back in Sherman's Court

Judge Phyllis Beck delivered the superior court's majority opinion on January 17, 1995. Beck's opinion focused on the key issue of whether and to what degree the right to self-determination can be exercised by surrogates after a principal has become incompetent. In finding in favor of Rosemarie Sherman, Beck noted that courts across the nation had agreed to allow the withdrawal of treatment from incompetent patients in every other case of this type, as long as the patient's desires could be determined. That is, "the right to self-determination has uniformly been held to survive incompetency" (Beck 1995: 12). The only sticking point, Beck noted, was the level of evidence required.

Those few states that require a high degree of certainty regarding the patient's wishes have done so for at least one of two reasons: (1) to prevent a wrong decision from leading to the withdrawal of life-sustaining treatment prematurely (the reality of medical uncertainty always leaves some sliver of hope for recovery), or (2) to prevent decisionmakers from acting in bad faith. Beck found both rationales wanting. First, she pointed out that public opinion research indicated most people would want life-sustaining treatments withdrawn if they were in a permanently vegetative state. Consequently, she said, the number of wrongful continuances of treatment that would occur if courts made presumptions in favor of life would far exceed the number of wrongful deaths that would occur if the courts allowed the discontinuance of such treatments.

Second, Beck pointed out that there was no evidence to suggest that surrogates act in bad faith or on the basis of conflicts of interest. The state's attorneys had earlier argued that the potential for abuse in decision making was a sound reason to apply the "clear and convincing evidence" test. But Judge Beck found that no such evidence could be sustained in this specific case or more generally.

Third, Judge Beck found fault with the entire concept of judicial involvement in cases like the one at hand. "The time of the decision to withdraw life sustaining treatment is one fraught with pain and anxiety for those who love the patient," she wrote. "To compound the suffering with a court proceeding is insensitive and unnecessary . . . overly intrusive, and violative of the individual's right to privacy" (Beck 1995: 14–15).

Beck went on:

> The patient's rights are adequately represented by the surrogate, in this case, the mother. She is clearly qualified to exercise substituted judgment and can express what Mr. Fiori would want. His mother, who has given her son devoted care for almost two decades, who has taken all those years to consider what should be done, who has consulted her religious advisors and her own heart, is here to tell us that at this point in time, "enough is enough" (Beck 1995: 15).

Judge Beck elaborated on the role of the family in such cases, leaving no question as to her general conclusions:

> Almost invariably the patient's family has an intimate understanding of the patient's medical attitudes and general world view and therefore is in the best position to know the motives and the considerations that would control the patient's medical decisions . . . because of their special bonds with him or her. . . . These decisions have been made by families, in consultation with doctors and other advisors, in privacy and without governmental interference. . . . The majority . . . believes the law should cherish and safeguard family integrity. The wisdom and decency of a family faced with life and death decisions do not need to be tested in court (Beck 1995: 17–18).[3]

Judge Wieand Emphasizes the "Best Interests" of the Patient

In a concurring opinion, Judge Donald Wieand agreed with Judge Beck that families should be deferred to without courts necessarily being involved. At the same time, he was concerned about cases that ended up in court because the patient's family disagreed with the physician, because family members disagreed among themselves, or because no family or close friends were available to help with decision making. These cases should be brought before the court, Wieand argued, and the court should be prepared to act in accordance with its *parens patriae* role.[4]

He explicitly rejected, however, the attorney general's contention that continued life should be the default rule for any situation in which the desire to be allowed to die had not been explicitly expressed. Rather, he argued, the parens patriae responsibility should be viewed as the responsibility to see that an incompetent individual's *interests* were advanced (Wieand 1995: 7–8). This approach would require the decisionmaker (in this case, the court) to carefully weigh such factors as the relief of suffering, the preservation or restoration of functioning, and the quality as well as the extent of life sustained in an effort to determine whether treatment should be continued or withdrawn.

What result would this approach have yielded if applied in the Fiori case? Wieand left little doubt about his opinion on this score: "To require someone to remain in [a persistent vegetative state] for perhaps decades cannot be in the best interest of that individual. Indeed it can be argued that to keep an individual in that condition, with no hope of recovery, is not only against the best interests, but inhumane" (Wieand 1995: 9–10, citation omitted).

Judge Popovich Emphasizes the Importance of the Court's Role as Parens Patriae

In his dissenting opinion, Judge Zoran Popovich appeared to be much more concerned than the judges in the majority about the ability of modern American families to act in good faith when it comes to end-of-life decision making. Popovich opined that "the deterioration of the family unit has contributed to the creation of a patchwork of single-parent homes, second and third marriages, establishing a step-parent environment and a straining of family bonding among non-blood relatives brought together by remarriage and alienated by divorce." Popovich argued that all this made the appointment of a surrogate difficult. Further, he questioned the degree to which a surrogate would act in good faith (Popovich 1995: 40).

Popovich was much more sanguine about the court's ability to play a useful role in end-of-life treatment decisions than were the judges in the majority. For example, he advanced the argument that "the state, as the *parens patriae* of its citizenry, is not to be dismissed as an intrusive, uninvited participant when the life of one of its own is at risk. In just such instances, the courts (as an extension of state government) have been a reservoir of wisdom and sound reflection when a life hangs in the balance" (Popovich 1995: 1).

For those concerned about the delay and publicity associated with court proceedings, Popovich asserted that expedited hearings could be arranged for court-supervised decision making concerning the sanctity of human life; furthermore, he said, those hearings would not be an invasion of anyone's privacy. "Rather," he suggested, "such a process would assure that all parties are truly acting with the best interests of the patient in mind and not motivated by any ulterior motive hidden from the light of scrutiny by veiled concerns for the patient's well-being" (Popovich 1995: 2).

Finally and perhaps most revealingly, Popovich confessed that "first and foremost, my actions are motivated by the desire to preserve life" (Popovich 1995: 37). As such, he advised that the court should "proceed slowly, on a case-by-case basis, while awaiting action by the state legislature" (Popovich 1995: 20). In the meantime, he advised employing procedural and substantive safeguards.

Procedurally, he recommended the court appointment of an impartial guardian to represent the patient's interests, an individual without potential conflicts of interest. Substantively, Popovich recommended that the decision to withhold or withdraw life-sustaining treatment should require clear and convincing evidence of the patient's wishes "and not merely the guesses of third parties about what he would have wanted or what was in his best interests."[5] He argued that such safeguards were in place when issues of less importance hung in the balance (e.g., the placement of an incompetent person's estate or the sterilization of an incompetent patient), so they should not be considered overly burdensome in circumstances where life itself was at stake (Popovich 1995: 15–16).

The Pennsylvania Attorney General's
Prolife Approach

The procedural and substantive themes touched on by Popovich in his superior court dissent were initially advanced by the state's lawyers in Judge Sokolove's courtroom in 1992. Those themes resurfaced in the attorney general's arguments before the three-judge and nine-judge panels of superior court justices, and they formed the foundation of the AG's argument before the Supreme Court of Pennsylvania in a brief filed on January 25, 1995. In all four venues, the attorney general's lawyers advanced the conservative, prolife approach articulated by Judge Popovich.

Ideologically, the Pennsylvania attorney general, Ernest D. "Ernie" Preate, was a staunch prolife advocate who had previously gained attention in the state and nationally for his role in defending Pennsylvania's relatively restrictive Abortion Control Act before the U.S. Supreme Court in 1992. This prolife leaning only partially explains why the AG's office plied such a conservative, prolife course on end-of-life decision making in the Fiori case, however. As one state official explained, although the attorney general himself was ideologically disposed to the conservative position, the stance his office adopted also flowed from an interest in facilitating the orderly development of case law.

The development of case law was important in this matter because the Fiori case had arisen in something of a legal vacuum. Pennsylvania had a living will law on the books that created an instrument to allow individuals to designate surrogates for purposes of making end-of-life decisions. But the statutory law was silent on the question of surrogate decision making when no living will existed and no surrogates had been identified. And no appellate-level decisions had been rendered in the state.

By adopting an adversarial stance vis-à-vis Rosemarie Sherman, members of the AG's team saw the opportunity to force policymakers—judges, in this case—to chart a legal course for others to follow, secure in the knowledge that the full range of issues and positions associated with such cases would be considered.[6] Just as it was the job of Sherman's lawyers to vigorously advocate her position in court, regardless of their personal views on the issues at hand, the AG's team of lawyers advocated the exact opposite position, hoping that the weight of arguments on either side would lead judges to decide fairly and appropriately which course to take—a course that would have the force of law in later cases.[7]

In building a foundation for rejecting the notion of substituted judgment, state attorneys Sue Ann Unger and John Knorr focused on the "liberty interest" a patient enjoys under the Fourteenth Amendment to the U.S. Constitution. The liberty interest is understood to go hand in hand with the requirement that each citizen be accorded due process. The brief authored by Unger and Knorr contended that failing to bring cases involving end-of-life treatment decisions to the courts would violate the patients' liberty interest in prolonged life without the benefit of due process.

For example, Unger and Knorr pointed out that the superior court's en banc decision left it to physicians "to decide, not just the medical facts about the patient's condition and prognosis, but whether there are 'extraordinary circumstances'—such as the bad faith of the relative seeking to terminate treatment—which require court involvement. This imposes upon physicians a responsibility which they are ill equipped to discharge, and abdicates to them a responsibility that is inherently judicial" (Unger and Knorr 1995: 13–14).

Relying on physicians to make determinations about the good faith of family members hardly constituted due process, they continued. Doctors were qualified to pass judgment on a patient's medical condition and prognosis. They were also qualified to suggest whether forgoing treatment made sense from a medical standpoint or whether it could reasonably be considered medically futile. But in the view of the AG's lawyers, physicians would *not* have the time, information, resources, skills, or predisposition needed to make judgments about the degree to which surrogates were acting in good faith. Rather, they argued, there was no reason

> to suppose that physicians have any special ability to "perceive" the many fac-
> tors—conflicts of interest, lack of good faith, disagreements among family
> members, and failure to abide by the patient's wishes—that might counsel hes-
> itation in rubber-stamping a self-elected surrogate's decision to withhold treat-
> ment. Such things are the proper responsibilities of *guardians ad litem* and
> courts, not physicians. . . . By excluding the court from its proper role, the Su-
> perior Court has compromised the integrity of the medical profession (Unger
> and Knorr 1995: 33, 34).[8]

The AG's lawyers used the details of the Fiori case to illustrate just how conflicts of interest could be overlooked. In 1981, Rosemarie Sherman became Fiori's legal guardian for purposes of prosecuting her malpractice action against the federal government after her son had suffered the seizure that put him in a PVS in 1976. The resulting settlement led to the establishment of a trust fund for Fiori's care and provided for an annuity to be paid to Mrs. Sherman should she survive her son. Although the AG's lawyers claimed they were not directly impugning Mrs. Sherman's integrity or motives, they argued that the conflict of interest (and potential for abuse) was clearly manifested in this case and that this should disqualify Sherman as a guardian of her son's interests.[9]

The AG's lawyers then moved on from Judge Beck's notion of "substituted judgment" (allowing a close family member to substitute his or her judgment for the decision of the principal, without court involvement) to critique Judge Wieand's "best interests" proposal, which was to take effect when substituted judgment could not be rendered. According to Unger and Knorr (1995: 30), not only did Mrs. Sherman fail to provide sufficient evidence that her son would wish to forgo continued life-sustaining treatments (in accordance with the substituted judgment approach), she also failed to present sufficient evidence that the forgoing of such treatments were in her *son's* best interest (as opposed to her own best interest or the interest of society). "Mr. Fiori was incapable of suffering pain or humiliation and unaware of his family," they argued, "[and] after well over a decade in a persistent vegetative state, Mr. Fiori's life could present no increased loss of dignity or intrusion on privacy." They went on to suggest that "under circumstances of no physical, psychological, or economic burden for his continued existence, immediate death could not be in the best interest of a patient such as Fiori" (Unger and Knorr 1995: 31).

More generally, the AG's lawyers argued that no one could accurately determine the value framework of an individual who had left no clear and convincing evidence of his or her wishes, making the entire notion of the patient's best interests suspect. Consequently, they said, "continued life" had to be the default decision rule when no clear and convincing evidence to the contrary was presented. In short, the state was bound to protect the life of one of its citizens when due process had not yielded clear evidence to suggest that the patient would prefer to die in a given set of circumstances.

The Prolife Argument of
the Pennsylvania Catholic Conference

Richard Connell and Maura Quinlan, representing the Pennsylvania Catholic Conference of Bishops, filed an amicus brief criticizing the superior court's decision on two seemingly contradictory grounds. First, Connell and Quinlan cited the 1990 case of Ruth Ragona, the only other case heard in the state of Pennsylvania to raise the same issues as raised by the Fiori case.

The sixty-four-year-old Ragona had clearly expressed the desire not to be kept alive by artificial means should she become permanently incapacitated. After two strokes left Mrs. Ragona in a vegetative state, her husband asked that his wife's nasogastric (NG) tube be removed. A panel of three Lackawanna County trial court judges agreed to apply the clear and convincing evidence standard, as advocated in that case by the attorney general's office, and approved the withdrawal of her feeding tubes since clear and convincing evidence of her wishes was available.

Although the *Ragona* decision would carry no weight as a precedent in case law (only appellate court decisions can do that), Connell and Quinlan indicated that the supreme court should endorse the *Ragona* ruling (Connell and Quinlan 1995: 8). They then buttressed the import of the patient's intentions by referencing Pennsylvania's Advance Directive for Health Care Act, which states that "the intent of the patient would appear to be the controlling determination with respect to the withdrawal of basic nutrition and hydration" (Connell and Quinlan 1995: 9).

However, the contradiction in the Catholic Conference's case became apparent when, after stressing the importance of self-determination through their citations of case and statutory law, the Catholic Conference's lawyers turned to the Pennsylvania bishops' definitive statement on the issue: "The patient in the persistent vegetative state is not imminently terminal. . . . The feeding—regardless of whether it be considered as treatment or as care—is serving a life-sustaining purpose. Therefore, it remains an ordinary means of sustaining life and should be continued" (Catholic Bishops of Pennsylvania 1991: 14). This latter, purely normative statement seems very much at odds with the case and statutory law cited earlier, both of which support the right of self-determination (assuming clear and convincing evidence exists).

Interestingly, the Connell-Quinlan brief did help bolster the attorney general's case in another way. Unger and Knorr picked up on the normative statement of the Pennsylvania bishops and used it to critique Mrs. Sherman's contention that her son would not want to be kept alive in his vegetative condition. Joey Fiori had been an altar boy through his high school years and was a devout Catholic, the AG's lawyers accurately pointed out. In doing so, they seemed to imply that Rosemarie Sherman could not even begin to suggest that her son would want life-sustaining medical treatment withdrawn when the position of the Pennsylvania Conference of Catholic Bishops was so much at odds with the notion of withdrawing treatment (Unger and Knorr 1995: 30).[10]

The Pennsylvania Medical Society Argues in Favor of Allowing the Withdrawal of Treatment

The Pennsylvania Medical Society position was advanced before the state supreme court, for both the society and Rosemarie Sherman, by PMS attorney Robert Hoffman. A central part of Hoffman's argument was devoted to questioning the presumption that life should be maintained as the default rule when clear and convincing evidence of the patient's wishes to the contrary was not available.

Hoffman drew on several sources to advance this argument. First, just as trial court judge Sokolove had done three years earlier, he cited public opinion polls and other research indicating that the vast majority of U.S. citizens would not want to be sustained in a permanently vegetative state. Second, he noted that doctors who had studied this issue closely had concluded that the use of aggressive medical therapy in such cases could be medically futile and perhaps even wasteful (see Multi-Society Task Force on PVS 1994b). Third, Hoffman noted that, in reality, most deaths today are already "managed" in some way. When considered together, he asserted, these factors showed that the AG's argument regarding the presumption in favor of life could not be sustained.

This was not to suggest, he added, that one should presume an individual would want life support withdrawn unless there was clear and convincing evidence to the contrary (although some have made this argument—see Cantor 1989, 1996). Rather, Hoffman proposed that rules be constructed so as not to bias treatment decisions in *either* direction (Hoffman 1995: 28). The goal, he argued, should be

> to implement, without preconception but with dignity, an individual's right to accept or reject life-sustaining treatment. Those rules should neither assume the patient desires treatment to be maintained nor discontinued and should treat as equals the right to life and the right to refuse life-sustaining treatment.

... Accordingly, while court proceedings, when utilized, must impose a "burden of proof," the selected standard should not skew the result unnecessarily in either direction (Hoffman 1995: 45).

The AG's lawyers erred, according to Hoffman, by presuming that life would be desired when the patient had left no explicit instructions either way. That "improperly converts silence into affirmance," Hoffman argued. He went on to characterize the attorney general's contention—that life-sustaining treatment should be continued—as "a very odd presumption indeed, given that most people when asked, indicate that they would not want to be sustained under these conditions with this prognosis" (Hoffman 1995: 44).

Hoffman also noted that

the decision maker must make a decision either to continue or to withdraw treatment; in either event, the patient's subjective views must be ascertained and applied as best they can. That the evidence as to personality, philosophy, value system, and life style may not always be definitive does not explain why it must be disregarded. . . . The Attorney General's complaint that this information was subject to "multiple interpretations" may be accurate as to persons who did not know Mr. Fiori. To Mrs. Sherman, who did, they were crystal clear. That is the fundamental point of this proceeding. Thus, Mrs. Sherman understood as others might not that the position of the Pennsylvania Catholic Conference would not control her son's views, even though he was Catholic (Hoffman 1995: 45).

Hoffman also criticized the attorney general's contention that the courts must always be involved in such cases (an idea that was also expressed in Popovich's dissent):

The Attorney General's position does not merely bring all such matters to court but relegates family members and their physicians to the periphery. . . . Thus, concerned family members are converted into overanxious heirs. This transformation is as insulting as it is erroneous, both in general and egregiously so under the facts of this case and Mrs. Sherman's incredible and longstanding devotion to her son. . . . Under the approach advocated by the Attorney General, these difficult and personal decisions will, of necessity, become adversarial proceedings, attracting the attention of the public, and will make family members and physicians participants, not decision makers. The surrogate decision maker, whether a court or guardian, will be someone with no established relationship to the patient and none of the understanding that relationships establish. Such a procedure makes no sense, invades the privacy of the patient and family, and should be soundly rejected by this Court (Hoffman 1995: 31–33, citations omitted).[11]

Lastly, Hoffman challenged the attorney general's argument regarding the lack of pain and awareness experienced by patients in a vegetative state.

If such patients did not feel pain and were unaware of the dire circum-stances in which they continued to exist, then what, if any, burdens of con-tinued life could be attributed to them? Hoffman dismissed this concern by citing the President's Commission report on end-of-life decision making:

> First, the few patients who have recovered consciousness after a prolonged pe-riod of unconsciousness were severely disabled [which] commonly included in-ability to speak or see, permanent distortion of the limbs, and paralysis. Being returned to such a state would be regarded as of very limited benefit by most patients. . . . Second, long-term treatment commonly imposes severe financial and emotional burdens on a patient's family, people whose welfare most pa-tients before they lost consciousness, placed a high value on (Hoffman 1995: 48, citing President's Commission 1983).

"Choice in Dying" Cites Trends in the States Favoring the Right to Choose

The amicus brief filed by Choice in Dying, drafted by attorneys Anna Moretti Kavolius and Ann Fade, pointed out that the clear and convincing evidence standard had been accepted in only three states (Missouri, in *Cruzan*; New York, in *O'Connor*; and Kentucky, in *DeGrella*).[12] It had been rejected everywhere else, they argued, because the test had been viewed as disadvantaging those who did not have the foresight, sophistica-tion, or access to information about advance directives necessary to make their wishes known. The CID attorneys pointed out that when families could not meet the clear and convincing evidence standard, they were forced to disregard the patient's lifestyle, ethical and religious beliefs, and general life preferences and accept the state's decision—that life should be maintained (Kavolius and Fade 1995: 6–7).

In fact, the CID lawyers pointed out that twenty-six states and the District of Columbia had already enacted surrogate decision-making statutes that authorized the kind of family and surrogate decision making being advo-cated by Mrs. Sherman's representatives (Kavolius and Fade 1995: 9).[13] Kavolius and Fade also echoed Hoffman and Sokolove's point regarding public opinion. They cited a 1991 *Boston Globe*–Harvard School of Public Health survey that found that 53 percent of the respondents thought fami-lies, in consultation with doctors, should be allowed to make treatment deci-sions for their incompetent loved ones and an additional 30 percent thought family members should make such decisions unilaterally. Overall, 83 percent of the survey respondents thought families should be making or helping to make end-of-life decisions for their loved ones without the interference of the courts. Significantly, only 2 percent of the respondents thought that such decisions should be left to the courts (Kavolius and Fade 1995: 9).

Kavolius and Fade referred to the clear and convincing evidence standard as unworkable. They indicated that a high percentage of the many requests for assistance received via Choice in Dying's hot lines came from family members in New York who were having trouble getting a loved one's treatment wishes honored (New York is the home of CID and one of the three states that use the clear and convincing evidence standard).[14] Apparently, institutions (especially New York institutions)—concerned about liability for withholding or withdrawing treatment—were regularly sending the family to court rather than reviewing the evidence and developing a consensus on treatment with members of the incompetent patient's family. The CID lawyers noted that even expedited proceedings were both expensive (in legal and medical terms) and taxing (emotionally and in terms of lost privacy). Certainly, they said, these were added reasons for rejecting the suggestion that the courts be routinely involved.

University Hospitals Cite Clinical Realities in Support of the Right to Choose

Alan Meisel and Betty Adler, attorneys for the University of Pittsburgh Center for Medical Ethics and the University of Pennsylvania Medical Center, joined the CID lawyers and PMS lawyer Robert Hoffman before the Pennsylvania Supreme Court to support Rosemarie Sherman's right to make an end-of-life decision for her son.[15] Like their colleagues, Meisel and Adler questioned the sagacity of requiring court proceedings in such cases on a number of grounds.

First, they cited the issue of costs. Even short delays caused by court proceedings—and there had to be some delays if the proceedings were to be substantive—would be expensive in medical terms, they argued. By way of example, they noted that the charges for services rendered in the medical intensive care unit (ICU) were running approximately $2,500 a day at the hospital of the University of Pennsylvania, where many end-of-life decisions were made on a regular basis, without court involvement (Meisel and Adler 1995: 28).

Every day of delay caused by court proceedings, the attorneys asserted, added these medical and other legal charges to the bill of the family (or some third-party payer). And at the same time, the emotional turmoil was extended and the loss of privacy felt by those having to grapple with what was inevitably a very tragic and privately painful situation was exacerbated. Meisel and Adler (1995: 26) cited the Florida Court of Appeals on this point, which noted that courts often delay the process so long that the patient expires long before the case is ever settled (as happened in the Fiori case).[16] The inescapable fact, they said, was that judicial proceedings, even expedited ones, made the patient's condition and the family decision-making process public, robbing them of their right to privacy in making such intimate choices (Meisel and Adler 1995: 12–14).

Next, the attorneys brought up the clinical reality—that end-of-life decisions were made in U.S. hospitals every day without clear and convincing evidence of the patient's wishes and without the involvement of the courts. In support of this claim, Meisel and Adler (1995: 29) noted that

> decisions not to further prolong the dying process are made by families in consultation with the attending physician at least five to ten times per week in the intensive care units of both the University of Pennsylvania Medical Center and the University of Pittsburgh Medical Center. Additionally, similar decisions are made daily throughout hospitals in this Commonwealth and elsewhere.

Meisel and Adler also noted that, according to the National Center for State Courts (NCSC), 70 percent of all deaths that "occur daily in the United States are somehow timed or negotiated with patients, families, and doctors quietly agreeing on not using death delaying technology. . . . It is obvious that there is a generalized society sanctioned practice that most of these life-sustaining medical treatment decisions are made without a [legally appointed] guardian or any court intervention" (NCSC 1992: 17–18; see also Lipton 1986: 1164). The same point, they added, was widely acknowledged by courts in a variety of states (see Meisel and Adler 1995: 19–20).[17]

Meisel and Adler pointed out that 70 percent of the 2.2 million deaths in the United States every year (that is, over 1.5 million deaths) were, in reality, managed in some way. Yet, they said, the only empirical study of court involvement in such cases estimated that, on average, only 200 to 450 such cases were argued in the trial courts in any given year. Put another way, at most only 450 of the 1.5 million cases per year in which life-sustaining medical treatment was either withheld or withdrawn at the end of life ever wound up in court. That meant that courts were involved in only 0.03 percent of all such cases annually and that 99.97 percent of life-sustaining medical treatment decisions were made without judicial assistance.

If the courts were actually involved in all such decisions, as the AG lawyers suggested, the courts would need to gird for an increase in their workload of more than 200,000 percent! In addition, Meisel and Adler noted that requiring routine involvement of the courts would "disrupt the work of doctors in ways that will detrimentally affect the treatment given to patients generally" (Meisel and Adler 1995: 28, citing *In re Cloyer*, 660 P. 2d 738, 745, 1983).

The simple fact, according to Meisel and Adler, was that it was already an accepted custom in medicine to turn to the next of kin when treatment decisions had to be made for an incompetent patient. Furthermore, this common practice had, in recent years, acquired legal recognition as something akin to common law. The slew of legal-medical manuals, handbooks, and articles advising physicians to obtain consent from the next of kin when considering which treatments, if any, a patient should receive testified to that reality (Meisel and Adler 1995: 19).

Meisel and Adler also took issue with the attorney general's contention that families and physicians could not be trusted to operate privately, beyond the glare of judicial scrutiny. They pointed out that, though several courts had raised this issue,[18] there simply was no evidence that abuse would occur if the courts were not routinely involved (Meisel and Adler 1995: 4). In fact, although family-based conflict of interest problems were regularly raised in the cases that did end up in court, a finding of "bad faith" had never been sustained by an appellate court in the twenty-year history of right-to-die litigation.[19]

Turning to the AG's argument that physicians were poorly equipped to act as a check on family decision making, Meisel and Adler contended that health care professionals "have a strongly inculcated professional bias in favor of continuing treatment [and] are also extraordinarily worried about potential civil or criminal liability and bad publicity. When these factors are combined, it is the experience of the amici [representatives from institutions filing this friend-of-the-court brief] that they sometimes serve as too strong a check on family members, rather than too weak a check." In other words, it is extremely difficult—not too easy—to get life-sustaining treatment stopped in many of today's hospitals and nursing homes. Of course, it *should* be difficult to terminate life-sustaining treatment—but not so difficult as to be impossible. According to Meisel and Adler (1995: 5–6), the fact that the Fiori case was litigated in the first place was stark testimony that it was, in fact, often impossible.

Families, not lawyers and judges, should make end-of-life decisions if at all possible, argued Meisel and Adler: "Our common human experience teaches us that family members and close friends care most and best for a patient. They offer support and concern, and have the best interests of the patient at heart. The importance of the family in medical treatment decisions is axiomatic" (Meisel and Adler, citing *In re Farrell*, 529 A. 2d at 414).

Meisel and Adler also suggested that surrogates wanted—and expected—family members to make such decisions. They cited public opinion polls and medical studies of patient preferences (Cohen-Mansfield et al. 1991; Gamble, McDonald, and Lichstein 1991) and the President's Commission report (1983: 128) in support of their claim:

> The family is typically most concerned about that patient's well being and most knowledgeable about the patient's wishes; the family deserves recognition as an important social unit—allowing family participation in decision making validates and bolsters that all-important social unit while protecting the privacy and preserving the autonomy of the patient who is no longer able to protect or preserve these things for him- or herself (Meisel and Adler 1995: 15–16).

Of the twenty-four jurisdictions in which decisions on the termination of treatment had been made at the appellate level, Meisel and Adler noted that courts in only three states had ever experimented with any form of routine judicial review: Massachusetts (the *Saikewicz* decision in 1977, which seemed to imply that courts would make all the final calls in life-sustaining treatment decision cases); New Jersey (*Quinlan* in 1976 and *Conroy* in 1985, both requiring incompetency and guardianship hearings); and Washington (*Cloyer* in 1983, requiring court involvement only for purposes of designating a guardian, who would be free to make decisions without court approval thereafter). In each case, appellate courts later reversed themselves and abandoned the notion of requiring routine court involvement as unworkable.

The medical center attorneys also pointed out that court review requirements were rejected both by the Uniform Law Commissioners (ULC) (see Chapter 2) and the National Center for State Courts (see Chapter 2; Meisel and Adler 1995: 32). The courts in all cases were urged to make themselves available to resolve irreconcilable disputes among family members and between the family and caregivers or when evidence suggested that the surrogate was motivated by concerns other than the best interests of the patient. But routine involvement of the courts was rejected as both unwise and impractical.

In sum, Meisel and Adler argued that the parens patriae power of the state, properly understood, did not require the state to preserve the life of an incompetent patient. Rather, it required the state to support decisions made in the patient's best interests, and those decisions often could be advanced best if the court was not involved directly in the proceedings. This is the way decision making works for the vast majority of patients who die in hospitals and nursing homes today, and it is the way the vast majority of Americans prefer that decisions be made for themselves. Because there was no evidence that this arrangement had led to abuse, the case for dramatic change, as proposed by Popovich and the attorney general, was weak indeed, according to Meisel and Adler.

Meisel and Adler wrapped up their presentation with a summary of what had become a widely shared consensus opinion among state court judges, common to at least twenty-four of the thirty or so appellate-level decisions on related cases that had been issued to date (Meisel and Adler 1995: 8). This consensus consisted of the following principles, all of which would support Sherman's contention and all of which ran counter—to one degree or another—to the position taken by Pennsylvania's attorney general (Meisel and Adler 1995: 9–10):

- Incompetent patients have the same common law and constitutionally protected rights as competent patients have to refuse life-sustaining treatment;

- The interests of the state in preserving life are virtually nonexistent when weighed against a competent individual's liberty interest in refusing life-sustaining treatment, and the state's interests are only a little less weak when weighed against an incompetent patient's rights to forgo life-sustaining treatment when the prognosis for recovery is very dim;
- The decision-making process should generally take place in the clinical setting among caregivers and family members (while courts remain available to assist when irreconcilable conflicts arise);
- Surrogate decisionmakers should attempt to make an informed substituted judgment for the incompetent patient; if unable to do so, they should resort to making a decision that would best serve the interests of the patient;
- Artificially supplied nutrition and hydration is a medical treatment that may be withheld or forgone like any other; and
- The decision to forgo life-sustaining medical treatment does not constitute active euthanasia or assisted suicide, both of which remain illegal.

The Pennsylvania Supreme Court Leaves No Doubt: "Sherman Was Right"

On April 2, 1996, the Pennsylvania Supreme Court issued a unanimous ruling in favor of Rosemarie Sherman and the Pennsylvania Medical Society. Justice Ralph J. Cappy, author of the court's opinion, argued simply that "the right to refuse medical treatment has deep roots in our common law" (Cappy 1996: 6) and that when the patient is no longer able to decide for him- or herself what treatments to accept or refuse, "a close family member is well-suited to the role of substitute decision-maker" (Cappy 1996: 13).

Cappy's opinion echoed Judge Sokolove's trial court decision in dismissing the four traditional state interests in such cases. With regard to the state's interest in the prevention of suicide, Cappy (1996: 7) wrote that withdrawing treatment could not be considered suicide because "in removing life-sustaining measures, the natural death process is allowed to continue." With regard to the protection of innocent third parties, Cappy (1996: 7) wrote that "the patient [Fiori] has no dependents who would be left emotionally and financially bereft."

When it came to preserving the integrity of the medical profession, Cappy (1996: 8) noted simply that "the medical community supports the withdrawal of life-sustaining treatment" in such cases. Finally, on the issue of the state's interest in the preservation of life, Judge Cappy (1996: 8) wrote that "the state's interest in maintaining the PVS individual in an endless twilight state between life and death is so weak that it cannot overcome the individual's right to self-determination."

The court was unswayed by the attorney general's argument that clear and convincing evidence had to be present before a decision to forgo life-sustaining treatment from an incompetent patient could be carried out. Instead, Judge Cappy (1996: 11–12) adopted the Choice in Dying position, arguing that "were this test [the clear and convincing evidence test] to be applied, all of those patients who did not have the prescience or the sophistication to express clearly and unmistakenly their views on this precise matter would not be able to have life support removed. . . . The only practical way to prevent the destruction of the PVS patient's right to refuse medical treatment is to allow a substitute decision maker to determine what measures the PVS patient would have desired in light of the patient's prognosis."[20]

Cappy went on to note that "in addition to the great knowledge of the PVS patient's personal views, close family members have a special bond with the PVS patient." Again parting ways with the attorney general, Cappy concluded that when physicians and close family members were in agreement on the course of action to take, there was no need for court involvement (Cappy 1996: 14).

Summary

The basic argument of the attorney general and those on the AG's side of the issue was straightforward: Because the state has an unqualified interest in preserving life, we should err on the side of life when it is not abundantly clear what the individual in the persistent vegetative state would want in terms of life-sustaining medical treatment. By contrast, Joey Fiori's mother, her attorney, those filing friend-of-the-court briefs on her behalf, and the superior and supreme courts of Pennsylvania held that although life may be sacred, the state's interest in preserving life does not automatically trump the right of a patient to have someone exercise on his or her behalf the right of self-determination, a right that flows from the common law right of privacy that protects one's body from unwanted intrusion. All parties agreed that this zone of privacy could not be violated without consent of the patient, but only those who supported Sherman's position agreed that someone very familiar with the patient should be able to decide what an incompetent patient would have wanted if competent.

The attorney general's approach to this issue, which is not widely supported in legal or medical circles, was not original. Lawyers representing the nursing home that cared for Nancy Jobes unsuccessfully adopted the same line of argument during the court fight to keep Jobes alive after an automobile accident and subsequent surgery left her, like Fiori, in a persistent

BOX 1.2   The Plight of Nancy Jobes

"Mrs. Jobes requires extensive care. While numerous medications, nutrition and hydration were initially provided through the use of a nasogastric tube, as a result of increasing difficulties with that tube's frequent removal and reinsertion, a gastrostomy tube was surgically inserted into Mrs. Jobes's stomach in December 1980. A life-threatening failure of this gastrostomy tube in June 1985 led to the closing of the gastric fistula, [and] a new cutting in her abdominal cavity [was created for] the establishment of a jejunostomy tube in her small intestine. Mrs. Jobes has been hospitalized at least three times since the performance of the jejunostomy for complications arising from its insertion and employment. It is through this tube that many medications, nutrition (a commercially produced synthetic, pre-digested nutritional formula) and hydration are provided. An automatic electrically driven pump provides a constant slow rate of liquid to the bowel where it is digested. Mrs. Jobes is incontinent and requires a catheter to continuously irrigate her bladder. She receives routine enemas for bowel evacuation. Mrs. Jobes also has a tracheostomy, which is covered with a plastic shield to which a flexible tube is attached. Through this tube she receives air from a compressor in order to afford moisture to the tracheotomy. The mist is driven by a mechanical air compressor. There is a suction machine adjacent to the bed available if necessary to remove her saliva. Mrs. Jobes cannot swallow. She is given antibiotics when necessary, as well as medication intended to prevent seizures. Mrs. Jobes's muscles have atrophied and her limbs are rigidly contracted. Her extremities cannot move. Her closely clenched fingers are padded to prevent the skin between them from breaking down.

"To summarize, Mrs. Jobes's physical condition is extreme: major organs and systems have failed; she is profoundly comatose; her body has atrophied, contracted, and deteriorated; she is totally incontinent. Her treatment is overwhelmingly burdensome and intrusive; she has been repeatedly hospitalized for more extended, extraordinary medical treatment; she requires two surgically implanted devices; she must be evacuated and irrigated; she must be handled constantly and prevented from self mutilation. Her prognosis is hopeless; she cannot live without massive, extraordinary medical and health care measures. One may fairly and reasonably ask whether these bodily intrusions and invasions upon a person in such dire condition and so close to death, undertaken for the best motives, have not reached a point that it is not possible to perpetuate her life without destroying her dignity and denigrating her humanity. . . . When cherished values of human dignity and personal privacy, which belong to every person living or dying, are sufficiently transgressed by what is being done to the individual, we should be ready to say: enough" (*In re Jobes* 529 A. 2d at 458–459).

vegetative state. In 1985, after Nancy Jobes had spent five years in a PVS, her husband and parents asked for and were granted the right to have artificial feeding terminated. The detailed characterization of Jobes's desperate clinical circumstances provided by Judge Alan B. Handler, author of a concurring opinion in the case, illustrated just how far medical technology is sometimes extended to save some individuals from death. These circumstances, presented in Box 1.2, are not uncommon for anyone in a PVS, Joey Fiori included.

Abstract reasoning cannot be separated from these clinical realities. When those who advocate the state's interest in preserving life fail to consider the medical and personal conditions of patients such as Jobes and Fiori, their pronouncements have the hollow ring of irrelevant platitudes. The condition of both Fiori and Jobes was nothing short of hopeless. And when loving family members stepped forward to ask that treatment be withdrawn, rejection of those reasonable and well-intentioned requests led to a continuation of treatment that was both degrading and dehumanizing.

When all agree that the patient is severely and irreversibly ill and someone who clearly has the patient's interest in mind makes a decision to prevent further "invasions of privacy," the state should step aside unless it intends to place its own interests above the interests of the individual. To do otherwise would be overly protective, paternalistic, and even oppressive, according to most medical, ethical, and legal organizations (see Chapter 2). Furthermore, forcing continued treatment would not resonate well with current religious pronouncements or popular opinion on this subject (see Chapter 3).

The fact is that, although the attorney general's arguments had some merit in the abstract, they simply did not play out well in reality. It is not simply the philosophical heft of the arguments made by those on Rosemarie Sherman's side of the case that makes this so. It is the concurring and broadly based body of literature, court decisions, statutes, professional association statements, and religious pronouncements that have been generated on the subject since the mid-1980s that help tip the balance clearly in Sherman's favor.

Chapter Two

The Emergence of Consensus

The adversarial nature of the judicial process in the United States is both its strength and its weakness. On the one hand, conflict forces participants to pursue a number of different lines of argument and present various types of evidence before allowing a judge (or a jury) to resolve an issue one way or the other. On the other hand, the conflict inherent in the American judicial process forces parties on either side of a question to stretch, distort, and convolute the evidence and arguments available in order to score points for their clients and, it is hoped, to ultimately win the case.

The same could be said for polemical treatments of controversial issues in both the popular and academic presses. Authors do what they can to advance their particular points of view, and the reader is often left to wonder whom and what to believe. Are the winners of the court battles—or the press battles—right? Or are they only the most clever? Surely, there is some way to sort through the morass of competing claims and counterclaims about what is appropriate with regard to making end-of-life decisions for those unable to make such decisions on their own.

One way to move beyond the adversarial judicial process and the personal opinions and biases of authors is to reference the positions of consensus groups. The term *consensus group* is used here to refer, loosely, to a diverse collection of individuals called together to find some sensible common principles that can provide practical and ethical guidance to others.

Although any single author (whether an ethicist, a physician, a lawyer, or a judge) may draw on the writings and thinking of others, the synthesis that results is still slanted, consciously or not, by the writer's own prejudices. Alternately, there is something more balanced about the conclusions of multidisciplinary consensus groups. These collective bodies tend to draw on a wide variety of professionals who bring a range of educational, training, clinical, and personal experiences to the table. These groups typically strug-gle mightily with tough questions in the process of finding some middle ground that all members of the group can accept. As such, their pronounce-ments represent a plurality of views that reach beyond individual opinion to achieve a more generalized and enduring statement of principles.

Often, consensus group reports are ratified, either formally by vote of an organization's members or informally through citation by others. When this happens, the reports in question take on even greater weight, impor-tance, and legitimacy. The consensus group reports referred to in this chap-ter have been chosen precisely because they have been legitimated in at least one of two ways: by being adopted by a professional organization or by be-ing widely cited in the writings of scholars, in the opinions of judges, and in the editorials of commentators.

This chapter focuses on the considered opinions of eleven consensus groups, including five health care associations (three physicians' groups, one association of nurses, and one religiously oriented hospital associa-tion), two independent nonprofit legal institutes, two task forces (one state and one federal), one not-for-profit bioethics institute, and one interdisci-plinary triad of authors who wrote a best-selling book on clinical ethics for medical school students.

The position statements cited here range from elaborate and extensively researched analyses of 500 pages or more (e.g., the President's Commission report) to brief, relatively straightforward statements of general principle (e.g., the compendium of statements issued by the American Nurses Associ-ation [ANA]). In each case, however, the statements that emerged from the deliberations of interdisciplinary teams reflect not only the opinions of the group members but also the general sense of the community the particular group was constituted to represent. Of course, not every member of every organization will endorse organizational position statements without dis-sent, but these statements can be taken as generally representative. It is in that spirit that they are abstracted in this chapter.

Most of these writings are referred to, paraphrased, and quoted in a vari-ety of places. But never has a comprehensive collection of such statements on the key issues associated with end-of-life decision making been collected for comparison, review, and consideration. For that reason and to the de-gree possible, the positions reported here have been abstracted verbatim. It is hoped that this will allow the reader to capture a fuller, richer sense of what was written and intended by the authors, with as little distortion as possible. For overall ease of reading, citations have been provided only to the statements themselves; citations that were embedded within these state-ments have been omitted. The full texts of all the statements are readily available (see Tables 2.1, 2.2, and 2.3).

TABLE 2.1   Medical Consensus Groups

The American Medical Association (AMA) 515 North State Street Chicago, Ill. 60610 (312) 464-5000	The AMA is among the oldest (founded in 1847), certainly the best known, and arguably the most influential medical organization in the United States today. Well over half of the approximately 460,000 physicians licensed to practice medicine in the United States currently belong to the AMA. The AMA—an organization that is often described (and criticized) as more conservative than the members it purportedly represents (Cummings and Wise 1989: 252)—periodically issues position statements authored by a standing multidisciplinary committee of physicians known as the Council on Ethical and Judicial Affairs.
American College of Physicians (ACP) Independence Mall West 6th Street at Race Philadelphia, Pa. 19106 (215) 351-2400	Founded in 1915, the American College of Physicians is a professional society of physicians specializing in internal medicine and closely related specialties. The ACP has 80,000 members and published the *Annals of Internal Medicine*. The ACP's Ethics Committee, composed of practicing internists, medical ethicists, educators, and lawyers, published the Physicians Ethics Manual in the *Annals of Internal Medicine* in 1989. The ACP updated the manual in 1992.
American Thoracic Society (ATS) 1740 Broadway New York, N.Y. 10019-4374 (212) 315-8700	The ATS was founded in 1905 and currently serves as the medical section of the American Lung Association. The ATS's 11,000 members include specialists in pulmonary diseases, thoracic surgeons, and researchers and public health workers concerned with diseases of the chest and lungs. The ATS publishes *The American Review of Respiratory Diseases*. The board of directors of the ATS approved formation of the ad hoc Bioethics Task Force, which, in 1991, issued an official statement that defines for ATS members acceptable standards of medical practice regarding the withholding and withdrawing of life-sustaining therapy. The consensus group that authored the statement consisted of thirteen doctors, one nurse, and five consulting specialists in law and ethics.
American Nurses Association (ANA) 600 Maryland Ave. SW Suite 100 W Washington, D.C. 20024-2571 (202) 554-4444	Founded in 1896, the American Nurses Association currently represents 2.3 million registered nurses nationwide and publishes the periodical *American Nurse*. The ANA's Task Force on the Nurse's Role in End-of-Life Decisions issued the *Compendium of Position Statements on the Nurse's Role in End-of-Life Decisions* in 1992 and added two new position statements, one on assisted suicide and one on active euthanasia, in 1994.

36

TABLE 2.2   Legal Consensus Groups

National Center for State Courts (NCSC) 300 Newport Avenue Williamsburg, Va. 23184 (804) 253-2000	The NCSC was founded in 1971 to provide assistance to state and local trial and appellate courts by compiling national statistics, conducting studies, and acting as a clearinghouse for the exchange of court-related information. In 1992, the NCSC issued what became a well-respected and widely cited treatise on the role of the state courts in end-of-life decision making, entitled *Guidelines for State Court Decision Making in Life-Sustaining Medical Treatment Cases.* More recently, the NCSC completed a three-year process of writing a follow-up report for caregivers with the publication of *Resolving Disputes over Life-Sustaining Treatment: A Health Care Providers Guide* (Hafemeister and Hannaford 1996). Those involved in formulating this document consisted of four judges, five lawyers, two ethicists, three physicians, and a registered nurse, all of whom had professional experience in end-of-life decision making. Additional input was solicited from other health care professionals, clinical social workers, administrators, legal counselors, and those involved with pastoral care. Input from patients and family members was also solicited.
Uniform Law Commissioners (ULC) 676 North St. Clair Street Suite 1700 Chicago, Ill. 60611 (312) 915-0915	The ULC, officially known as the National Conference of Commissioners on Uniform State Laws, is an organization of judges, law school deans, professors, and practicing attorneys appointed by the state governors to promote unity in state laws on subjects in which uniformity is deemed desirable and practical. In past years, the ULC has created model statutes that have updated state administrative procedures acts and standardized the commercial and civil codes of the states. In 1985, the ULC adopted the Rights of the Terminally Ill Act, and it amended this model law with its Uniform Rights of the Terminally Ill Act in 1989. More recently, the ULC has issued the Uniform Health-Care Decisions Act, which updates and expands on the first two model statutes.
New York State Task Force on Life and the Law (NYSTFLL) 5 Penn Plaza New York, N.Y. 10001-1803	The NYSTFLL was created in 1985 to devise policies on a host of ethically challenging issues arising from advances in medical technology. Currently, it claimsto be "the only standing government commission in the United States with a mandate to recommend public policy on a range of medical/ethical issues"

(continues)

TABLE 2.2 *(continued)*

(212) 613-4303	(NYSTFLL 1992: 1). The interdisciplinary group responsible for publishing *When Others Must Choose: Deciding for Patients Without Capacity* consisted of nine physicians (including the commissioner of health for New York State), a hospital president, a medical school dean and provost, two medical school professors, seven clerics (including a Roman Catholic monsignor, an Episcopal bishop, and two rabbis), four lawyers, and three registered nurses.
Alan Meisel Center for Medical Ethics, University of Pittsburgh 3900 Forbes Avenue Pittsburgh, Pa. 15260 (412) 648-1384	Alan Meisel is the only independent author cited here. Meisel's *The Right to Die* is the most comprehensive and extensively researched source of information on the legal issues on death and dying currently available. The basic text, together with its *Cumulative Supplement,* covers nearly 1,000 pages and includes several thousand citations to the 160 or so important cases that have been argued in the state courts to date. Although Meisel's writings do not reflect the deliberations of any particular organization, his work is widely cited by a variety of authors and consensus groups as *the* authoritative source of legal information on such issues. In addition to publishing *The Right to Die* and a number of related articles, Meisel served as coauthor of an amicus brief accepted by the Pennsylvania State Supreme Court in the Fiori case, discussed in Chapter 1. That brief was filed jointly under the auspices of two respected consensus groups: the University of Pittsburgh Center for Medical Ethics and the Ethics Committee of the University of Pennsylvania Medical Center. Meisel's writings can be considered to carry greater weight than the works of other independent authors whose thinking has not been so extensively legitimated by external groups. Most of Meisel's analysis presented here is drawn from a 1991 article published (by the American College of Physicians) in the *Archives of Internal Medicine,* entitled "Legal Myths About Terminating Life Support."

TABLE 2.3   Ethics Consensus Groups

Deciding to Forego Life-Sustaining Treatment President's Commission for the Study of Ethical Problems in Medicine and Biomedical and Behavioral Research Library of Congress #83-600503	The President's Commission report entitled *Deciding to Forego Life-Sustaining Treatment* (1983) has stood the test of time as probably the most important and authoritative source of ethics-oriented information on end-of-life decision making published to date. This report has served as an important point of reference to which lawyers, judges, health care providers, and ethicists have returned time and again for their bearings. The group of approximately two dozen physicians, ethicists, and lawyers who contributed to the research and writing of this 550-page report charted, in very clear and prescient fashion, the outlines and many of the details of the consensus positions that were to emerge over the ensuing years. Not only is this report widely cited, it is widely—maybe even universally—accepted as the definitive word on the ethics of end-of-life decision making.
The Hastings Center 255 Elm Road Briarcliff Manor, N.Y. 10510 (914) 762-8500	Founded in 1969, the Hastings Center is one of the oldest and most respected bioethical organizations in the country. Its 11,500 members are individuals concerned with medical and professional ethics, including physicians, nurses, lawyers, administrators, academics, and other professionals in health-related fields. The Hastings Center conducts research and provides consultant services on a wide variety of issues related to ethics. The center's *Guidelines on the Termination of Life-Sustaining Treatment and Care of the Dying* is among the most widely cited documents in the medical and ethical literature. It is also well represented in the texts of legal briefs and court decisions. The document was constructed by a multidisciplinary group consisting of specialists in medicine, law, philosophy, nursing, and health care administration. The report draws on state law (statutory law, constitutional law, and common law), government commission reports, statements of principles issued by professional, religious, and patient advocacy organizations, and medical, legal, and ethical literature on the subject to provide a comprehensive summation of the current state of ethical affairs relevant to the care of the dying.

(continues)

TABLE 2.3 *(continued)*

Clinical Ethics: A Practical Approach to Ethical Decisions in Clinical Medicine (1992, 3rd ed.)
 	
New York: McGraw-Hill
 	
ISBN 0-07-105392-1
	Clinical Ethics: A Practical Approach to Ethical Decisions in Clinical Medicine is the product of a collaboration among a professor of medical ethics, a professor of internal medicine, and a professor of philosophy. The writings of these three authors do not reflect the official position of any particular policy-making group or professional organization. The book is included here because it is one of the top-selling medical school books on clinical ethics in the United States today. As such, it has the tacit endorsement of a wide variety of medical schools. In addition, it reflects well the state of the medical, legal, and ethical dimensions of the right-to-die debate in generally straightforward terms.
	
	    Albert R. Jonsen, Ph.D., professor of ethics in medicine, University of Washington Medical School, Seattle, Wash.
	
	    Mark Siegler, M.D., professor of internal medicine, University of Chicago's School of Medicine, Chicago, Ill.
	
	    William J. Winslade, Ph.D., J.D., professor of philosophy, University of Texas Medical Branch, Galveston, Tex.

Catholic Health Association (CHA) 4455 Woodson Road St. Louis, Mo. 63134-0889 (314) 427-2500	The CHA, founded in 1915, serves as the professional association for Catholic hospitals, extended care facilities, and health care systems in the United States. With 1,200 member organizations, the CHA is the largest association of not-for-profit health care facilities in the country. After several task forces of theologians, clergy, health caregivers, and ethicists deliberated over how suffering, pain management, and the dying process should be viewed in light of the Catholic tradition, the CHA issued a definitive statement on the subject, entitled *Care of the Dying: A Catholic Perspective.*

Building Blocks of Consensus

Position statements from a variety of mainstream medical, legal, and ethical organizations and authors are provided in this chapter as evidence that the modern consensus on the critical questions of end-of-life decision making is both broad and deep. From the medical realm, the positions of the American Medical Association (AMA) Council on Ethical and Judicial Affairs are provided together with the statements of the American College of Physicians (ACP), the American Thoracic Society (ATS), and the American Nurses Association.

From the legal world, position statements from the National Center for State Courts, the Uniform Law Commissioners, and the New York State Task Force on Life and the Law (NYSTFLL) are abstracted along with the legal analysis of Alan Meisel, the country's preeminent and probably its most widely cited expert in this area of jurisprudence.[1] A medical-ethical position of a religious orientation is provided by the statement on end-of-life decision making published by the Catholic Health Association (CHA), and secular versions of ethical considerations are supplied by the President's Commission for the Study of Ethical Problems, the Hastings Center, and the writings found in a leading text on the subject, entitled *Clinical Ethics: A Practical Approach to Ethical Decisions*.

The statements of each of the groups and individuals listed in Tables 2.1 (medical consensus), 2.2 (legal consensus), and 2.3 (ethical consensus) have been parsed and sorted according to five critical issues, each of which was raised in the case of Joey Fiori. First and most sweeping is the general category of *decision making*: Who should be allowed to make decisions for incompetent patients, and how should these decisions rightfully be rendered? Second is the question of *forgoing treatment versus suicide*: Does complicity in the forgoing of treatment or the provision of pain medication sufficient to hasten death involve the patient or clinician in suicide or active euthanasia?

Third is the distinction between *withholding and withdrawing treatment*: Is the distinction important or irrelevant? Can one withhold treatment but not withdraw it, or are the two actions morally equivalent? Fourth is the issue of *terminal illness*: Must a patient be terminally ill before end-of-life decisions can be made directly or through a surrogate? Fifth and finally comes perhaps the most troubling aspect of this debate for many Americans, *artificial nutrition and hydration and the ordinary-extraordinary distinction*: Is there anything special about artificially provided food and water that would lead decisionmakers to believe that ANH must always be provided, or should ANH be treated as just another medical procedure?

Decision Making

The consensus position is that competent adults can make any decisions they want regarding their own medical treatment. Surrogates, preferably close family members, may be deferred to, without the involvement of the courts, in making any decision that an incompetent patient could have made if he or she were competent. Surrogates should rely on the incompetent patient's wishes, expressed and implied, when making decisions—a process referred to as "substituted judgment." If there is insufficient information to make a substituted judgment, surrogates should weigh the benefits and burdens of various scenarios in an effort to decide which course of action would serve the patient's best interests. The courts need only be involved as a last resort to deal with irreconcilable conflicts within a family or between the family and the patient's caregivers.

American Medical Association

The principle of patient autonomy requires that competent patients have the opportunity to choose among medically indicated treatments and to refuse any unwanted treatment (Council 1992: 2230). The obligation to respect a competent patient's right to self-determination includes the obligation to follow the instructions of an advance directive (Council 1991: 67). When a patient does not have an advance directive . . . the surrogate should base treatment decisions on what the patient would likely decide if he or she were capable of making the decision. This standard, or guiding principle, is called substituted judgment. . . . If there is no reasonable basis upon which to interpret what a previously competent patient would have decided, or if the patient never possessed decision-making capacity, the surrogate decision maker should base treatment decisions on which outcome would most likely promote the patient's well-being. This guiding principle is referred to as the "best interests" standard (Council 1991: 68). . . .

Factors that should be considered when weighing harms and benefits of treatment include the expected duration of life with and without treatment, pain and suffering associated with the treatment, and the amount of incapacitation and ability to interact with others if life is sustained. When using the best interests standard, the subjective perspective of the surrogate decision maker will unavoidably enter into judgments about the quality of life that would exist for the patient with life-sustaining treatment. "Quality of life" here is defined as the worth to the individual whose life is in question, and not as a measure of social worth. . . . One way to help ensure that a decision is not inappropriately influenced by the surrogate's own values is to determine whether the decision is one that most reasonable persons would choose for themselves in similar circumstances (Council 1991: 68).

The family should be relied upon to make treatment decisions [for incompetent patients] because family members are generally best suited to determine what the patient who lacks decisionmaking capacity would have chosen. Family members are most likely to have had conversations with the patient specifically about the withdrawal of life-prolonging treatment [and] family members have the most intimate understanding of the patient's perspective. . . . Moreover, family members are generally the most concerned with the patient welfare. . . . Those who are outside the family, such as the state or health care institutions, should be wary to intrude upon family decisions particularly when the decisions are within a reasonable range of choices (Council 1991: 70–71).

While certain aspects of judicial decisionmaking are attractive . . . the slow and cumbersome nature of the judicial process makes routine judicial review for decisions regarding life support impossible. In addition, the public, adversarial and tremendously time-consuming and costly nature of the judicial process would create significant hardship for the patients and families involved. Furthermore, routine judicial review would remove the decisionmaking process from families, thereby devaluing the family's role in decisionmaking (Council 1991: 72).

American College of Physicians

The basic principles of informed consent, shared decision making, and the use of surrogate decision makers when necessary . . . apply to end-of-life decisions as well. Principles are manifest as follows: Patients who have decision-making capacity and should have been adequately informed of their clinical situation and options usually have the right to accept or refuse any recommended medical treatment, including life-sustaining treatment. . . . This right of the patient is based on the philosophical concept of autonomy, the common-law right of self-determination, and the more recently enunciated constitutional right of privacy. The crux of the issue is that the competent patient's (rather than the physician's) assessment of the benefits and burdens of treatment should determine what treatment is administered or withheld. . . . Surrogate or proxy decision-makers . . . should know the patient's values well and be free of obvious fiscal or emotional conflicts with the patient. The physician should take reasonable care to ensure that the surrogate's decisions are motivated by respect for the patient's interests and values. . . . Whenever possible, these decisions should be reached in the clinical setting by responsible physicians, family, and other caregivers (ACP 1989: 330–331).

American Thoracic Society

An adult person who no longer has decision-making capacity should continue to have the right to refuse all forms of medical therapy: However, this right must be exercised on the patient's behalf by an appropriate surrogate decision maker. . . . If no such person exists, the physician should help to identify one or more close family members or close friends of the patient to be the surrogate decision maker, primarily on the basis of their knowledge of the patient's preferences, values, and goals and their commitment to supporting the patient's rights and best interests. Whenever possible, out of respect of the patient's autonomy, the surrogate decision maker should make the same decisions about the patient's care as the patient would have made if capable of doing so. . . . If circumstances arise in which the surrogate decision maker cannot make a decision based on knowledge either of the patient's prior statements or of the patient's values and goals, he or she should collaborate with the patient's physician and other health care providers to make decisions for the patient based on what is determined to be in the patient's best interests (ATS 1991: 479–480).

American Nurses Association

In the case of the incompetent or never competent patient, any existing advance directives or the decisions of surrogate decision makers acting in the patient's best interest should be determinative (ANA 1992: 13).[2] In cases where a patient is unable to make his wishes known . . . the decision of a surrogate should be relied upon. A surrogate decision maker, preferably designated by the patient, is one who makes decisions in the best interest of the patient and without self interest (ANA 1992: 9).[3]

National Center for State Courts

It is increasingly certain . . . that family members usually may serve as the patient's surrogate, even without statutory authorization or court appointment. . . . First, as a general rule, family members are in the best position to know the patient and have reliable information about the patient's wishes. Second, the interests of the family members are likely to coincide with those of the patient. . . . Finally, most individuals want a family member to serve as their surrogate. . . . If the patient has not expressed his or her wishes, the surrogate should use . . . the "substituted judgment" standard. . . . This process involves the surrogate's good faith inquiry into the patient's values, beliefs, and lifestyle . . . to determine what the patient would have wanted if he or she had sufficient decision-making capacity to express treatment preferences. . . . Unfortunately, a patient's wishes and values may not always be clear. . . . Under these circumstances, the usual practice is to permit surrogates to use . . . the "best interests" standard. . . . Determining a patient's best interests generally includes evaluating objective medical criteria such as the patient's diagnosis and prognosis, the amount of enjoyment and suffering the patient is likely to experience, and the likelihood that the use of life-sustaining medical treatment will restore the patient to his or her previous quality of life. This determination is not a purely clinical one, however. Often it is an almost intuitive determination that requires evaluation of what a reasonable person in the patient's situation would want (Hafemeister and Hannaford 1996: 16–19).[4]

Uniform Law Commissioners

The [Uniform Health-Care Decisions] Act acknowledges the right of a competent individual to decide all aspects of his or her own health care in all circumstances, including the right to decline health care or to direct that health care be discontinued, even if death ensues. . . . Unless limited by the principle, an agent has the authority to make all health-care decisions which the individual could have made. . . . The Act requires an agent or surrogate . . . to make those decisions in accordance with the instructions and other wishes of the individual to the extent known. Otherwise, the agent or surrogate must make those decisions in accordance with best interests of the individual but in light of the individual's personal values. . . . (ULC 1993: 1). A health-care decision made by an agent for a principal is effective without judicial approval (ULC 1993: 5).

New York State Task Force on Life and the Law

After consulting with health care professionals, surrogates should decide about treatment based on the patient's wishes or, if the patient's wishes are not reasonably known and cannot be reasonably ascertained, based on the patient's best interests. Assessments of a patient's best interests should be patient-centered and should include consideration of the dignity and uniqueness of every person; the possibility and extent of preserving the patient's life; preservation, improvement, or restoration of the patient's health or functioning; relief of the patient's suffering and other such concerns and values as a reasonable person in the patient's circumstances would wish to consider. . . . By and large, decisions made in accordance with the proposed law will be private bedside decisions by those closest to the patient. . . . The courts should not be the avenue of first resort, either as the sole alternative to address conflict or as the primary decision maker for all patients who are neither terminally ill nor permanently unconscious (NYSTFLL 1992: XI). . . .

Over the past decade, two standards for surrogate decision making, "substituted judgment" and "best interests," have been embraced by commentators, policy makers, and the courts. . . . The Task Force proposes that these standards should guide surrogate decisions for health care generally (NYSTFLL 1992: 103).

The study's findings do not . . . support the notion that individuals outside the patient's circle of family or close friends should be designated to act as surrogate. Although family members do not always approximate the patient's wishes, they are more likely than others to do so. Studies have shown that family members are more familiar with the patient's health care wishes than physicians or other health care professionals. They also know far more about the patient than state-appointed representatives, judges, or others who will otherwise be called upon to make surrogate decisions. Family members are also generally those most concerned about and dedicated to the patient's well-being. Connected to the patient by bonds of kinship and caring, family members often play a crucial role as advocate for the patient (NYSTFLL 1992: 94).

Alan Meisel

Every day, and with limited legal guidance, families and doctors are making decisions for patients unable to do so themselves (Meisel 1991: 1498). . . . As everyone associated with a hospital, nursing home, or hospice knows, efforts at prolonging the lives of dying patients are frequently tapered off or halted at the request of patients still possessing decision making capacity or families of patients who have lost the capacity to make decisions (Meisel 1991: 1500). The acceptance of virtually all courts considering . . . the principle that incompetent patients must be accorded the same substantive rights as competent patients has been at the root of the widespread judicial acceptance of the substituted judgment standard. [The best interests standard] has been relegated by most courts to a secondary status, to be applied when the evidence necessary for applying the substituted judgment standard is lacking. When it is applied, the surrogate decision maker assesses what medical treatment would be in the patient's best interests as determined by such objective criteria as relief from suffering, preservation or restoration of functioning, and quality and extent of sustained life (Meisel 1989: 265–266).

President's Commission Report

When a patient lacks the capacity to make a decision, a surrogate decision maker should be designated. Ordinarily this will be the patient's next of kin, although it may be a close friend or another relative if the responsible health care professional judges that this other person is in fact the best advocate for the patient's interests (President's Commission 1983: 126–127).

The decisions of the surrogates should, when possible, attempt to replicate the ones that the patient would make if capable of doing so. When lack of evidence about the patient's wishes precludes this, decisions by surrogates should seek to protect the patient's best interests (President's Commission 1983: 5–6). . . .[5]

The two values that guide decision making for competent patients—promoting patient welfare and respecting patient self-determination—should also guide decision making for incompetent patients. . . . These values are reflected, roughly speaking, in the two standards that have traditionally guided decision-making for the incapacitated: "substituted judgment" and "best interests." . . . The substituted judgment standard requires that a surrogate attempt to reach the decision that the incapacitated person would make if he or she were able to choose (President's Commission 1983: 132). In assessing whether a procedure or course of treatment would be in a patient's best interests, the surrogate must take into account such factors as the relief of suffering, the preservation or restoration of functioning, and the quality as well as the extent of the life sustained. . . . The impact of a decision on an incapacitated patient's loved ones may be taken into account in determining someone's best interests, for most people do have an important interest in the well-being of their families or close associates (President's Commission 1983: 134–135).

Hastings Center's Guidelines

If the patient receiving life-sustaining treatment is incompetent, a surrogate decision maker should be identified. Without an advance directive that designates a proxy, the patient's family should become the surrogate decision maker. . . . Decisions regarding withholding or withdrawing life sustaining treatment should be based on substituted judgment (what the patient would have decided) when there is evidence of the patient's preferences and values. In making a substituted judgment, decision makers may consider the patient's advance directive (if any); the patient's values about life and the way it should be lived; and the patient's attitudes towards sickness, suffering, medical procedures, and death. If there is not adequate evidence of the incompetent patient's preferences and values [e.g., in the case of lifelong incompetents or if no suitable surrogates exist], the decision would be based on the best interests of the patient (what outcome would most likely promote the patient's well-being). . . . When there are disputes among family members or between family and health care providers, the use of ethics committees specifically designed to facilitate sound decisionmaking is recommended before resorting to the courts (Hastings Center 1987: 28).

Clinical Ethics

Traditionally, next of kin have been considered the natural surrogates and medical providers have turned to family members for consent. This practice appears to have been tacitly accepted in Anglo-American law, but until recently, was rarely expressed in statutes. In recent years, many states have enacted legislation that gives specific authority to family members and ranks them in priority. . . . When someone other than the patient is granted authority to decide on behalf of the patient, their decision must promote the patient's welfare. This is determined in two ways:

(a) If the patient has been able to express preferences in the past and has done so, the surrogate must use knowledge of these preferences, or at least of the known values of the individual, in making the decision. This is called "substituted judgment" and has been favored by many legal decisions.

(b) If the patient's own preferences are unknown or are unclear, the proxy must consider the "best interests" of the patient. This requires that the surrogate's decision promote the welfare of the individual. Welfare is defined as those choices about relief of suffering, preservation or restoration of function, extent and quality of life sustained that reasonable persons in similar circumstances would be likely to choose (Jonsen, Siegler, and Winslade 1992: 69–70).

Catholic Health Association

The degree to which the court should be active in resolving decisions about treatment is an issue of great importance. Put simply, the issue is whether the court should be making decisions that should rightfully be made by the patient (or by his or her surrogate). Patient self-determination, then, is properly exercised when the patient (or surrogate), in consultation with the physician, decides what is best. Programs provided by health care ethics committees or pastoral care staffs can also help support the primary decision maker and, if necessary, mediate conflicts (CHA 1993: 24).

Forgoing Treatment Versus Suicide

The consensus position holds that forgoing life-sustaining medical treatment or providing palliative care with the intent of relieving suffering are both entirely ethical acts. Neither act should be confused with mercy killing, active euthanasia, or assisted suicide.

American Medical Association

Assisted suicide and euthanasia should not be confused with the provision of palliative treatment that may hasten the patient's death ("double effect").[6] The intent of the palliative treatment is to relieve pain and suffering, not to end the patient's life, but the patient's death is a possible side effect of the treatment. It is ethically acceptable for a physician to gradually increase the appropriate medication for a patient, realizing that the medication may depress respiration and cause death (Council 1994a: 92).

Assisted suicide also must be distinguished from withholding or withdrawing life-sustaining treatment, in which the patient's death occurs because the patient or the patient's proxy, in consultation with the treating physician, decides that the disadvantages of treatment outweigh its advantages and therefore the treatment is refused (Council 1994a: 92). Physicians have an obligation to relieve pain and suffering and to promote the dignity and autonomy of dying patients in their care. . . . Even if the patient is not terminally ill or permanently unconscious, it is not unethical to discontinue all means of life-sustaining medical treatment in accordance with a proper substituted judgment or best interests analysis (Council 1994b: 36–37).

American College of Physicians

Physicians should distinguish among withdrawing life-sustaining treatment, allowing the natural process of death to occur, and taking deliberate actions to shorten a patient's life. Objections to assisted suicide and active euthanasia should not deter physicians from withholding or withdrawing medical interventions in appropriate situations (ACP 1992: 955).

American Thoracic Society

Physicians and other health providers have a responsibility to respect patient autonomy by withholding or withdrawing any life-sustaining therapy as requested by an informed and capable patient (ATS 1991: 478). . . . An adult patient who no longer has decision making capacity should continue to have the right to refuse all forms of medical therapy; however this right must be exercised on the patient's behalf by an appropriate surrogate decision maker (ATS 1991: 479). . . . Helping a patient forego life support under these circumstances is regarded as distinct from participating in assisted suicide or active euthanasia, neither of which is supported by this statement (ATS 1991: 478).

American Nurses Association

Honoring the refusal of treatments that a patient does not desire, that are disproportionately burdensome to the patient, or that will not benefit the patient is ethically and legally permissible (ANA 1994a: 1). The profession's opposition to nurse participation in active euthanasia does not negate the obligation of the nurse to provide proper and ethically justified end-of-life care which includes the promotion of comfort and the alleviation of suffering, adequate pain control, and at times, foregoing life-sustaining treatments (ANA 1994a: 2). . . .

While it is well known that pain medications often have a sedative or respiratory depressant side effect, this should not be an overriding consideration in their use for dying patients as long as such use is consistent with the patient's wishes. . . . Nurses should not hesitate to use full and effective doses of pain medication for the proper management of pain in the dying patient (ANA 1992: 7). . . .

Withholding or withdrawing life-sustaining medical therapies or risking the hastening of death through treatments aimed at alleviating suffering and/or controlling symptoms are ethically acceptable and do not constitute active euthanasia (ANA 1994a: 1).

National Center for State Courts

In general, increasing the dosage level of medication to achieve adequate symptom control—even when the secondary effect may be to hasten death—is ethically justified when this practice is in accord with the patient's wishes (Hafemeister and Hannaford 1996: 64–65). . . . There are significant moral and legal distinctions between letting die (including the use of medications to relieve suffering during the dying process) and killing (assisted suicide/euthanasia). In letting die, the cause of the death is seen as the underlying disease process or trauma. In assisted suicide/euthanasia, the cause of death is seen as the inherently lethal action itself (NCSC 1991: 145).

Uniform Law Commissioners

The [Uniform Health-Care Decisions] Act acknowledges the right of a competent individual [or designated surrogate] . . . to decline health care or to direct that health care be discontinued, even if death occurs (ULC 1993: 1). The withholding or withdrawing of health care in accordance with the [Act] does not for any purposes constitute a suicide or homicide (ULC 1993: 22).

New York State Task Force on Life and the Law

The Task Force . . . distinguishes active measures such as lethal injection from legitimate, reasoned decisions to withdraw or withhold treatment made in accord with appropriate standards. The Task Force's proposal addresses the need for policies to provide sound, responsible decisions for patients who cannot decide for themselves. It is not intended either as a step on the road to assisted suicide or as a vehicle to extend the authority of the family beyond the traditional boundaries of consent to provide treatment or not to treat (NYSTFLL 1992: 222).

Alan Meisel

Courts have recognized an important distinction between killing and letting die and have unanimously concluded that termination of life support is neither murder, suicide, nor assisted suicide. Judicial opinions provide three reasons why this is so. (1) A patient's death due to the termination of life support is not criminal because the patient's medical condition—rather than the termination of life support—is the cause of death. The removal of life support merely allows death to take its course. (2) When life support is terminated . . . the intent is to relieve suffering. . . . (3) Such conduct involves the exercise of a patient's legal right to refuse treatment (Meisel 1991: 1498).

President's Commission Report

Although not all decisions to omit treatment and allow death to occur are acceptable, such a choice, when made by a patient or surrogate, is usually morally acceptable and in compliance with the law on homicide (President's Commission 1983: 61). . . . When some patients are dying of a disease process that cannot be arrested, physicians may, for example, write orders not to provide resuscitation if the heart should stop, forego antibiotic treatment of pneumonia and other infections, cease use of respirators, or withhold aggressive therapy from overwhelmingly burdened patients. Although declining to start or continue life-sustaining treatment is often acceptable, health care providers may properly refuse to honor a patient's request to be directly killed (President's Commission 1983: 63).

Hastings Center's Guidelines

Under the rubric of "termination of treatment" we do not include active euthanasia ("mercy killing") or assisted suicide. These guidelines have been formulated in the belief that a reasonable, if not unambiguous, line can be drawn between foregoing life-sustaining treatment on the one hand, and active euthanasia or assisted suicide on the other.

Our society forbids assisting suicide or active euthanasia, even if the motive is compassionate. . . . Respecting the individual's liberty to direct his or her own life requires, however, that patients generally be allowed to refuse medical interventions, even if others feel that this is contrary to the patient's best interests. Likewise, when a person is suffering greatly, medication and other medical interventions may be used to give relief. This relief may foreseeably lead to an earlier death. Yet it may still be morally and legally acceptable, if the intention is not to kill but to relieve the suffering, if the intervention proposed serves the patient's needs better than would an alternative, and if the patient or surrogate consents (Hastings Center 1987: 6).

Clinical Ethics

[In cases of euthanasia,] the physician employs a means that will rapidly and definitely interrupt an organic process that is necessary to continued life. This fact distinguishes these cases from the cases [of forgoing treatment], where the physician stopped, or did not provide, some intervention for the support of failing vital processes. . . . The ethical distinction lies in the fact that in the cases [of forgoing treatment] described . . . the duty to continue treatment has been extinguished by the patient's request or by the inability to achieve any of the goals of medicine. In the cases [of euthanasia], the physician acts directly to kill the patient: this does not correspond to any recognized duty of physicians (Jonsen, Siegler, and Winslade 1992: 107).

Catholic Health Association

It is necessary to examine the distinction between killing and allowing to die. "Killing" is an intentional action or omission bringing about the death of another; the cause of death is the human intervention or omission. . . . "Allowing to die" refers to stopping treatment which is burdensome or offers no reasonable hope of benefit so that the underlying pathology, which called for the use of the treatment in the first place, will run its course and eventually cause the patient's death. . . . Catholic teaching asserts that allowing a person to die by omitting useless and/or burdensome treatment is permissible and morally different from killing (CHA 1993: 48). . . . The effective use of narcotics to alleviate or suppress pain is the prudent thing to do, even though they may eventually cause loss of consciousness or a quicker death. In all cases, the use of pain relief should be as much as possible under the control of the patient, who must decide what level of pain is tolerable and how much medication is beneficial (CHA 1993: 50).

Withholding Versus Withdrawing Treatment

The consensus position here is that although it may be easier psychologically for surrogates and caregivers to withhold a treatment than to stop a treatment, there is no ethically or morally important difference between withholding and withdrawing life-sustaining medical treatment.

American Medical Association

There is no ethical distinction between withdrawing and withholding life-sustaining treatment. Withdrawing life support may be emotionally more difficult than withholding life support. . . . However, as most bioethicists now recognize, such a distinction lacks ethical significance (Council 1992: 2231).

American College of Physicians

The same reasons that justify not starting treatment also justify stopping treatment. Indeed, the reasons for withdrawing a treatment may be more compelling, because it may have proved unsuccessful or because the patient's prognosis and wishes may have been clarified. . . . Court rulings and most ethicists have found no legal or ethical difference between withdrawing and withholding treatment (ACP 1992: 953).

American Thoracic Society

Physicians and other health care providers have a responsibility to respect patient autonomy by withholding or withdrawing any life-sustaining therapy as requested by an informed and capable patient [or appropriate surrogate decisionmaker]. In this regard, there is no ethical difference between withholding and withdrawing (ATS 1991: 478).

American Nurses Association

There is no ethical or legal distinction between withholding or withdrawing treatments, though the latter may create more emotional distress for the nurse and others involved (ANA 1994a: 1).

National Center for State Courts

No significant legal or ethical distinctions can be made between decisions to withdraw (stop) and to withhold (not start) life-sustaining medical treatment (Hafemeister and Hannaford 1996: 13).

Uniform Law Commissioners

The [Uniform Health-Care Decisions Act] lets you give specific instructions about any aspect of your health care. Choices are provided for you to express your wishes regarding the provision, withholding or withdrawal of treatment to keep you alive (ULC 1993: 8).

New York State Task Force on Life and the Law

The Task Force believes that withholding and withdrawing treatment are morally equivalent and should not be distinguished. The Task Force urges health care facilities to review their policies and practices about life-sustaining treatment and to abandon distinctions based on the difference of whether or not a treatment has already been started (NYSTFLL 1992: 222). Decisions to forego treatment are an integral part of medical practice; the use of many treatments would be inconceivable without the ability to withhold or stop the treatments in appropriate cases (NYSTFLL 1992: 10).

Alan Meisel

Although it may be psychologically more difficult for health care professionals to stop the treatment of a critically ill patient than not to start it, it is a myth that there is a legal requirement to continue treatment if it is properly refused (Meisel 1991: 1499).

President's Commission Report

The distinction between failing to initiate and stopping therapy—that is, withholding versus withdrawing treatment—is not itself of moral importance. A justification that is adequate for not commencing treatment is also sufficient for ceasing it. Moreover, erecting a higher requirement for cessation might unjustifiably discourage vigorous initial attempts to treat seriously ill patients that sometimes succeed (President's Commission 1983: 61–62). . . . Little if any legal significance attaches to the distinction between withholding and withdrawing. Nothing in law—certainly not in the context of the doctor-patient relationship—makes stopping treatment a more serious legal issue than not starting treatment (President's Commission 1983: 77).

Hastings Center's Guidelines

Many health care professionals and others seem to believe that withholding life-sustaining treatment may be morally permissible, but that withdrawing treatment is wrong. This categorical distinction between withholding and withdrawing treatment seems to us mistaken. There certainly are psychological differences between withholding and withdrawing treatment. But these differences are only the starting point of ethical reflection; they do not determine its conclusions (Hastings Center 1987: 5–6).

Clinical Ethics

Some believe that there is an ethical difference between starting and stopping, the former being more permissible than the latter. There may be psychological or emotional differences: Some physicians find it more troubling to stop an ongoing intervention than not to initiate a new one. . . . In withdrawing treatment, the physician may feel responsible (in a causal sense) for the events that follow, even though he may bear no responsibility (in the sense of ethical or legal accountability) either for the disease process or for the patient succumbing to the disease. . . . It is the common position of medical ethicists, supported by many judicial decisions, that the distinction between stopping and starting is neither ethically nor legally relevant. It is our position that there is no significant ethical difference between stopping and starting, if the essential considerations regarding medical indications, patient preference, and quality of life are the same (Jonsen, Siegler, and Winslade 1992: 97–98).

Catholic Health Association

[There is] no moral distinction between withholding or withdrawing treatment (whether it be a mechanical respirator, a cardiac pacemaker, a renal dialysis machine, antibiotics, or medically dispensed nutrition and hydration) when its use is futile or would produce burdens disproportionate to the benefits the patient could appreciate (CHA 1993: 49).

Terminal Illness

The consensus position regarding when life-sustaining treatment decisions can be made deals directly with the false assumption that such decisions can only be made for those who are terminally ill. The consensus position holds that a patient need not be terminally ill for that patient (or a surrogate) to make decisions involving the forgoing of life-sustaining medical treatment.

American Medical Association

Even if death is not imminent but a patient is beyond doubt permanently unconscious, and there are adequate safeguards to confirm the accuracy of the diagnosis, it is not unethical to discontinue all means of life-prolonging treatment (Council 1990: 429).

American College of Physicians

The question of discontinuing support for persons who are permanently unconscious but are not terminally ill or brain dead (such as persons in a persistent vegetative state) remains a perplexing one. ... The best clinical recommendation in these difficult cases is for the physician to elicit the opinions of the patient's family, friends, clergy, primary-care physician, and other caregivers in an effort to determine what the patient would wish in these circumstances (ACP 1989: 332).

American Thoracic Society

The U.S. Supreme Court's 1990 decision in the Nancy Cruzan case in effect recognized a constitutional right of capable adults, even those not terminally ill or facing imminent death, to refuse any medical therapy including life-sustaining therapy and artificially provided hydration and nutrition (ATS 1991: 478).

American Nurses Association

ANA position statements do not directly address this issue.

National Center for State Courts

The use of terms such as "terminal illness," "terminal condition," and "imminently dying" often create more confusion than clarity in life-sustaining medical treatment decisions. Regardless of the patient's condition, the overriding concerns for the health-care provider in the foregoing of life-sustaining medical treatment are: (a) respecting patient autonomy (self-determination), and (b) improving patient well-being (the weighing of benefits and burdens of one plan of care in comparison with alternatives). Health care professionals have a duty to promote the welfare of their patients. However, this does not necessarily include the duty to preserve life at all costs. Where life-sustaining medical treatment fails to promote a patient's welfare, there is no longer an ethical obligation to provide it, and treatments no longer beneficial to the patient may be stopped (NCSC 1991: 143–144).

Uniform Law Commissioners

The "individual instruction" [concerning a health care decision] may but need not be limited to take effect in specified circumstances, such as if the individual is dying. . . . The authority of an agent . . . may extend to any health-care decision the principal could have made while having capacity (ULC 1993: 5–6).

New York State Task Force on Life and the Law

Family members or others close to the patient should be authorized to consent to withhold or withdraw life-sustaining treatment, if the treatment would be an excessive burden to the patient and one of the following conditions is satisfied: (I) the patient is terminally ill; (II) the patient is permanently unconscious; (III) the patient's attending physician confirms that the decision satisfies the substituted judgment/best interests, and an interdisciplinary review committee approves (NYSTFLL 1992: 109). . . . Permanently unconscious patients include those in a persistent vegetative state, patients who are completely unresponsive after brain injury or hypoxia and fail to stabilize in a vegetative state, [and] patients who are in the end stage of degenerative neurological conditions such as Alzheimer's disease (NYSTFLL 1992: 109–110, note 7). . . .

Although the Task Force members hold differing views about whether permanently unconscious individuals can benefit from continued treatment, they agree that society should grant family members and others close to the patient the authority to decide to forego treatment for patients who are either terminally ill or permanently unconscious, in accord with the standards proposed (NYSTFLL 1992: 110).

Alan Meisel

After the Supreme Court's *Cruzan* decision, it is virtually indisputable that competent patients have a right to refuse treatment whether terminally ill or not . . . as long as the patient is incurably and critically ill, such as patients in a persistent vegetative state (Meisel 1991: 1499).

President's Commission Report

The decisions of patients' families should determine what sort of medical care permanently unconscious patients receive. Other than requiring appropriate decisionmaking procedures for these patients, the law does not and should not require any particular therapies to be applied or continued, with the exception of basic nursing care that is needed to ensure dignified and respectful treatment of the patient (President's Commission 1983: 6).

Hastings Center's Guidelines

Patients who are permanently unconscious are unaware of benefits or burdens. The only possible benefit to them of life-sustaining treatment is the possibility that the diagnosis of irreversible unconsciousness is wrong and they will regain consciousness. Accordingly, the major considerations are whether a reasonable person, in the patient's circumstance, would find that this benefit, as well as the benefits to the patient's family and concerned friends (such as satisfaction in caring for the patient and the meaningfulness of the patient's continued existence) are outweighed by the burdens on those loved ones (such as financial cost or emotional suffering) (Hastings Center 1987: 29).

Clinical Ethics

Since persons in a persistent vegetative state retain some reflex activities, they may have some eye movement, swallowing, grimacing, and pupillary adjustment to light. This is naturally quite disturbing to observers, leading them to hold out much more hope for recovery than is actually warranted by the clinical facts. Medical interventions promise no benefit beyond sustaining organic life. . . . [Consequently,] if no preferences of the patient are known . . . in our judgment, it is ethically permissible to discontinue respiratory support and all other forms of life-sustaining treatment. In the state of irreversible loss of cognitive and communicative function, the individual no longer has any "interests," that is, nothing that happens to the patient can in any way advance his or her welfare [and] no goals of medicine other than support of organic life are being, or will be, accomplished (Jonsen, Siegler, and Winslade 1992: 96–97).

Catholic Health Association

The proper respect for the sanctity of life lies between two extremes. One extreme is "physical vitalism," which advocates the absolute value of maintaining biological life regardless of other values, such as loss of independence, loss of dignity, preventing pain, or saving resources. Physical vitalism can lead to the abuse of overtreatment, that is, doing everything possible to prolong physical life while believing that no cost is too great and no chance too remote to save life. The other extreme is "utilitarian pessimism" which values life for its social usefulness and advocates ending life when it becomes frustrating, useless, or burdensome. . . . Between these two extremes, the Catholic principle of sanctity of life affirms that life is a basic good, but not an absolute one to be preserved at all costs. . . . Just as one must not sacrifice life as long as there is reasonable hope for its well-being, one also must not sacrifice hope when life has reached its reasonable limits. When the dying patient can no longer appreciate treatment as a benefit, and creative living becomes impossible, then hope should focus on the eternal life after death (CHA 1993: 46–47).

ANH and the Ordinary-Extraordinary Distinction

The consensus position regarding artificially provided nutrition and hydration holds that classifying such a treatment as either "ordinary" or "extraordinary" is not particularly helpful and may even generate confusion. Rather, ANH should be classified as a medical intervention that can be waived, like any other, in accordance with a patient's preferences, expressed either directly (through informed consent or an advanced directive) or indirectly (through a substituted judgment determination or a best interests analysis).

American Medical Association

The distinction between "ordinary" and "extraordinary" treatments has been used to differentiate ethically obligatory vs. ethically optional treatments. In other words, ordinary treatments must be provided while extraordinary treatments may be withheld or withdrawn. Varying criteria have been proposed to distinguish ordinary from extraordinary treatment. Such criteria include customariness, naturalness, complexity, expense, invasiveness, and balance of likely benefits and burdens of the particular treatment. The ethical significance of all these criteria essentially are subsumed by the last criterion—the balance of likely benefits vs. burdens of the treatment (Council 1992: 2230). . . .

For example, artificial nutrition and hydration has frequently been cited as an objectively ordinary treatment which, therefore, must never be foregone. However, artificial nutrition and hydration can be very burdensome to patients. Artificial nutrition and hydration immobilizes the patient to a large degree, can be extremely uncomfortable (restraints are sometimes used to prevent patients from removing nasogastric tubes), and entails serious risks. . . . It is far from evident that providing nutrition through a nasogastric tube to a patient for whom it is unwanted is comparable to the typical human ways of feeding those who are hungry (Council 1992: 2230–2231).

In some cases, terminally ill patients voluntarily refuse food or oral fluids. In such cases, patient autonomy must be respected, and forced feeding or aggressive parenteral rehydration should not be employed. Emphasis should be placed on renewed efforts at pain control, sedation, and other comfort care for the associated discomfort (Council 1994a: 96).

American College of Physicians

It is not unethical to discontinue or withhold fluids and nutritional support under certain circumstances. An emerging clinical and judicial position is that enteral and parenteral nutrition and hydration should be likened to other medical interventions and may be withheld or withdrawn according to general principles for decision making outlined above (ACP 1989: 333).

American Thoracic Society

The right to refuse treatment applies equally to withholding therapy that might be offered, such as cardiopulmonary resuscitation (CPR), and to withdrawing therapy that is already under way, such as mechanical ventilation or artificially provided hydration and nutrition. This right is based on the ethical principle of autonomy and self-determination (ATS 1991: 478).

American Nurses Association

Artificial nutrition and hydration should be distinguished from the provision of food and water. . . . The provision of nourishment and hydration by artificial means (i.e., though tubes inserted into the stomach, intestines, or blood vessels) is qualitatively different from merely assisting with feeding. Like all other interventions, artificially provided hydration and nutrition may or may not be justified. . . . As in all other interventions, the anticipated benefits must outweigh the anticipated burdens for the intervention to be justified. . . . In cases where a patient is unable to make his wishes known, or is unable to evaluate the benefits and harms of refusing artificial nutrition and hydration, the decision of a surrogate should be relied upon (ANA 1992: 9).

National Center for State Courts

Artificial nutrition and hydration are forms of medical treatment that should be governed by the same practices and policies that apply to other forms of medical treatment (Hafemeister and Hannaford 1996: 13). . . . Although issues involving artificial nutrition and hydration are often presented more emotionally, from a moral and legal standpoint, they raise the same questions as do other forms of medical treatment (NCSC 1991: 145). . . .

Life-sustaining medical treatment can take many forms, from something as simple as a penicillin pill to something as complex as a respirator, depending upon the patient's circumstances. It is these circumstances that are important in making life-sustaining medical treatment decisions and the potential benefit to the patient, and not labels such as "extraordinary," "ordinary," and "heroic," which are of little value in actually making the life-sustaining treatment decision. Indeed, they tend to confuse the decision making (NCSC 1991: 144).

Uniform Law Commissioners

An agent shall make a "health-care decision" in accordance with the principal individual's instructions, if any, and other wishes to the extent known to the agent (ULC 1993: 5). . . . "Health-care decision" means a decision made by an individual or an individual's agent, guardian, or surrogate, regarding the individual's health care, including . . . directions to provide, withhold, or withdraw artificial nutrition and hydration and all other forms of care (ULC 1993: 3).

New York State Task Force on Life and the Law

Ideally, adults will sign a health care proxy or provide guidance about their wishes. Our laws must also recognize decisions to withhold or withdraw artificial nutrition and hydration for those patients whose wishes cannot be identified or who never were able to formulate their own values or preferences (NYSTFLL 1992: 221).

Alan Meisel

It is a myth that only extraordinary treatment may be foregone but that a patient is obliged to accept ordinary treatment. Physicians may no more compel a patient to accept ordinary treatment than extraordinary treatment, assuming that the difference between them is even meaningful. . . .

Some contend that artificial nutrition and hydration is not a medical treatment at all, and that its termination results in a patient starving to death and constitutes active euthanasia. However, it is largely a myth that stopping tube feeding is legally different from stopping other treatments (Meisel 1991: 1499).

President's Commission Report

Whether care is "ordinary" or "extraordinary" should not determine whether a patient must accept or may decline it. The terms have come to be used in conflicting and confusing ways. . . . [To avoid misunderstanding, public discussion should focus on the underlying reasons for or against a therapy rather than on a simple categorization as "ordinary" or "extraordinary." . . . This line of reasoning suggests that extraordinary treatment is that which, in the patient's view, entails significantly greater burdens than benefits and is therefore undesirable and not obligatory, while ordinary treatment is that which, in the patient's view, produces greater benefits than burdens and is therefore reasonably desirable and undertaken. The claim, then, that the treatment is extraordinary is more of an expression of the conclusion than a justification of it (President's Commission 1983: 88). . . . The Commission has . . . found no particular treatments—including such "ordinary" hospital interventions as parenteral nutrition or hydration, antibiotics, and transfusions—to be universally warranted and thus obligatory for patients to accept (President's Commission 1983: 90).

Hastings Center's Guidelines

Among the most effective and widely used methods of sustaining life are medical procedures for supplying nutrition and hydration by tubes, catheters, or needles inserted into the patient's body. . . . We have concluded that it is wisest and most plausible to understand these methods as medical interventions that may be foregone in some cases. Therefore, the standards to be used for decisions concerning termination of these procedures are essentially those that apply to the termination of other forms of medical treatment. . . . In reaching these conclusions, we have recognized that food and water undeniably have symbolic and psychological importance. They symbolize our caring for and nurturing of one another, and can be a means for the patient to obtain comfort and satisfaction. In certain circumstances, however, the patient experiences more comfort, caring, and satisfaction from foregoing medical procedures for supplying nutrition and hydration, and instead receiving supportive care to keep him or her comfortable (Hastings Center 1987: 59).

Clinical Ethics

The traditional discussions of the ethics of foregoing life-sustaining treatment have turned on certain distinctions, such as . . . ordinary/extraordinary care. . . . Recent study has shown these distinctions to be confused and confusing.

They are little more than summary statements of elaborate, and sometimes faulty arguments, rather than justifications. Unfortunately, these terms are often substituted for careful attention to details and to analytic thinking. We recommend that decisions to forego intervention not be based on invocation of these classic distinctions. In place of these distinctions, the "principle of proportionality" has recently been endorsed by many ethicists. This principle states that a medical treatment is ethically mandatory to the extent that it is likely to confer greater benefits than burdens upon the patient. . . . The principle of proportionality states that no . . . absolute duty exists: Preservation of life is an obligation that binds only when life can be judged more a benefit than a burden by and for the patient (Jonsen, Siegler, and Winslade 1992: 31–33). . . .

In certain cases, it is ethically correct to discontinue artificial nutrients and hydration. The circumstances that justify this decision are: no significant medical goals other than maintenance of organic life is possible, the patient is so mentally incapacitated that no preferences can be expressed now or in the future, and no prior preferences for continued sustenance in such a situation have been expressed (Jonsen, Siegler, and Winslade 1992: 101).

Catholic Health Association

The familiar terms "ordinary" and "extraordinary" can be very misleading when explaining the substance of this teaching. . . . The *Vatican Declaration on Euthanasia* has recognized the ambiguity of these terms and suggests that we might more effectively refer to "proportionate" and "disproportionate" treatment. . . . The moral focus [of the revised distinction] is not on the category of disease, the state of medical science, the type of treatment itself, or whether the treatment is simple, customary, non-invasive, or inexpensive. Rather, the true ethical considerations focus on the proportion between the benefit the patient would be able to appreciate from the treatment and the burden the patient would endure. For this reason, the principle is sometimes referred to as the burden/benefit principle. To make proper use of this moral principle, we need to measure the proportionate benefits and burdens for each particular patient, and from the patient's perspective . . . in order to determine whether [the proposed treatment] provides a benefit proportionate to the burden the patient will have to bear. If the reasonably foreseen benefits to that patient (such as cure, reduced pain, restored consciousness and bodily functions) outweigh the burdens to the patient or to others, then the treatment is morally obligatory. But the treatment is not obligatory if it would be disproportionately burdensome or futile. . . . A treatment is futile when it offers no probable hope of success to restore the patient to a state of reasonable well-being (CHA 1993: 48–49). . . .

The burden/benefit principle makes no moral distinction between withholding or withdrawing life-sustaining treatment (whether it be a mechanical respirator, a cardiac pace-maker, a renal dialysis machine, antibiotics, or medically dispensed nutrition and hydration) when its use is futile or would produce burdens disproportionate to the benefits the patient could appreciate (CHA 1993: 49).

Summary

In sum, there can be little doubt about what is ethically, legally, and medically acceptable regarding the key issues of end-of-life decision making if the writings reviewed here can be taken as generally representative of professional sentiment (and there is every indication that they are). Clearly, the *Fiori* opinions rendered by Judge Leonard Sokolove (in the Bucks County trial court), Judge Phyllis Beck (in the Pennsylvania Superior Court), and Judge Ralph Cappy (in the Pennsylvania Supreme Court) all fall squarely in the mainstream described here. This extraordinarily broad-based consensus—summarized in Table 2.4 and referred to from this point forward as the "consensus position"—appears to provide a firm foundation upon which future public policies can be constructed and private decisions can be made.

At the same time, one might criticize the consensus position for failing to more fully incorporate religious concerns (the CHA being the only religiously oriented group cited). One might also criticize the consensus position as elitist, for the statements reviewed here are largely the product of interdisciplinary teams of highly trained medical, legal, and ethical professionals who, generally speaking, took little explicit accounting of public opinion in formulating their conclusions. As important as the consensus position is, we should not proceed further before addressing its inadequacies in this regard. With that end in mind, Chapter 3 will offer a discussion of the two missing links in the consensus position: religious teachings and public opinion.

TABLE 2.4   The "New Consensus"

Consensus Group	Issue 1[a]	Issue 2[b]	Issue 3[c]	Issue 4[d]	Issue 5[e]
American Medical Association (AMA): Council on Ethical and Judicial Affairs (1990, 1991, 1992, 1994a, 1994b)	Yes	No	No	No	No
American College of Physicians (ACP): *Physicians Ethics Manual* (1989, 1992)	Yes	No	No	No	No
American Thoracic Society (ATS): Bioethics Task Force report (1991)	Yes	No	No	No	No
American Nurses Association (ANA): *Nurse's Role in End of Life Decisions* (1992, 1994)	Yes	No	Not covered	No	No
National Center for State Courts (NCSC): *Guidelines for State Court Decision Making* (1992), and Hafemeister and Hannaford:	Yes	No	No	No	No

(continues)

TABLE 2.4 *(continued)*

Consensus Group	Issue 1[a]	Issue 2[b]	Issue 3[c]	Issue 4[d]	Issue 5[e]
Resolving Disputes Over Life-Sustaining Treatment: A Health Care Provider's Guide (1996)					
Uniform Law Commissioners (ULC): "Uniform Health-Care Decisions Act" (1993)	Yes	No	No	No	No
New York State Task Force on Life and the Law: *When Others Must Choose* (1992)	Yes	No	No	No	No
Allan Meisel, University of Pittsburgh Center for Medical Ethics, *The Right to Die* (1989, 1992)	Yes	No	No	No	No
President's Commission for the Study of Medicine and Bio-medical and Behavioral Research (1983)	Yes	No	No	No	No
The Hastings Center, *Guidelines on the Termination of Life-Sustaining Treatment and Care of the Dying* (1987)	Yes	No	No	No	No
Clinical Ethics: A Practical Approach, 3d ed. (Jonsen, Seigler, and Winslade 1992)	Yes	No	No	No	No
Catholic Health Association (CHA): *Care of the Dying* (1993)	Yes	No	No	No	No

[a]Issue 1: Can members of the family make end-of-life decisions for an incompetent patient based on what the family perceives to be the patient's best interests?

[b]Issue 2: Do caregivers participate in "assisted suicide" when they are involved in (1) the forgoing of life-sustaining treatment, or (2) the provision of pain medication that hastens death as an unintended side effect?

[c]Issue 3: Is there any ethically important distinction between withholding and withdrawing life-sustaining medical treatment?

[d]Issue 4: Must patients be terminally ill before end-of-life treatment decisions can be made?

[e]Issue 5: Must artificially administered food and water always be provided?

Chapter Three

A Broader Consensus

The formulators of the consensus position can rightly be criticized for failing to give explicit, systematic attention to religious sentiments and public opinion in their deliberations. At the same time, in spite of this oversight, the consensus position is very much in line with current views of the religious community, attitudes of the mass public more generally, and sentiments of bedside caregivers in particular.

Religion

Although religious teachings on end-of-life decision making have tended to be overlooked in the secular literature, empirical evidence suggests that one religion in particular—Catholicism—has played a preeminent role in the evolution of end-of-life decision-making policies. The role of the Catholic Church in these questions can be traced to Pope Pius XII who, in 1958, resurrected the long dormant "ordinary-extraordinary" distinction and advised that it be used as something of an acid test in deciding whether it is moral to forgo a particular medical treatment (Pope Pius XII 1958).[1] Thereafter, the pope's distinction was regularly interjected into the mainstream secular discussion of the ethical, medical, and legal aspects of end-of-life decision making (though the pope was not always credited as the source). The Catholic Church—the largest religious denomination in the United States (28 percent of Americans claim to be Catholic)—has been a moral force to reckon with in medical-ethical debates over end-of-life decision making ever since.

The Catholic perspective has served as an important beacon for religious and secular decisionmakers alike since the 1950s, although that influence has waned substantially since the mid-1980s. The weight of Catholic teaching in this area is evidenced by the fact that the President's Commission report, a treatise of over 500 pages and probably the most important and comprehensive document on end-of-life decision making published to date, included one and only one religious position statement: the 1980 Vatican statement on euthanasia (see Sacred Congregation 1980).

In addition, the testimony of Catholic theologians has regularly been solicited by courts or accepted in the form of friend-of-the-court briefs (just as the Pennsylvania Catholic Conference's brief was accepted by the Pennsylvania Supreme Court in the Fiori case). In short, the essentially Catholic ordinary-extraordinary distinction and other essentially Catholic positions on end-of-life decision making have influenced lawyers, judges, physicians, and ethicists for years. To some extent, the ordinary-extraordinary distinction survives to this day, years after the church, together with the courts, ethics groups, and various medical associations, backed away from it as misunderstood and confusing.[2]

Catholic representatives in the state legislatures and state conferences of Catholic bishops have also played an important role in the debate through direct political action. Most notably, Catholic politicians and Catholic Conference lobbyists have successfully worked together in a number of states to slow or stop the development of statutory laws that pertain to the right to die. Catholics have been most influential in states such as New York, Massachusetts, New Jersey, and Pennsylvania, which have a high percentage of Catholics within the population and a high percentage of Catholic politicians in the state legislatures.[3]

The Catholic Church's position on end-of-life decision making, coupled with the positions of other organized religions in the United States, promises to continue shaping the understanding that Americans bring to the bedsides of their sick and dying loved ones. This chapter begins, then, with a review of the current positions of organized religions in the United States regarding end-of-life decision making—the framework Americans are told they can work within when they solicit clerical guidance as death approaches.[4]

Catholic Teachings

Although it would be accurate to characterize the Catholic influence as conservative when it has come to end-of-life decision making, the degree of this conservatism has ebbed substantially over time. Now, most mainstream Catholic organizations have abandoned their obstructionism of years past and joined forces with more progressive elements of the debate, within and outside the church, in an effort to ensure that Catholic teachings remain relevant in the modern world of high-tech medicine and are not entirely swept away with the winds of secular change.

Jesuit theologians are leading the way in this regard, most notably John Paris and Richard A. McCormick,[5] though others have contributed along these lines as well.[6] The Catholic Health Association has also played an important role in moving the church in a more progressive direction.[7] The U.S. Catholic Conference of Bishops and its various state-level affiliates also have moved in the progressive direction in recent years, although this shift has varied from imperceptible to substantial depending on the particular conference.

To be sure, some state conferences remain staunchly conservative (e.g., those in Pennsylvania and New Jersey).[8] But others (such as those in Florida, Minnesota, Oregon, Rhode Island, Texas, and Washington) have assumed a much more liberal approach, consistent with positions taken by the Catholic Health Association and the consensus position itself (see Eastburn and Schaeffer 1994: 26; Paris 1992; McCormick 1992).

The Vatican and the U.S. Conference of Catholic Bishops find themselves between these two poles, closer to the Pennsylvania and New Jersey Catholic Conferences perhaps but moving slowly but surely in the direction of the CHA, Paris and McCormick, and other state conferences. Evidence of this movement can be found in the Vatican's 1980 *Declaration on Euthanasia*, which states that one has no obligation to accept a medical technique

> which is already in use but burdensome. Such a refusal would not be equivalent to suicide, according to this statement. On the contrary, it should be considered as an acceptance of the human condition, or a wish to avoid the application of a medical procedure disproportionate to the results that can be expected, or a desire not to impose excessive expenses on the family or community (Sacred Congregation 1980; reprinted in Wildes, Abel, and Harvey 1992: 223).

This same declaration is also notable for its own critique of the ordinary-extraordinary distinction advanced by Pope Pius XII.[9] In its place, the *Declaration on Euthanasia* suggests the adoption of a "proportionate means–disproportionate means" test that would make it clearly permissible "to refuse forms of treatment that would only secure a precious and burdensome prolongation of life" (Sacred Congregation 1980; reprinted in Wildes, Abel, and Harvey 1992: 223). This is a much more flexible and accommodating approach than might have been expected of the Vatican prior to the 1980s.

The U.S. Conference of Catholic Bishops seems to have softened its position as well. One might reasonably expect a clear, doctrinaire, and staunchly conservative expression of right-to-life principles from the U.S. Conference's Pro-Life Committee (PLC), a group that has charted a staunchly conservative, prolife course with regard to the abortion issue. But even within the PLC, there apparently is a fair amount of ambiguity and room for individuals to maneuver on right-to-die questions. For example, the PLC's eight-page statement on euthanasia and end-of-life decision making opens with the following disclaimer:

Our Catholic tradition has developed a rich body of thought on these questions, which affirms a duty to preserve human life but recognizes limits to that duty. Our first goal in making this statement is to reaffirm some basic principles of our moral tradition. . . . These principles do not provide clear and final answers to all moral questions that arise as individuals make difficult decisions. Catholic theologians may differ on how best to apply moral principles to some questions not explicitly resolved by the church's teaching authority (U.S. Bishops' Pro-Life Committee 1992: 705).

The bishops further soften their position on the second page of the statement: "We are fully aware that such guidance is not necessarily final, because there are many unresolved questions related to these issues and the continuing development of medical technology will necessitate ongoing reflection" (U.S. Bishops' Pro-Life Committee 1992: 706). The statement closes with more along this line:

It is not easy to arrive at a single answer to some of the real and personal dilemmas involved in this issue. In study, prayer and compassion we continue to reflect on this issue and hope to discover additional information that will lead to its ultimate resolution. . . . We . . . offer tentative guidance on how to apply these principles. . . . We recognize that this document is our first word, not our last word, on some of the complex questions involved in this subject (U.S. Bishops' Pro-Life Committee 1992: 711).

There is even more ambiguity in the body of the text. Here, amid a series of statements that reaffirm a strong "sanctity of life" position, the bishops draw directly from the Vatican's document:

In the final stage of dying one is not obliged to prolong the life of a patient by every possible means: "When inevitable death is imminent in spite of the means used, it is permitted in conscience to take the decision to refuse forms of treatment that would only secure a precarious and burdensome prolongation of life, so long as the normal care due to the sick person in similar cases is not interrupted" (U.S. Bishops' Pro-Life Committee 1992: 706).

With regard to artificial nutrition and hydration, the bishops' advice is very much in sync with the consensus position described in Chapter 2 (and very much unlike the more conservative position taken by the Pennsylvania Catholic Conference) (see Note 7 in this chapter):

Although the shortening of the patient's life is one foreseeable result of an omission (of artificially provided food and fluids), the real purpose of the omission was to relieve the patient of a particular procedure that was of limited usefulness to the patient or unreasonably burdensome for the patient and the patient's family or caregivers. This kind of decision should not be equated with a decision to kill or with suicide . . . sometimes even food and fluids are no longer effective in providing this benefit [sustaining life] because the patient has entered the final stage of a terminal condition. At such times we should make the dying person as comfortable as possible and provide nursing care and proper hygiene as well as companionship and appropriate spiritual aid. . . . Initiating medically assisted feeding or intravenous fluids in this case may increase the patient's discomfort while providing no real benefit. . . . A person may legitimately refuse even procedures that effectively prolong life if he or she believes they would impose excessively grave burdens on himself or herself, or on his or her family and community. Burdens might be physical pain, psychological pain (damage to the patient's self image), and even burdens associated with financial concerns (familial or societal) (U.S. Bishops' Pro-Life Committee 1992: 707–708).

In the words of Richard Doerflinger, a spokesperson for the National Conference of Catholic Bishops: "It can be good medicine and good morality to forego artificial feeding when it can only impose addition burdens on a patient who is imminently dying from a progressive terminal illness" ("Study Backs" 1994). This puts the U.S. conference well on its way toward reconciling its position with that of progressive state conferences, many Catholic theologians, and the Catholic Health Association, which advances the following position:

We need not cling fearfully to life as the last thing we possess. . . . While a struggle for health can be meaningful, a struggle against death at all costs—an effort that becomes a torment—is nonsense (CHA 1993: VII). . . . We have all heard reports of hopelessly ill patients who lie tethered by tubes to machines employed beyond the point of being beneficial. The machines merely prolong dying. This behavior is prompted, in part, by the mistaken moral conviction that human beings have an obligation to use whatever treatments and technologies are available to prolong physical existence (CHA 1993: XIII). . . . All those involved, caregivers and patient, should humbly accept the inherent limitation of the human condition. When this moment arrives, it is also time to begin celebrating the life which is coming to its completion (CHA 1993: 49).

Other Religious Positions

The Catholic Church is exceptional because of its vocal, long-standing involvement in the right-to-die debate at the level of both clinical specifics and theological generalities. In addition and unlike the other denominations, the Catholic Church has a sprawling complex of health care institutions that bring the church into contact with clinical realities and real-life moral dilemmas on a regular basis. The church also has a web of politically active state conferences that regularly issue specific statements on medical ethics for general consumption. In addition, the conferences lobby on specific legislative provisions in the state and federal capitols.

In recent years, other denominations have begun to emulate the Catholic Church by issuing statements of their own on the ethics of end-of-life decision making. Although their pronouncements have tended to be general statements of principle and have garnered much less popular attention, they do inform us about broader trends in the religious community—trends that will probably disturb those concerned primarily with the "sanctity of life" position and assuage those more concerned with the principles of "patient self-determination" and "death with dignity."

Baptists

The American Baptist Church, which counts 20 percent of the U.S. population among its followers, is second only to the Catholic Church in size. The Baptist Church does not issue general statements of social principles as a rule, however. Unlike the relatively hierarchical Catholics, Baptists have no overarching, governing framework that presumes to represent the rank-and-file churches of the Baptist persuasion. Not only are the Baptists split into several associations, each church within each association is also considered an independent piece of the whole (Urofsky 1994: 25). Consequently, it sometimes seems that there are as many answers to end-of-life decision-making questions as there are Baptist churches and Baptist clerics.

Nonetheless, one statement, issued in the *Social Principles* booklet published by the General Association of General Baptists, gives some general indication about the predisposition of Baptists: "We believe life and death belong in the hands of God. . . . We oppose euthanasia, sometimes referred to as mercy killing. . . . We affirm the right of every person to die with dignity. We reject efforts made to prolong terminal illnesses merely because the technology is available to do so" (cited in Urofsky 1994: 25).

One should not put too much stock in such a statement, given the plurality of sentiment represented in the Baptist fold. At the same time, this pronouncement does suggest that at least some Baptists would be sympathetic to the consensus position discussed in Chapter 2.

United Methodist Church

One in every ten Americans is a Methodist, and statements drawn from the United Methodists Church's (UMC's) *Book of Resolutions* indicate that end-of-life decision-making guidance for this 10 percent of the population probably falls well within the boundaries of the mainstream consensus position. This is particularly true with regard to the "benefits-and-burdens"— or "proportionality"—approach advocated by the Catholic Church and supported by the consensus position, both of which promote judicious (but not judicial) application of the best interests standard.

For example, according to the UMC, "Christian theological and ethical reflection shows that the obligations to use life-sustaining treatments cease when the physical, emotional, financial, or social burdens exceed the benefits for the dying patients and the care givers" (United Methodist Church 1992: 14). The UMC resolution argues that

> when a person is dying and medical intervention can at best prolong a minimal level of life at great cost to human dignity, the objective of medical care should be to give comfort and maximize the individual's capacity for awareness, feeling, and relationships with others. In some cases of patients who are without any doubt in an irreversibly comatose state, where cognitive functions and conscious relationships are no longer possible, decisions to withhold or withdraw mechanical devices which continue respiration and circulation may justly be made by family members and guardians, physicians, hospital ethics committees, and chaplains (United Methodist Church 1992: 14).

Lutheran Church

Six percent of Americans claim the Lutheran religion as their own. To grasp the Lutheran approach to end-of-life decision making, one might look first to the Evangelical Lutheran Church in America, the organization that has been most vocal on these issues. The Evangelical Lutheran Church filed a friend-of-the-court brief with the U.S. Supreme Court in the case of Nancy Cruzan, on behalf of the Cruzan family.[10] The brief criticized the Missouri courts' decisions rejecting the Cruzan family's request to remove life-sustaining treatment from their daughter. The church reasoned that the courts' actions "sever family ties . . . substituting the moral and religious judgment of the state for that of the person" (Gibbs 1990: 68). More to the point, according to its "Message on End-of-Life Decisions," the Evangelical Lutheran Church holds that

> food and water are part of basic human care. Artificially-administered nutrition and hydration move beyond basic care to become medical treatment. Health care professionals are not required to use all available medical treatment in all circumstances. Medical treatment may be limited in some instances, and death allowed to occur. Patients have a right to refuse unduly burdensome treatments which are disproportionate to the expected benefits. When medical judgment determines that artificially-administered nutrition and hydration will not contribute to an improvement in the patient's underlying condition or prevent death from that condition, patients or their legal spokespersons may consider them unduly burdensome treatment. In these circumstances it may be morally responsible to withhold or withdraw them and allow death to occur. This decision should not be taken to mean that family and friends are abandoning their loved one (Evangelical Lutheran Church 1992: 3).

Episcopal Church

The Episcopal Church, the religious home of 2 percent of Americans, has also spoken out clearly in terms that locate it well within the mainstream consensus described in the previous chapter. According to its 1991 statement "Life-Sustaining Treatment," Episcopal teaching holds that

> although Human life is sacred, death is part of the earthly cycle of life. . . . It is morally wrong and unacceptable to take human life in order to relieve the suffering caused by incurable illness. . . . However, there is no moral obligation to prolong the act of dying by extraordinary means and at all costs if such a dying person is ill and has no reasonable expectation of recovery. . . . The decision to withdraw life-sustaining treatment should ultimately rest with the patient, or with the patient's surrogate decision-maker in the case of a mentally incapacitated patient. We therefore express our deep conviction that any proposed legislation on the part of the national or state governments regarding the so-called "right to die" issues (a) must take special care to see that the individual's rights are respected . . . , and (b) must also provide expressly for the withholding or withdrawing of life-sustaining treatment. . . . Palliative treatment to relieve the pain of persons with progressive incurable illness, even if done with the knowledge that a hastened death may result, is consistent with theological tenets regarding the sanctity of life (Episcopal Church 1991).

United Church of Christ

The 2 percent of Americans who are affiliated with the United Church of Christ (UCC) are given general guidance on end-of-life decision making in the proceedings of the UCC's eighteenth general synod. This guidance is similar in many respects to the statements issued by other churches in the United States:

> We affirm individual freedom and responsibility to make choices in these matters. It is not claimed that euthanasia is the Christian position, but that the right to choose is a legitimate Christian decision. It is contended that governmental powers and entrenched custom have made life and death decisions, closing off options which more properly belong to individuals and families. . . . When illness takes away those abilities we associate with full personhood, leaving one so impaired that what is most valuable and precious is gone, we may feel that the mere continuance of the body by machines or drugs is a violation of the person. . . . Therefore, be it resolved, the Eighteenth General Synod supports the rights of individuals, their designees and their families to make decisions regarding human death and dying. Be it further resolved, the Eighteenth General Synod affirms the right of individuals to die with dignity and not have their lives unnecessarily prolonged by extraordinary measures if so chosen (United Church of Christ 1991).

Two central themes emerge from this review of religious positions. First, it is evident that these religions are sympathetic to the struggles and ambiguity that surround end-of-life decision making. Yet none of these religious bodies offer direct, doctrinaire guidance on what treatments can be withheld or withdrawn under what specific circumstances. Aside from the admonition to care for and respect the patient, which is common to all the statements, there is very little in the way of specific guidance in these pronouncements. Rather, it seems that clerics are saying that decisions about terminating treatment, including decisions about forgoing food and fluids (even when death is not imminent), can and should be left up to individuals acting in good faith.

Second, none of these statements support active euthanasia, and they do not confuse euthanasia with the decision to forgo life-sustaining treatment. In both these ways, the emerging religious consensus on end-of-life decision making appears to mirror quite closely the consensus position charted in Chapter 2.

Public Opinion

A wealth of survey data, largely collected in the early 1990s (when the case of Nancy Cruzan was prominent in the national news), suggests that the relatively progressive positions on end-of-life decisions expressed by religious bodies and adopted by mainstream medical, ethical, and legal thinkers resonate well with the sentiments of the general public. Moreover, this resonance appears to persist across a broad range of demographic subgroups.

For example, in one 1990 Gallup poll, 84 percent of the respondents indicated they would like life-sustaining treatment withheld if they "were on life support systems and there was no hope of recovering" (Lindgren 1993: 233). It is significant that this high level of support holds up well even when groups are broken down by age, education level, income level, gender, religion, region of the country, political affiliation, and ideology (see Table 3.1). In fact, the only distinguishing characteristic seems to be race: Fewer blacks and other nonwhites favor the withdrawal of treatment as compared to whites (64, 71, and 87 percent, respectively).[11]

Even though a relatively low percentage of nonwhite respondents said they would like life-sustaining medical treatment withheld, there was still strong support among nonwhite respondents for the withdrawal of treatment at the end of life. Meanwhile, none of the other twenty-seven subgroups of respondents in any of the other eight demographic categories fell below the 78 percent mark when it came to expressing the desire to have life-sustaining treatment withdrawn when there is no hope of recovery.

The survey questions in this Gallup poll might be criticized for being too vague regarding what specific treatments the public would prefer to forgo. This is a potentially valid critique, but it cannot be sustained since other survey research indicates that there is also strong support among nursing home residents, physicians, and the general public for withdrawing *specific* treatments, including feeding tubes, when one is dying or permanently unconscious. Table 3.2 summarizes some of these findings.

TABLE 3.1   Preferences for Withholding Treatment, by Demographic Group

Question: If you, yourself, were on life support systems and there was no hope of recovering, would you like to remain on life support systems or would you like treatment withheld so that you could end your life? [Numbers refer to the percentages of people who said they would like treatment withheld.]

Age	18–29	30–49	50 or older	
	85	84	82	
Education	less than high school	high school graduate	some college	college graduate
	82	86	83	82
Income	under $20,000	$20,000 to $29,000	$30,000 to $49,000	over $50,000
	83	83	86	86
Gender	Male	Female		
	82	85		
Race	White	Black	Other	
	87	64	71	
Religion	Catholic	Protestant	Jewish	None
	85	84	91	80
Region	East	Midwest	South	West
	78	87	83	88
Party Identification	Democrat	Independent	Republican	
	82	86	84	
Ideology	Liberal	Moderate	Conservative	
	86	91	84	

SOURCE: Selections from Gallup poll, 1990, cited in Lindgren 1993: 233–234.

As the table reveals, the desire to refuse artificial feeding varies somewhat from poll to poll. It appears to be weakest among nursing home residents (68 percent) and strongest among the group that is presumably most knowledgeable about the costs and benefits of tube-feeding therapy in cases of serious and irreversible illness: physicians (92 percent). Overall, it is obvious that whatever relatively minor differences exist among polls regarding the refusal of tube feeding and other life-sustaining treatments, there is strong, broadly based support for the option of forgoing treatment.

Table 3.3 provides an even more detailed look at patient preferences. This table summarizes the results of a study of 507 individuals (405 hospital outpatients and 102 members of the general public) in which six specific therapies (antibiotics, IV fluids, ANH, kidney dialysis, mechanical respiration, and CPR) were described. Overwhelming majorities of respondents

TABLE 3.2   Attitudes About Refusing Life-Sustaining Treatment for Oneself

Survey Population	Hypothetical Condition[a]	Treatment That Could Sustain Life[a]	% Who Would Refuse Treatment	Source and Date of Poll
Nursing home residents	About to die of natural causes	Drugs, fluids, food by tubes, breathing machines, heart massage	68	Diamond et al. 1989
Physicians	Permanent unconscious-ness in a PVS	Artificial feedings	92	Brunetti, Carperos, and Westlund 1989
General public	Terminally ill or in an irreversible coma	Life support systems, including food and water	73	Gallup 1990
General public	Coma with no brain activity	Feeding tube	85	CBS News— *New York Times* 1990
General public	On life support systems, no hope of recovery	Life support systems	84	Gallup 1990
General public	In a coma with no hope of recovery, suffering no pain	Life-sustaining treatment	75	KRC Communi-cations/ Research 1991

[a]Language in these columns is extracted exactly as stated in the survey question.
SOURCE: Data summarized and cited in Lindgren 1993:231–232, 254.

indicated that, if they were in a persistent vegetative state, they would pre-fer to refuse each of the six proposed treatments even though each of these treatments would tend to prolong life. Only one respondent in six said he or she would want antibiotics, and only one in ten would opt for CPR. Ar-tificial nutrition, kidney dialysis, and mechanical respiration would be flatly refused by four out of five respondents.

Table 3.4 summarizes the results of eight different surveys regarding atti-tudes about what rights others should enjoy in making end-of-life medical treatment decisions. Once again, the level of support for individual auton-omy and the right to forgo life-sustaining treatment was quite high across the board. In all cases, more than 70 percent of the population appeared to

TABLE 3.3   Choices Regarding the Use of Life-Sustaining Treatments, If in a PVS

Proposed Treatment	% Who Would Want This Treatment If in a PVS[a]	% Who Would Want a Trial of This Treatment If in a PVS	% Undecided	% Who Would Not Want This Treatment If in a PVS
Antibiotics	16	[b]	8	76
Intravenous (IV) fluids	9	7	7	77
Artificial nutrition	8	5	7	80
Kidney dialysis	8	6	6	80
Mechanical respiration	7	6	7	80
CPR	10	[b]	7	83

[a]Respondents were 405 outpatients of 30 primary care physicians at Massachusetts General Hospital and a cohort group of 102 members of the general public from the Boston area.

[b]A trial of treatment was not an option in this case.

SOURCE: Data summarized and cited in Emanuel et al. 1991: 893.

support the right of others to make medical treatment decisions for themselves at the end of life. This was true even in the four surveys in which *food and water* or *feeding tubes* were mentioned as the kinds of treatments that others might elect to forgo. In fact, the average percentage of those saying that others should have the right to refuse treatment was 77 percent in the four surveys in which food was mentioned and about 82 percent in the four surveys in which food was not specifically referenced. Even if this difference of 5 percentage points is statistically significant, a margin this small hardly seems substantively important.

Who should make end-of-life decisions? Most polls suggest that there is overwhelming support for advance directives among the general public. For example, Linda Emanuel, Michael Barry, John Stoeckle, Lucy Ettelson, and Ezekiel Emanuel (1991: 889) found that some form of advance directive was desired by 89 percent of those surveyed.[12] If no advance directive has been executed (and the evidence suggests that in four out of five cases, none has), then the overwhelming majority of Americans appear to prefer that families be centrally involved in making the final determinations regarding life-sustaining medical treatment (see Table 3.5; also see Cohen-Mansfield et al. 1991: 290).

Two nearly identical studies were conducted in 1991, one by KRC Communications and one by the *Boston Globe* (in conjunction with the Har-

TABLE 3.4   Attitudes About the Rights of Others to Refuse Life-Sustaining
Treatment

Condition	Treatments That Others Might Choose to Refuse	% of Respondents Favoring the Right of Others to Refuse Treatment	Source and Date of Poll
Terminally ill	Life-sustaining medical treatment	81	Gallup 1985
Hopelessly ill or irreversibly comatose	Life-support systems, including food and water	73	Kane, Parsons, and Associates 1986
Hopelessly ill or irreversibly comatose	Life-support systems, including food and water	78	Gallup 1990
Terminally ill	Life-sustaining medical treatment	86	*Los Angeles Times* 1989
Terminally ill	Life-sustaining medical treatment	89	*Los Angeles Times* 1990
In a coma with no brain activity	Feeding tube	81	CBS–*New York Times* 1990
Terminal disease	Medical treatment	71	Princeton Survey Research Associates 1990
Hopelessly ill or irreversibly comatose	Life-support systems, including food and water	76	KRC Communications 1991

SOURCE: Data summarized and cited in Lindgren 1993: 237, 240–246.

vard University School of Public Health). Both sets of researchers found the same proportion of respondents—30 percent—wanted families alone to be the decisionmakers; 53 percent of the respondents in each study said these decisions should be made by families in conjunction with doctors. Combining these two categories yields a total of 83 percent of respondents who preferred that families be involved in the decision-making process. The KRC survey, which provided more options for respondents to choose from, indicated only minimal interest in having doctors or the courts act unilaterally (3 percent in each case) and no interest at all in having hospital administrators serve as decisionmakers.[13]

Table 3.5 shows that the overwhelming majority of Americans hope families will be involved in end-of-life decision making, usually in collaboration

TABLE 3.5   Attitudes About Who Should Be Permitted to Make End-of-Life Decisions[a]

Family Members Alone	Family Members and Doctors	Doctors Alone	Hospital Personnel	Courts	Legislatures	Source and Year
b	80[b]	b	b	7	2	Yankelovich, Clancy, and Shulman 1986
b	85	b	b	b	b	Yankelovich, Clancy, and Shulman 1986
88	b	8	b	1	0	National Law Journal 1990
30	53	3	0	3	b	KRC Communications 1991
30	53	b	b	b	b	Boston Globe–Harvard University 1991

[a]Numbers in the table represent the percentages of respondents who agreed that the category of individuals identified at the top of the chart should be the primary decisionmakers regarding life-sustaining medical treatment.

[b]Indicates that no data were reported for that category of response or that the response category was not available as an option respondents could choose.

SOURCE: Yankelovich and KRC studies are summarized and cited in Lindgren 1993; the *Boston Globe*–Harvard survey is cited in Kavolius and Fade 1995: 9; the *National Law Journal* study is cited in Coyle 1990: 1.

with physicians. Meanwhile, there is little support for any other category of potential decisionmakers (e.g., doctors alone, hospital administrators, judges, or legislators).

In sum, then, the consensus position advanced by medical, legal, and ethical groups and tacitly endorsed by religious groups is by and large supported by the public. All are in general agreement on the key points. First, individuals should have the right to make end-of-life decisions for themselves. Second, members of the patient's family should help make end-of-life decisions when an individual has become incompetent and has left no instructions about life-sustaining treatment. And third, it is entirely acceptable and, from the public's perspective, perhaps even desirable to forgo life-sustaining medical treatment, including ANH (and antibiotics, for that matter, according to the 1991 study by Emanuel et al.), when the end of life is near or when one's ability to enjoy conscious life becomes irreversibly compromised.

Physicians

Many physicians may not be particularly well versed on the current consensus group positions on end-of-life decision making (a point discussed in greater detail at the end of this chapter). Yet their attitudes and behaviors suggest that doctors at the bedside are moving in the same direction that consensus groups, religious associations, and public opinion polls seem to be headed. As such, physicians must be considered part of the quiet, grassroots movement that promises, like public opinion, to legitimate the consensus position from the bottom up over time.

It has become almost a cliché to suggest that physicians tend to overtreat their patients, even (and perhaps especially) at the end of life. Whatever the accuracy of this characterization, it tends to mask a significant shift in attitudes among rank-and-file physicians since the early 1970s regarding the use of tube feeding, mechanical respiration, and cardiopulmonary resuscitation. Advances in medical technology have made it possible to extend life, to be sure. But increasingly, physicians have become aware that extending life sometimes carries a great cost in terms of medical resources, patient suffering, and patient autonomy. As a result, doctors are now warming to the idea of waiving life-sustaining treatment—an idea that may have been rejected as profoundly unethical just a few short decades ago. Dr. Charles Sprung (1990: 2211) summarizes the situation precisely:

> Only 30 years ago, it was believed a physician "must do everything" for a patient. This theory was in concert with the western ethical system, which provided for the infinite worth of a human being. The primary goal of medical practice was to prevent death at all costs. . . . [Today,] physicians are forced to make extremely difficult decisions in allocating society's scarce health care resources. They have to decide who shall live when not all can live.

Physicians are making these decisions with increased sensitivity to the consensus position notion that, though comfort care is always mandatory, one is not obliged to do everything medically possible for those patients for whom meaningful life is at an end. They have also turned to the family members of patients to help them make these difficult decisions. Again, physicians seem to be acting in accordance with the consensus position, even if they are doing so unwittingly.

Withholding and Withdrawing Treatment

One example of this transformation in medical ethics occurred over the course of just one decade. In the beginning of the 1980s, the removal of artificially provided food and fluids "was considered a gross deviation from legal and ethical standards" (Sprung 1990: 2213). By the end of the decade, however, research demonstrated that between 85 and 90 percent of critical care professionals were withholding and withdrawing this and other kinds of life-sustaining medical treatment from patients suffering from irreversible disease (Sprung 1990: 2213; also see Faber-Langendoen and Bartels 1992; Smedira et al. 1990). By the mid-1990s, a national survey of 879 physicians practicing in adult intensive care units revealed that 96 percent of them had either withheld or withdrawn life-sustaining treatment with the expectation that the patient would die as a result, and most reported doing so "frequently" during the course of the preceding year (Asch, Hansen-Flaschen, and Lanken 1995: 288).

Obviously, the withholding and withdrawing of treatment from patients—once a fringe exercise of questionable ethics—has become a fully accepted aspect of critical care medicine in U.S. hospitals today. The same kind of transformation may have taken place in the specialty of geriatrics. According to Dr. Leo Cooney (cited in Nuland 1994: 71),

> Most geriatricians are at the forefront of those who believe in withholding vigorous interventions designed simply to prolong life. It is geriatricians who are constantly challenging nephrologists [kidney specialists] who dialyze very old people, pulmonologists [lung specialists] who intubate people with no quality of life, and even surgeons who seem unable to withhold their scalpels from patients for whom peritonitis would be a merciful mode of death.[14]

Researchers also report relatively high levels of anxiety in the physician population regarding the issue of overtreatment. In one study of 687 physicians and 759 nurses, conducted by a team of researchers led by Mildred Solomon (Solomon et al. 1993: 17), only 12 percent of the caregivers agreed with the statement "sometimes I feel we give up on patients too soon," but over half (55 percent) agreed that "sometimes I feel the treatments I offer my patients are overly burdensome." Nearly that many respondents—47 percent—said that they acted against their conscience in

BOX 3.1   The Hippocratic Oath

One might wonder how physicians can reconcile their increasingly common predisposition to forgo potentially life-sustaining medical treatment in light of the Hippocratic oath's "do no harm" principle. The answer is that this time-honored pledge is beginning to be reinterpreted more broadly in the context of current medical realities. There was a time in the not-too-distant past when the do no harm principle was simply understood to most to mean "do nothing that will allow death to occur." Today, many are beginning to interpret do no harm in more flexible, patient-centered terms, to mean "do nothing that is not in the best interests of the patient."

At its core, writes Sherwin Nuland (1994: 246), "the Hippocratic philosophy of medicine declares that nothing should be more important to the physician than the best interests of the patient who comes to him for care." The Hastings Center, in its text on clinical guidelines (1994: 9), makes much the same point, arguing that the norms of medical practice from their Hippocratic origins (for both physicians and nurses) have rested on the duty to act in the best interest of the patient. "Maintaining biological function may not be identical with acting in the best interests of the patient. Technological capacities . . . may create seemingly irresistible imperatives to go ahead and use treatment" in ways that subvert or overlook the best interests of the patient (Hastings Center 1994: 9).

Attention to the best interests of the patient allows physicians the opportunity to weigh the do no harm part of the Hippocratic oath with another tenet from Corpus Hippocratum, one that directs that physicians "refuse to treat those who are overmastered by their disease, realizing that in such cases, medicine is powerless" (cited in President's Commission 1983: 15–16).

providing care to the terminally ill. Sixty-seven percent thought that mechanical ventilation was used inappropriately at times for critically and terminally ill patients. Almost as many, 64 percent, thought CPR was overused, and 54 percent thought the same was true for ANH.

These data suggest that physicians no longer subscribe to the notion that continued aggressive treatment is a good thing, by definition, in all cases. Rather, the behavioral data cited in studies led by Asch (Asch, Hansen-Flaschen, and Lanken 1995), Faber-Langendoen and Bartels (1992), Sprung (1990), and Smedira (Smedira et al. 1990) suggest that significant portions of the physician population have begun to move beyond a simplistic reading of the Hippocratic oath's "do no harm" pledge and now consider withholding or withdrawing treatment to be acceptable and maybe even desirable in cases of hopeless illness (see Box 3.1).

Providing Patients and Surrogates with Options

The management of death, in which physicians, patients, and surrogates collaborate on a decision to forgo potentially life-prolonging procedures, has become a fact of life in U.S. hospitals and nursing homes today. The American Hospital Association (AHA) estimates that four out of five hospital deaths result from conscious and open decisions to withhold or withdraw some potentially life-sustaining medical treatment (Meier 1994: 14). Increasingly, physicians are operating in an environment where they and their patients decide to limit treatments that may have been provided as a matter of course in years past.

Perhaps the most often refused treatment is cardiopulmonary resuscitation. Cardiac arrest happens, at some point, in everyone's death. But several decades of experience with the techniques and outcomes of CPR suggest that for many patients (e.g., the elderly, the frail, and the seriously ill), attempts at resuscitation are painful, wrenching exercises in futility. The "do not resuscitate" (DNR) order was introduced in the 1970s with this reality in mind, as a way to give patients the option of forgoing resuscitation efforts when, in their own minds (or in the minds of their surrogates), CPR would not be worth the effort.[15] Today, no attempt is made to resuscitate approximately 75 percent of hospital heart attack patients because these patients have DNR orders written on their charts (Lindgren 1993: 186).[16]

The withholding of treatment extends well beyond CPR, however. Terri Fried and Muriel Gillick (1994: 304–305) found that diagnostic tests (such as barium X rays, ultrasounds, and biopsies) were refused by patients 40 percent of the time in the last six months of life and 89 percent of the time during a patient's final illness. Hospitalization for surgery (rejected 29 percent of the time) and nonsurgery hospitalizations (e.g., for pneumonia, congestive heart failure, kidney failure) were rejected 22 percent of the time overall. Ultimately, not only did 89 percent of the home care patients (or their proxy decisionmakers) in this study reject potentially life-prolonging treatment during their final illness but a substantial minority of them (40 percent) also chose to reject treatment well *before* their final illnesses.

Family Members as Surrogates

Most individuals who die become incompetent to make medical treatment decisions for some period of time,[17] and even though there are usually no advance directives to guide decision making, decisions about life-sustaining medical treatment must be made. The medical management of death is a reality in the United States today. The only real questions that remain are: Who will do the managing, and how will it be done?

The need for surrogate decision making is especially prevalent in nursing homes. One study indicated that 58 percent of the 2 million nursing home residents in the United States were suffering from mental disorders (mostly dementia) (Eckholm 1990). Another study involving 170 New York nursing homes found that the decision-making capacity of 73 percent of the patients was somehow compromised. Nearly half of all residents (47 percent) were completely incapable of making decisions about their own medical care even though only 2 percent of the residents had "officially" been declared incompetent to make decisions about their care in judicial proceedings (Miller and Cugliari 1990: 464).

From a technically legal standpoint, a person is presumed competent to make decisions until a court declares otherwise and appoints a guardian (OTA 1988: 172). But legal competency proceedings are rarely initiated for medical reasons. Instead, according to Kapp and Lo (cited in OTA 1987b: 72),

> if an elderly person is deemed incompetent by caregivers, they usually turn to family members to make decisions on behalf of the patient. It is not clear why clinical practice so diverges from legal standards. Physicians may be ignorant about the precise legal definition of competency or may regard legal proceedings as too cumbersome and time consuming, with insufficient benefit to justify the cost. . . . Furthermore, families resist going through the trial, trauma, and expense of competency proceedings, especially when there are no fundamental disagreements between family and staff regarding the status of the patient's decisionmaking capability and the proposed treatment plan.[18]

The point here is that physicians, who are finding they can keep patients alive well past the point of competence, are increasingly turning to family members to act as decisionmakers, without the help of the courts. This behavior is very much in line with the consensus position on surrogate decision making, the position of mainstream religious organizations in the United States, and the will of the American public.

Cracks in the Consensus

The consensus-building process that has progressed deliberately among professional health care organizations, legal experts, and ethicists appears to be very much in sync with the looser, more ad hoc evolution toward consensus that has developed among religious organizations, frontline physicians, and the general public. Yet everyone seems to be in concordance on all the key issues associated with end-of-life decision making:

1. Surrogates can withhold or withdraw treatment for patients using the substituted judgment standard or, failing that, a best interests analysis;
2. Forgoing treatment is ethically distinct from suicide, assisted suicide, and euthanasia;
3. There is no ethically, medically, or morally important distinction between withholding and withdrawing life-sustaining medical treatment;

4. Treatment my be withheld from patients who are seriously ill (e.g., those who are persistently vegetative), even though these patients are technically not considered to be "terminal";

5. Artificial nutrition and hydration is a medical procedure that can be withheld or withdrawn like any other.

Arguments of the Pennsylvania attorney general to the contrary, the consensus on these five basic points is stable, broad-based, and deeply seated in the cultural and professional fabric of modern American society. Medical associations and physicians, ethics specialists, experts in the field of law, religious organizations, and the vast majority of the general public are all parties to the consensus. Given this broad agreement, one might well wonder what possible controversy exists. If most individuals and groups agree on the critical principles of end-of-life decision making, then why does the process not go more smoothly for people like Rosemarie Sherman?

The answer is that there are significant cracks in the consensus at several important locations. First, there is the attitude-behavior dichotomy within the general public. The overwhelming majority of Americans claim to be interested in advance directives, yet most never act on those convictions. Moreover, although many people say that life-sustaining medical treatment is generally undesirable in cases of terminal illness, family members often ask that everything possible be done for their dying loved ones when death is near.[19] The difference between attitude and behavior in these instances is symptomatic of the more general problem Americans have in dealing with death.

The second crack in the consensus is created by the doctors themselves. Physicians may continue to overtreat, even though they would prefer to pull the plug. Concerns about legal liability are often at the root of this behavior, but other motivations exist as well.[20]

The third crack in the consensus involves the conservative judges (e.g., in New York and Missouri), conservative Catholic Conferences (e.g., in Pennsylvania, New Jersey, New York, and Massachusetts), and prolife attorneys general (e.g., in Pennsylvania, with the Fiori case). There are also conservative state legislatures to consider in Missouri, North Dakota, and other states where at least a portion of the consensus position is rendered illegal by statute. Sometimes and maybe frequently, these policy outliers receive more attention than those supporting the mainstream sentiment, leading the general public and clinical practitioners to be overly cautious because they overestimate the degree to which controversy exists on right-to-die issues.

Fourth and finally, some institutions—usually for religious reasons—refuse to honor decisions made according to the consensus position. No discussion of consensus would be complete without some elaboration on these significant elements of dissent.

Public Recalcitrance

Although the overwhelming majority of Americans think advance directives are a good idea and should be honored, only a small minority actually follow up on this sentiment and complete advance directives for themselves. Table 3.6 illustrates this dichotomy between thought and action.

Linda Emanuel and her colleagues (Emanuel et al. 1991: 892) identified a number of reasons for this discrepancy between belief and action in regard to advance directives. The most common reason given by respondents from the general public was that advance directives were thought to be relevant only to the sick or the old (32 percent). The most common reason cited by patients was that they were waiting for physicians to initiate a discussion about advance directives, a discussion that never occurred (29 percent). Twenty-four percent of the patients said they thought that advanced directives were only relevant for those sicker or older than they, and another 14 percent said they just never thought to raise the topic (Emanuel et al. 1991: 891–892). These individuals may think about death regularly, just as 65 percent of Americans do generally (Shapiro 1992: 42), but they apparently are not giving much thought to how they will handle death when it draws near.

Although completing advance directives may be a useful exercise, it is not necessary to complete a legal document to have control over end-of-life decision making should one become incompetent. Most states would honor fairly broad statements made by an individual about what he or she would want at the end of life. And apparently all states would honor an individual's oral directions about how end-of-life decisions should be made, as long as those statements clearly and convincingly express what should be done.

Even here, however, patients seem loath to act on their convictions. One study of 103 nursing home residents found that 90 percent of those interviewed would like a close relative to make decisions for them about life-sustaining treatment should they become incompetent (Cohen-Mansfield et al. 1991: 290). But only 40 percent of the group had discussed their feelings about their future medical care with anyone (Cohen-Mansfield et al. 1991: 291), and only 25 percent had executed a durable power of attorney for health care to ensure that their choice of surrogate would be honored.

For whatever reason, Americans seem profoundly reluctant to act on their stated beliefs about end-of-life decision making. And when individuals do not complete advance directives or even discuss their desires with members of their families, the burden of making decisions falls to surrogates (after the designation of a surrogate or surrogates has been sorted out). These individuals must then divine the proper course of action through an exercise in substituted judgment or a determination of the patient's best interests.

TABLE 3.6   Attitude Versus Behavior Regarding Advance Directives

% Who Think Advance Directives Are a Good Idea	% Who Actually Complete an Advance Directive	Study Source and Date	Citation
68	[a]	Lou Harris 1982	Lindgren 1993: 239
84	[a]	Lou Harris 1987	Lindgren 1993: 241
[a]	9	Steiber 1987	Emanuel et al. 1991
[a]	20	Gallup 1990	Lindgren 1993: 251
93	16	Emanuel et al. 1991	Emanuel et al. 1991
70	15	Hare and Nelson 1991	Hare and Nelson 1991
89	18	Emanuel et al. 1991	Emanuel et al. 1991
81	24	KRC Communications 1991	Lindgren 1993: 250
[a]	17	ABC News– Washington Post 1991	Lindgren 1993: 250
70	15	Hare, Pratt, and Nelson 1992	Hare, Pratt, and Nelson 1992
[a]	10 to 25[b]	poll data uncited	U.S. GAO 1995b
79%[c]	17%[c]		

[a]No data reported.

[b]Since the GAO published a range here, these data are not included in calculating averages.

[c]This number is an average figure.

When Americans fail to execute advance directives and/or fail to discuss their treatment preferences with loved ones, they force the action into an arena where doubts persist about what should be done. And when individuals fail to exercise their right to guide future decision making by making advance directives or having explicit family conversations about end-of-life decisions, there is always a possibility that a judge, a statute, or a caregiver will step into the breach and force continued life on one who would prefer that nature take its course.

Physician Recalcitrance

Members of the lay public are not alone in their inability to act with the courage of their convictions. Physicians often find themselves in the same predicament, albeit for different reasons. A portion of the physician's reluctance to let mortally ill patients die can be attributed to a failure of understanding; most of the rest can be attributed to a fear of liability.

According to Alan Meisel (1991: 1497), "The practice of medicine requires more than a competence of medical technique and procedures. At least a passing knowledge of the law and medical ethics is required, especially when it comes to the care of dying patients." Unfortunately, this knowledge is sometimes lacking. As the New York State Task Force on Life and the Law (1992: 11) noted, "Studies and experience have shown that health care professionals are often ill-informed about the law on treatment decisions as it applies to them and their patients."

Perhaps the shallow understanding of medical ethics is nowhere more apparent than in the use and abuse of the phrase *do no harm*. Doctors in the Western world have been guided by the Hippocratic oath for nearly two millennia. Over that period, one phrase from the oath—*do no harm*—has repeatedly been understood to explain the physician's most fundamental responsibility regarding the care and treatment of patients. The problem is that recent advances in medical technology may have stretched the do no harm principle beyond its limits. Today, that principle may be (and often is) used as a rationale for doing everything medically possible for patients, regardless of considerations such as the cost of treatment, the medical efficacy of the procedure, and, perhaps most important, the expected posttreatment quality of life for the patient (where quality of life is judged from the patient's perspective). The predisposition to treat every affliction aggressively may be on the wane as interest in the notion of patient self-determination waxes, but the do no harm principle remains a strong motivation for some physicians who, as a result, continue to do too much in certain cases (Blank 1988: 13).

In addition, some specific misunderstandings create significant cracks in the consensus position. For example, the New York State Task Force on Life and the Law (1992: 231) reported that many health care providers in New York erroneously believed they could withhold—but not withdraw—life-sustaining treatment. Mildred Solomon's research team found that only 34 percent of the 1,446 caregivers surveyed (687 physicians and 759 nurses) agreed with the consensus position that there is no ethically important distinction between withholding and withdrawing treatment (Solomon et al. 1993: 18).

In addition, despite the fact that the consensus has rejected the ordinary-extraordinary distinction in favor of a best interests standard, 74 percent of the respondents in the study indicated that this linguistic distinction was still helpful in making decisions to terminate treatment (Solomon et al. 1993: 20). The General Accounting Office has also reported evidence along these lines. According to one recent study, a significant proportion of caregivers continue to find the terms *ordinary care* and *extraordinary care* useful (U.S. GAO 1995b: 16), even though nearly every authoritative body that has visited this question in recent years (including the Catholic Church) has rejected this language as confusing and misleading.

Robert Weir and Larry Gostin (1990: 1846) explain the gap between the consensus position and the behavior of some (or perhaps many) physicians by noting that doctors usually do not read the medical ethics literature and are often unaware of the consensus that has been reached in recent years regarding life-sustaining treatment for the terminally ill. Physicians also get very conservative legal advice from institutional counsels and may be worried about potential exposure to liability if they do anything less than provide aggressive treatment to the end.

Institutions

Certain ideologies also help to undermine the consensus position. Health care institutions that reject the consensus position on ethical or moral grounds (typically but not always, these would be religiously affiliated institutions) are especially important in this regard, for they can determine, within some limits, what kinds of care and treatment options are provided as a matter of course.[21] Data collected by the New York State Task Force on Life and the Law (1992: 288) are illustrative (see Tables 3.7 and 3.8).

Cracks in the consensus position are made manifest by these data. First of all, it appears that nursing homes, with an average overall objection rate of 23 percent vis-à-vis forgoing life-sustaining treatment (Table 3.8), are less likely to accede to a patient's wishes than hospitals, which show an average overall objection rate of 14 percent (Table 3.7). This is true even though there is nothing in the consensus position to suggest that a patient's rights should be dependent on the nature of the facility in which he or she is being treated.

Second, in the case of each proposed treatment, objection rates tend to increase as one moves from the "terminal illness" prognosis (with a combined average objection rate of 14 percent), through the "permanently unconscious" condition (with a combined average objection rate of 17 percent), to the "severely debilitated" condition (with a combined average objection rate of 24 percent).[22] The consensus position suggests that a patient's rights to forgo treatment are not dependent on his or her condition,

TABLE 3.7   Institutional Objections to Withholding or Withdrawing Treatment: Hospitals

Hospital Responses	Scenario 1: Terminally Ill	Scenario 2: Permanently Unconscious	Scenario 3: Severely Debilitated	Averages
% that would object to withholding artificial respiration	1	4	14	6
% that would object to withdrawing artificial respiration	5	11	15	10
% that would object to withholding ANH[a]	15	17	24	19
% that would object to withdrawing ANH[a]	16	20	24	20
Averages	9	13	19	14

[a]ANH refers to artificially provided nutrition and hydration.
SOURCE: Data drawn from NYSTFLL 1992: 288.

but the attitudes of some clinicians seem to be at odds with this notion. Third, there is more resistance to withdrawing treatment than there is to withholding treatment in every case but one (where there was no difference), even though the consensus position holds that there is no meaningful distinction between the two.

Finally, there appears to be an increased reluctance on the part of institutions when it comes to forgoing ANH. Only 8 percent of hospitals, on average, would object to forgoing artificial respiration across the three patient condition scenarios presented, but about 19 percent—more than twice that proportion—would object to forgoing ANH. The situation is even more pronounced in nursing homes, where 13 percent would object to forgoing artificial respiration but nearly a third—about 32 percent—would object to forgoing ANH.[23] Obviously, these institutions are making distinctions between artificial feeding and artificial respiration—distinctions that have no significance according to the consensus position, religious pronouncements, and general public sentiment.

State Legislatures

The last element of dissent involves the few conservative state legislatures around the country that have passed laws, wittingly or otherwise, that run counter to the positions taken by the vast majority of clinicians, clerics, judges, and ethicists. For example, as recently as 1995, living will statutes

TABLE 3.8   Institutional Objections to Withholding or Withdrawing Treatment: Nursing Homes

Nursing Homes Responses	Scenario 1: Terminally Ill	Scenario 2: Permanently Unconscious	Scenario 3: Severely Debilitated	Averages
% that would object to withholding artificial respiration	7	8	18	11
% that would object to withdrawing artificial respiration	12	12	21	15
% that would object to withholding ANH[a]	26	29	38	31
% that would object to withdrawing ANH[a]	29	33	39	34
Averages	29	21	29	23

[a]ANH refers to artificially provided nutrition and hydration.
SOURCE: Data drawn from NYSTFLL 1992: 288.

in seven states excluded from coverage (either explicitly or implicitly) those who are diagnosed as permanently unconscious. Three other states have laws that are ambiguous on this matter. The number of jurisdictions dissenting on this issue has shrunk from thirty-two states in 1992, so the trend is clearly in the direction of the consensus position (U.S. GAO 1995b: 42; Hoefler 1994: 194). Still, should residents of the seven holdout states be stricken permanently unconscious, their rights to self-determination may well be supported everywhere but where it counts—in the statute books of the states where they reside.

Coverage of artificial nutrition and hydration under living will laws is another area where legislative cracks in the consensus appear. One state (North Dakota) flatly rules out ANH as a treatment that can be waived in accordance with a living will (five states took this stance in 1992), and another state (Missouri) restricts the withholding or withdrawing of ANH to a limited set of circumstances (seven states took this position in 1992). Perhaps more important, twelve state laws are silent on the ANH question (down from eighteen states in 1992), and two (New York and Massachusetts) do not recognize living wills by statute for any purpose (down from four in 1992) (U.S. GAO 1995b: 42; Hoefler 1994: 201). Once again, it appears that certain state legislatures have not been able (or willing) to keep up with the trends in ethics, law, and medicine, though they have collectively tended to move in the direction of the consensus in recent years.

Summary

Overall, the consensus position described in Chapter 2 appears to be alive, well, and widely embraced by religious groups, physicians, and the general public. Still, pockets of dissent force some unfortunate families into court (e.g., the families of Karen Quinlan, Nancy Cruzan, and Joey Fiori), where other forces are sometimes allowed to take control.

Whether the consensus position is allowed to inform decision making is an issue whose significance reaches far beyond the population of patients in a persistent vegetative state. Although there are only about 25,000 patients in the United States today who would technically be considered to be persistently vegetative, there are nearly 2 million elderly Americans alive today who are so severely demented that they exist in quasi-conscious states that resemble the PVS. These individuals have irreversibly lost nearly every shred of consciousness and awareness that higher brain functions allow us. Will these individuals be treated in accordance with consensus rules, or will the existence of cracks in the consensus mean that that they will be subjected to ultimately futile medical treatment until death prevails? Chapter 4 will address this all-important question.

Chapter Four

Beyond the PVS: Severe Dementia

The case of Joey Fiori was, of course, important for the relatively small circle of individuals who knew him, who cared for him, and who were involved in litigating his case. But Fiori's situation was not unique. At any given time, between 15,000 and 35,000 U.S. citizens are being sustained in a persistent vegetative state (Council 1990: 426). Consequently, the number of people involved in and concerned about the issues raised by the Fiori case extends well beyond those directly involved in his situation.

The circle of affected parties extends even further because we all have a stake in the treatment of patients in a PVS, connected as we are to these individuals through shared understandings of social values and ethical standards. In addition, we all help to underwrite the health care expenses incurred by these individuals, estimated to be between $1 and $7 billion annually.[1]

Potentially, we are all affected by the issues raised in the Fiori case in a more direct way as well. Most patients become incompetent to make medical decisions at the end of life, just as Fiori did. Most do not have an advance directive, just as Fiori did not. And most Americans will die, like Fiori, only after a decision to forgo life-sustaining treatment is made by someone else. Given this reality, it follows that most deaths in the United States will raise, to one degree or another, the same questions that were raised in *Fiori* and addressed by consensus groups both before and after the case was decided: Who should make end-of-life treatment decisions—courts or families and caregivers? When should these decisions be made—only when the patient is terminal, or also when he or she is seriously and irreversibly ill? And on what basis should decisions be rendered—on the basis of clear and convincing evidence, substituted judgment, the best interests standard, or something else?

Most of us will die having lost the ability to make decisions for ourselves, and many of us will also pass through a protracted vegetative state. Joey Fiori's situation was sui generis, then, in only a very narrow sense.[2] It is true that patients rarely linger in a persistent vegetative state for twenty years as Fiori did. But clinicians have come to realize that the persistent vegetative state is *not* an isolated syndrome. Rather, the PVS is a point on a continuum of brain functionality that begins with a healthy brain and runs through the stages of mild, moderate, and severe dementia before passing through the PVS and ending with brain death at the other extreme.

Many Americans continue living, with the assistance of tube feeding and other life-supporting technologies, in a severely demented, quasi-vegetative state that is similar to the PVS in many important respects (see Multi-Society Task Force on PVS 1994a, 1994b). This large and growing class of patients deserves our attention, for life-sustaining treatment decisions will have to be made for them at some point, just as they were for Joey Fiori. Even a decision not to make a decision has costs and consequences for all parties involved.

Pathogenesis of Severe Dementia

Alzheimer's disease, often referred to as senile dementia of the Alzheimer's type (DAT), is by far the most common cause of chronic dementia in the United States, accounting for approximately two-thirds of all cases. Dementia in the remaining cases is caused by related illnesses, such as Pick's, Huntington's, and Parkinson's diseases. Dementia is also common in the end stages of acquired immunodeficiency syndrome (AIDS). Regardless of their origin, most chronic neurological disorders lead to death—on average, seven to eight years after the onset of the disorder and four to five years after diagnosis (most progressive neurological disorders are not diagnosed until several years after onset).

At the turn of the twentieth century, when the average life span was only forty-eight years or so, approximately 600,000 of the 78 million U.S. citizens alive at the time (or 1 in every 130 people) suffered from disorders like Alzheimer's. Since then, as the population of the country has grown by about 350 percent, the number of citizens with progressive neurological disorders has increased 1,000 percent.

Today, Alzheimer's disease or one of its related pathologies afflicts one in every forty-five Americans overall, one in every eight Americans over the age of sixty-five, and nearly half (47 percent) of the population over eighty-five (U.S. Senate 1991: XXII). Demographers predict that the population of patients suffering from Alzheimer's or Alzheimer's-like disorders will mushroom from 6 million to 30 million by the middle of the next century (OTA 1987b: 3). It is no wonder, then, that Patricia Hanrahan and Daniel Luchins (1995: 56) refer to dementia as an "epidemiological time bomb."

Alzheimer's disease was first brought to the attention of the medical community in 1907 by German neuropathologist Alois Alzheimer. The pathology involves the progressive degeneration and loss of nerve cells associated with memory, learning, and judgment in the brain's cortex. Early symptoms of the disorder may be limited to impaired short-term memory, but as the disorder progresses to the moderate stage, those suffering from DAT may exhibit mood swings and personality changes that can be confounding and even frightening to the patient and to the patient's family and friends. Behavioral symptoms also become more pronounced and may include angry outbursts, violence, depression, paranoia, hallucinations, delusions, and wandering. Thought, judgment, perception, language, and functional abilities continue their slow but steady deterioration as the disease progresses.

The moderate phase of DAT may be the most difficult to manage. Family members often experience shame, embarrassment, denial, frustration, anger, depression, and guilt as they care for an Alzheimer's patient who may not recognize them, who may physically or verbally abuse them and others, and who inevitably becomes totally dependent on others for care and sustenance.

Dementia progresses to the severe state in one in every seven Americans over sixty-five and one in every four Americans past eighty-five. Over time, the condition inexorably degenerates and inevitably begins to mimic the PVS. The current population of 2 million severe dementia sufferers is projected to double to 4 million by the mid-2020s as members of the baby boom generation advance into old age (OTA 1987b: 15; see Table 4.1).

There are no standard or commonly accepted criteria that reliably establish the existence of severe dementia. Instead, clinicians look for the presence of one or more of the following conditions as a signal that the dementia has reached the "severe" stage: (1) incontinence, (2) the inability (or lack of desire) to speak (language in the severely demented often consists of only one or two words or cries), (3) significant decreases in mobility, and (4) loss of the ability to swallow (OTA 1987b: 67). These problems force many families of severely demented patients to turn to nursing homes where around-the-clock care can be provided, care that may often include the use of chemical and physical restraints. A large study of nursing home procedures in New York led researchers to estimate that between 53 and 60 percent of nursing home residents were receiving psychotropic medication and that anywhere from 25 to 85 percent were being physically restrained for their own safety and the safety of other residents (NYSTFLL 1992: 13–14).

Whether restrained or not, severely demented patients typically end up bedfast, and they require assistance for most if not all the daily living tasks they had typically completed on their own since childhood, including bathing, feeding, dressing, and toileting (Enck 1994: 69). According to the U.S. Office of Technology Assessment (OTA), two out of three patients with severe dementia need assistance with eating, 87 percent have to be dressed by others (many wear bed gowns most of the time), and 99 percent

TABLE 4.1   Actual and Projected Growth of the Elderly and Demented
Populations in the United States

	Americans 65 Years Old and Older		Americans 85 Years Old and Older		Cases of Severe Dementia
	(million)	*(%)*	*(million)*	*(%)*	*(million)*
1900	3.1	4.0	0.1	0.2	a
1910	4.0	4.3	0.2	0.2	a
1920	4.9	4.7	0.2	0.2	a
1930	6.6	5.4	0.3	0.2	a
1940	9.0	6.8	0.4	0.3	a
1950	12.3	8.1	0.6	0.4	a
1960	16.6	9.2	0.9	0.5	a
1970	20.0	9.8	1.4	0.7	a
1980	25.6	11.3	2.2	1.0	1.3
1990	31.6	12.6	3.3	1.3	1.9
2000	34.9	13.0	4.6	1.7	2.4
2010	39.4	13.9	6.1	2.2	2.8
2020	52.1	17.7	6.6	2.3	3.3
2030	65.4	21.8	8.2	2.7	4.0
2040	68.1	22.6	12.3	4.1	5.1
2050	68.5	22.9	15.3	5.1	a

[a]No data available.

SOURCE: Aging data are derived from OTA 1987a: 7. Dementia data are extrapolated from OTA 1988: 3.

need total assistance in bathing and personal hygiene. Over half of severely demented patients are diapered, and 98 percent are totally dependent on others for toileting (OTA 1987b: 501, 502).

Mercifully, psychological problems become less pronounced in the later stages of dementia as patients become less purposeful and communicative. At the same time, the manifestations of severe dementia put patients at greater risk for physiological problems that exacerbate their condition. The lack of mobility means patients with severe dementia are more likely to contract pneumonia and develop bedsores. The use of tube feeding increases the chances that patients will contract aspiration pneumonia. And incontinence increases the chances of contracting urinary tract infections. To treat these infections effectively, caregivers must do the necessary diagnostic tests (e.g., blood draws and sputum suctioning), which may cause discomfort and may also serve to confuse and upset the patient.[3]

Similarities Between PVS and Severe Dementia

It is not radical to suggest that severely demented and PVS patients be considered part of the same class of patients in terms of end-of-life decision making, for medical researchers have been comparing the two groups and blurring the lines of distinction between them for years. Dr. Ronald Cranford, probably the most prolific writer on the subject and the most widely cited clinician in the subspecialty that deals with neurological disease, states that "from a strictly medical standpoint—in terms of consciousness and the capacity for experiencing suffering—there is not a major difference between no consciousness at all (the persistent vegetative state) and only minimal consciousness (profound dementia) (Cranford 1991a: 20).[4] Both the PVS and profound dementia "are of recent vintage," notes Cranford, and both are "creatures of modern medical technology. . . . Not only can modern medicine rescue these individuals, it can perpetuate their life for extended periods of time, even though those characteristics that make them uniquely human—thinking, feeling, talking, interacting with others—are permanently lost" (Cranford 1991a: 17; see also Tresch et al. 1991: 930).[5]

Similarly, Judith Ahronheim and M. R. Gasner (1990: 278) note that "patients with end-stage dementia are not far from the PVS state." Thomas Walshe and Cheri Leonard (1985: 1045, 1047) are equally direct: "The PVS is a feature of the terminal phase of several progressive neurological disorders. . . . The clinical features of PVS in the chronic diseases, although they arrive slowly, are much like those described in patients who develop the syndrome after acute injury."

The New York State Task Force on Life and the Law, criticized by some as too cautious and conservative on certain right-to-die issues, has also found it appropriate to draw parallels between PVS and advanced dementia: "Permanently unconscious patients include those in a persistent vegetative state [and] patients who are in the end stage of degenerative neurological conditions such as Alzheimer's disease" (NYSTFLL 1992: 160). Even the authors of the President's Commission report (1983: 180), a document formulated well before consensus had begun to take shape on this and related issues, adopted this position: "Another group that might be classified as permanently unconscious are end-stage victims of degenerative neurological conditions such as Alzheimer's."

Certainly, a number of clinical characteristics lead one to conclude that the two syndromes are similar in several important ways (see Table 4.2). As Cranford has pointed out, both syndromes are relatively new, made possible by medical technology that enables us to rescue and then sustain pa-

TABLE 4.2   Similarities Between PVS and Severe Dementia

Contemporary phenomena	Both syndromes have emerged only recently, largely due to the advances of modern technology, including CPR, defibrillators, ventilators, ICUs and trauma centers, artificial feeding, and dialysis.
The vegetative functions persist	Breathing, heartbeat, and respiration remain essentially intact, while the cognitive functions (e.g., feeling, thinking, and interacting) are either severely degraded or entirely absent.
Circadian rhythm persists	Both PVS and severely demented patients exhibit sleep-and-wake cycles. During waking hours, these patients have eyes open and may blink, cry, grunt, or move the limbs sporadically.
Other clinical characteristics	Incontinence; inability to swallow; sometimes there is bloating and facial swelling (from tube feeding), causing patients to lose their distinctive facial features; some exhibit severe contractures of the extremities and may tend to curl up into a fetal position.
Not technically terminally ill	Though very seriously ill, these patients would not be considered terminally ill in the conventional sense of the term as long as aggressive medical treatments are employed. If medical interventions continue, life can be prolonged for years or even decades.

SOURCE: Information for this table is drawn primarily from Cranford 1991a: 14–16.

tients who would have died just a few decades ago. In both syndromes, the ability to understand or interact with one's surroundings is either profoundly degraded (in severe dementia) or completely absent (in a PVS), while the vegetative functions (e.g., breathing, heartbeat, and respiration) remain essentially intact.

The circadian rhythm is another commonality between these two syndromes. Sleep-and-wake cycles persist in both classes of patients. When "awake," they may open, blink, and move their eyes in a way that suggests at least a minimal level of consciousness (even though little if any consciousness exists). Both classes of patients also tend to be incontinent (usually requiring diapering or catheterization), both tend to have lost their ability to swallow (usually requiring tube feeding), and both tend to exhibit some contracture in the extremities (sometimes requiring patients to wear mittens to keep their fingernails from cutting into the skin of the wrists).

Finally, neither dementia nor PVS patients are terminally ill in the classic sense of that term. As a matter of fact, patients in both classes can be sustained for many years with continued life support and attentive nursing care.

Taken together, these similarities are sufficient to lead Ladislav Volicer and his colleagues (Volicer et al. 1986), Walshe and Leonard (1985), Cranford (1991a), and others to make a dramatic proposal: Since PVS and severe dementia are essentially equivalent, patients in both classes should be treated similarly, in accordance with the guidelines of the consensus position described in Chapters 2 and 3. This proposal stands up quite well even after considering the major differences that exist between the two syndromes. In fact, the proposal may even be strengthened by considering the differences.

Differences Between PVS and Severe Dementia

Although severe dementia is similar to the PVS in many important respects, there also are significant differences between the two syndromes (see Table 4.3). First, most of the 25,000 or so patients currently in a PVS developed the condition shortly after the brain suffered an insult—either an interruption in the supply of oxygen (e.g., from a heart attack, stroke, suffocation, or a near drowning) or from a blow to the head (usually in a traffic accident or a serious fall). As a result, these individuals moved quickly from a normal, healthy state of consciousness to the PVS (usually in a matter of seconds if there was head trauma or minutes if there was a loss of oxygen to the brain).[6]

By contrast, severe dementia results from an incremental loss of brain function over the course of years. Severely demented individuals pass through the various stages of dementia after Alzheimer's disease or some other progressive neurological disorder begins robbing them of their ability to think, feel, remember, and interact with others. Many of these "biologically tenacious" (Callahan 1989: 63) individuals survive long enough to become "severely demented"—the last stage before the PVS and a phase of brain impairment in which many if not all of the end-of-life decision-making issues raised by the PVS apply.

A second and more important difference between severe dementia and PVS exists at the level of diagnosis. Generally, the PVS can be reliably diagnosed after three months to one year of observation and diagnostic testing. There are, however, no particularly reliable diagnostic tests that can accurately determine the degree of dementia that may exist in a patient suffering from a chronic brain disorder. The term itself—*severe dementia*—is not clearly defined in the medical literature in a universally acceptable and clinically determinable way.

Although it is fairly easy to diagnose the existence of an organic brain disorder, it is harder to pin down the specific level of dementia that exists as time goes on, for the lines between mild, moderate, and severe dementia are not always easily discerned.

The prospect of recovery is a third important area of difference between PVS and severe dementia. Patients in a PVS have, on occasion, had recoveries of sorts, though there is no documented evidence of a "good" recovery

TABLE 4.3 Differences Between PVS and Severe Dementia

	Persistent Vegetative State (PVS)	Severe Dementia
Onset and course	Sudden, caused by an interruption in the supply of oxygen to the brain or resulting from a blow to the head	Gradual onset of progressive neurological deterioration over years or decades
Diagnosis	Relatively straightforward and reliable after one to three months	Ascertaining various stages of dementia can be difficult at times
Prospects of recovery	A good recovery has never been documented in an adult after one to three months; a few recoveries have been documented after the three-month point, but patients are left severely impaired	None
Gradations of consciousness	None; all PVS patients are completely insensate	Extremely low levels of consciousness, progressing toward the vegetative state over time
Self-awareness	None; all PVS patients are completely insensate	Patients are largely unaware of themselves as unique individuals after passing the point of moderate dementia
Sensation of pain	None; all PVS patients are completely insensate	Present but to a decreasing degree as the dementia becomes more advanced
Number of cases nationwide	15,000 to 35,000	Approximately six million Americans suffer from dementia; as many as two million suffer from severe dementia
Landmark court cases (state)	*Quinlan* and *Jobes* (N.J.), *Brophy* (Mass.), *Delio* (New York), *Cruzan* and *Busalacchi* (Mo.), *Fiori* (Pa.)	*Conroy* (N.J.), *O'Connor* (N.Y.), *Dinnerstein* (Mass.), *Rasmussen* (Ariz.)

SOURCE: Information for this table is drawn primarily from Cranford 1991: 14–16.

after a patient has been in a PVS for more than a few months.[7] Patients with severe dementia, however, never recover (Multi-Society Task Force on PVS 1994b: 1574).

A fourth important difference between the two syndromes has to do with levels of awareness. On the one hand, patients in a PVS are completely unaware of themselves and their surroundings. As such, they have no capacity to sense physical or emotional distress of any kind. On the other hand, patients who are severely demented but not entirely vegetative may retain some ability to sense physical pain, emotional strain, or both. Physically painful stimuli may cause severely demented patients to wince or cry out. These patients may also retain some vague awareness of their debilitated condition, an awareness that may prove to be a source of significant emotional distress (Meyers and Grodin 1991: 527).

Finally, with only 15,000 to 35,000 cases at any given time, the PVS can be considered a relatively rare phenomenon (1 case per 13,000 U.S. citizens), and no one predicts any dramatic increases in these statistics. But severe dementia is widespread and promises to become substantially more prevalent over the next several decades. The OTA's estimate that there are some 2 million cases of severe dementia in United States today means that approximately 1 in every 135 Americans suffers from this affliction (OTA 1987b: 7), a proportion that will increase dramatically as the baby boomers begin entering their retirement years shortly after the turn of the twenty-first century. As Daniel Callahan puts it, we can expect to see "a substantially larger number of people in the future who are going to be in a vegetative, semi-vegetative, or otherwise terribly debilitated state but simply will not die" (Callahan 1989: 63).

In sum, there are four important differences between patients in a PVS and patients who are severely demented. One of those differences—the problem with diagnosing severe dementia with medical certainty—tends to weaken the proposition that the two classes of patients are similarly situated. How can we treat severely demented patients as if they were persistently vegetative when we cannot be sure if they are severely demented or not? The flaw in this critique has to do with the term *medical certainty*, which is something of an oxymoron. In fact, very few things of significance in medicine are certain.

More typically, physicians and medical researchers speak in terms of probabilities. And though the probability of making a mistake in diagnosing the PVS is lower than it is with severe dementia, errors in diagnosing either syndrome are uncommon. Dementia usually progresses slowly and relatively predictably over the course of years, giving clinicians plenty of time to observe and adjust their diagnoses along the way. In most cases, then, it is unlikely that the diagnosis of severe dementia, which typically would come years after the initial diagnosis of a dementing disorder, will be wildly off the mark (Walshe and Leonard 1985: 1045). Consequently, although problems with diagnosis continue to be a concern, they are not of a magnitude sufficient to exempt all those diagnosed with severe dementia from coverage under the consensus principles laid out earlier.

The other three differences between a PVS and severe dementia, by contrast, tend to strengthen the "death with dignity" claims some have made regarding the importance of including severely demented patients under the consensus position's umbrella of principles and guidelines. First, even though some confusion persists over the incidence and degree of recovery that certain PVS patients have experienced, there is no ambiguity whatsoever about the chances of a patient recovering from a degenerative brain disorder such as Alzheimer's. It may be difficult to tell exactly when a patient passes from the "moderately demented" to the "severely demented" category, but one thing can be reliably conveyed to the family regardless of the level of dementia: The patient will never recover.

Second, since some severely demented patients may retain marginal levels of consciousness, continued existence may be more burdensome for them than it is for the PVS patient, who is entirely unaware of his or her plight. Pain and discomfort may also be felt by the severely demented patient; the PVS patient suffers no such sensations.

Third, there are a hundred severely demented patients for every one PVS patient. Thus, severely demented patients as a group consume many more public resources, strain many more family budgets, cause much more emotional trauma within families, and suffer far more personally than PVS patients, as a group.

In the end, there may be considerable merit to providing families of severely demented patients with the same life-sustaining treatment options and protections that families of PVS patients enjoy under the consensus position laid out in Chapter 2 and bolstered in Chapter 3. Certainly, the public seems supportive of this notion, as Table 4.4 reveals.

This table summarizes the results of a study of 507 individuals (405 hospital outpatients and 102 members of the general public) in which seven specific therapies (antibiotics, IV fluids, ANH, kidney dialysis, mechanical respiration, CPR, and pain medication) were proposed under three different scenarios (dementia, PVS, and dementia with terminal illness). Consistently high percentages of respondents indicated that they would prefer to refuse the six proposed treatments that would tend to prolong life (antibiotics, IV fluids, ANH, dialysis, respiration, and CPR). The only treatment that respondents seemed interested in was pain management, a treatment that, as explained in the survey, also has the potential to hasten death.[8]

For each therapy proposed, the percentage of respondents saying they would refuse the treatment was lowest within the dementia scenario and highest within the dementia with terminal illness scenario; the PVS refusal

TABLE 4.4 Choices Regarding the Use of Life-Sustaining Treatments[a]

Treatment Decision	% Who Would Agree If Suffering from Dementia	% Who Would Agree If in a Persistent Vegetative State	% Who Would Agree If Suffering from Dementia and Terminal Illness
Would *refuse* antibiotics	69	76	79
Would *refuse* intravenous (IV) fluids	73	77	82
Would *refuse* artificial nutrition	76	80	82
Would *refuse* kidney dialysis	75	80	83
Would *refuse* mechanical respiration	75	80	84
Would *refuse* CPR	72	83	84
Would *accept* pain medication, even if it would bring about an earlier death	77	[b]	79

[a]Respondents were 405 outpatients of 30 primary care physicians at Massachusetts General Hospital and a cohort group of 102 members of the general public from the Boston area.

[b]Patients in a persistent vegetative state are unable to sense pain, making pain medication irrelevant.

SOURCE: Data summarized and cited in Emanuel et al. 1991: 893.

rates fell somewhere in between. Even in the dementia scenario, however, the desire to forgo life-sustaining treatments was overwhelming, even though the level of dementia (e.g., mild, moderate, or severe) was not specified. More than two out of every three respondents said they would forgo relatively simple treatments—such as antibiotics (69 percent) and intravenous fluids (73 percent)—if they were demented. More than three-quarters of the respondents said they would refuse tube feeding, and four out of five said they would forgo mechanically assisted respiration.

Whatever subtle nuances exist in the desire for refusing various treatments in these three patient scenarios, it is clear that, as a rule, the vast majority of respondents would prefer to forgo everything except pain medication when their ability to enjoy conscious life has been compromised and the prospects for recovery are slim. A closer look at dementia-related costs and case studies only strengthens the arguments of those who contend that severely demented patients and PVS patients are alike for purposes of making life-sustaining treatment decisions and should therefore be covered by the consensus position outlined in Chapter 2.

Resources

In addition to the issues associated with the physical and emotion distress and deterioration suffered by demented patients, issues of resource allocation might reasonably be raised. Anecdotal and quantitative evidence abounds that, generally speaking, perhaps too much in the way of medical procedures are provided to demented patients who are at or near the end of their lives.

Ezekiel and Linda Emanuel (1994: 543) estimate that 3.3 percent of all health care spending (close to $33 billion in 1998 dollars) might be saved if each of the approximately 2 million Americans who die every year were to choose hospice care, use advance directives, and refuse aggressive, in-hospital interventions toward the end of life (cited in Scitovsky 1994: 585–586). P. A. Singer and F. H. Lowery estimate that the cost of caring for dying patients could be cut in half, saving approximately $55 billion annually, if the decision to forgo life-sustaining medical treatment was made more regularly, through the use of advance directives, for example (cited in Maksoud, Jahnigeen, and Skibinski 1993: 1250; see Box 4.1). It is possible that a fair proportion of these savings could be realized if the severely demented were not treated so aggressively.

Aggressive Care and Spending Patterns

Perhaps the extravagance of current medical practices regarding treatment at the end of life is best represented by the use—some would argue overuse—of the intensive care unit for treating elderly patients. According to Dr. David Finley, director of a hospital's critical care services, the fact that many U.S. hospitals have ICUs filled with the frail elderly is deplorable. "End-stage care is not what [the ICU] is intended for," argues Finley. "It was originally supposed to be for people with treatable illnesses and a reasonable chance of recovery" (cited in Clark 1992).

In a similar vein, Dr. Steven Schroder, an internist, noted the differences between ICU patients in the United States and Europe after touring a number of European facilities. ICUs in European countries, he reported, were smaller, accounting for between 1 and 5 percent of all hospital beds. In the United States, ICUs typically account for 15 to 20 percent of all beds (Stout 1993). Schroder also noted that "the patients there were different. They were healthier and they were younger. The common patient in an ICU in a

---

BOX 4.1   Saving Money Using Advance Directives

Increased use of advance directives may be one way to begin realizing savings in caring for patients at the end of life. A recent study of 476 Medicare patients who died in private, university-based hospitals over a three-year period revealed that the 132 patients who had advanced directives incurred average total inpatient charges of $30,478. The 342 patients in the study who did not have advance directives had average total inpatient charges of $95,305 (Chambers 1994: 541)—more than three times as much. In two of the three years of the study, there were no appreciable differences in the severity of illness between the two groups of patients, those with advance directives and those without. And the difference in spending levels was maintained even after controlling for demographic characteristics (e.g., age, race, and gender), use of the ICU, and the number of procedures employed, suggesting that it was not only the sickest of the patients who had advanced directives (Chambers 1994: 545).

A second study, conducted in 1993 by Alfred Maksoud, Dennis Jahnigeen, and Christine Skibinski (1993: 1250), found much the same thing. The 12.5 percent of patients who were admitted to the hospital with DNR orders in place and subsequently died had average final inpatients charges of $10,631; the remaining 87.5 percent of the patients who entered the hospital without DNR orders and subsequently died had average total bills of approximately $68,000 (Maksoud, Jahnigeen, and Skibinski 1993: 1249). One significant finding of this study was that when advance directives were executed after admission, they often came too late to save much if any money. In fact, Maksoud, Jahnigeen, and Skibinski (1993: 1249) found that DNR orders executed in the hospital were written, on average, only two days before a patient's death, and the average charge for these patients was actually *higher* (approximately $73,000) than it was for patients who died in the hospital without ever having executed DNR orders (approximately $57,000).

---

major U.S. hospital is an eighty-five-year-old whose heart is failing, whose lungs are failing, who is in need of artificial respiration." Schroder asked one European physician about the difference, and the reply he received was telling: "'I trained in the U.S.,'" his colleague explained, "'Your teaching hospitals are excellent, your technology is superb, but you don't know when to stop'" (cited in Stout 1993).

Care outside the ICU is extensive as well. According to one study, nursing home residents who suffer from dementia have medical charges between 25 and 40 percent higher than charges for patients without mental disorders (Short, Feinleib, and Cunningham 1994: 13). Another study involving fifty-one vegetative nursing home residents (Tresch et al. 1991) found that residents were regularly hospitalized for acute care. In fact, nearly two out of three residents in the study were hospitalized at least once, and half of that group underwent surgical procedures during hospitalization.[9] Overall, the annual cost of caring for the demented elderly has been estimated at between $24 and $48 billion when costs of supervision and assistance—often provided by family members and counted as lost wages—are added to the medical costs (OTA 1987b: 447; Nuland 1994: 103).

Treatment—or perhaps overtreatment—of elderly demented patients probably helps to explain the skewed patterns in health care spending data for the elderly. According to the Health Care Finance Administration (HCFA), although only 5 percent of Medicare beneficiaries die in any given year, 28 percent of the Medicare budget (about $20 billion) is spent in attempting to address the health care needs of this group. About half of this amount ($10 billion, or 1 out of every 7 Medicare dollars) is spent on patients in the last two months of life, and about a third of this amount ($7 billion, or 1 of every 14 Medicare dollars) is spent in the patient's last thirty days. Overall, 6 Medicare dollars are spent on those who die in the hospital for every dollar spent on elderly patients who survive hospitalization (Scitovsky 1994: 562, 578).[10] Will Rogers once said that in the world of politics, it costs a fortune just to get beat. Perhaps it could also be said that in today's world of medicine, it costs a fortune just to die.

Comparing utilization patterns across age groups raises even more questions. Although the elderly in the United States make up only about 13 percent of the general population, they account for 34 percent of all health care expenditures (63 percent of those dollars come from the public sector). The 13 percent of the population over the age of sixty-five also occupy 40 percent of the nation's hospital beds and consume 67 percent of all medications prescribed (U.S. Senate 1991: 133). The uninsured rate among the elderly—another measure of resource distribution in society—is essentially zero, thanks to Medicare and Medicaid, but the uninsured rate hovers around 15 percent for the rest of the population and approaches 15 percent among U.S. children.

Medicaid, the program designed to address the health care needs of poor Americans, spends seven dollars per capita, mostly on long-term care for "apparently poor" elderly, blind, and disabled individuals (some really are poor, but others have sheltered their resources to appear poor), for every dollar spent on health care for "actually poor" children (U.S. GAO 1995: 1–2). This disparity in spending between the young and the old has become more pronounced in recent years. According to Victor Fuchs, overall spending on health care for the elderly has outpaced spending for those under sixty-five by an average of 4 percent per year (1984: 149). Fuchs explains that only about half of the difference in spending can be explained away by the increase in the size of the elderly population relative to those under sixty-five. The rest of the increase represents a real net shift in spending on the elderly relative to younger Americans (Fuchs 1984: 149–150).[11]

This shift in spending across age groups is taking place at a precarious time, demographically speaking, for the ratio of working-age Americans to

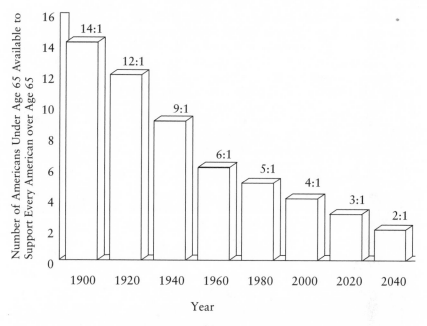

FIGURE 4.1 Elderly Support Ratio

elderly Americans has been decreasing dramatically ever since the turn of the twentieth century. In 1900, there were more than fourteen working-age adults available to support every person over sixty-five. Today, there are only about four working-age adults for every elderly American. Between now and the middle of the next century, demographers predict that the ratio will drop even further, leaving only two-and-a-half workers to support every one elderly American (see Figure 4.1).

Utilization and Spending Patterns in Perspective

This overview of spending trends is not presented to suggest that the demented elderly are taking advantage of the rest of society by overusing health care resources (although some would be happy to draw this conclusion). Indeed, the elderly pay for about 30 percent of their general health care costs and approximately half of all long-term care out of their own pockets (OTA 1987b: 172–173). In addition, older members of our society should be expected to consume more in the way of health care resources, given the multitude of medical problems that commonly attend the aging process. The data provided here are meant only to stimulate discussion, not end it.

Nonetheless, long-term care for the elderly, especially the severely demented elderly, is an important and often overlooked economic and ethical concern. As Anne Scitovsky notes (1994: 588–589):

In the many studies of medical care at the end of life, the emphasis has been almost exclusively on high-cost, high technology care. Largely ignored has been the problem of patients dying in nursing homes. . . . As the population ages, this group of decedents will become increasingly important and may well pose greater economic problems than the high-cost decedents on whom most of the research has focused. . . . They also present ethical problems different from, and possibly more difficult than, those posed by critically ill patients. Chronically ill patients present us with the dilemma not so much of when to forego "heroics," but rather or when to halt ordinary care (such as treatment with antibiotics in case of infection) and sustenance.

The authors of the President's Commission report (1983: 96–97) sound a similar chord when they suggest that one must be cautious when factoring the costs of care into the balance, for strict rationing along these lines may lead to ethically tenuous consequences. Individuals place different values on sustained life, and there is a danger in creating hard-and-fast rules about what costs can be incurred under what circumstances; to do so could lead to discrimination and devaluation of the lives of society's most vulnerable members. Yet according to the President's Commission report (1983: 96–97),

allowing decisions about life-sustaining care to be made with total disregard for the costs they impose on others has equally serious implications. Enormous expenditures may be made for very limited benefits, such as sustaining a painful and burdened life of someone who has little or no capacity to enjoy it. . . . The fact that a therapy is life-sustaining does not automatically create an obligation to provide it.

In the end, cutting health care costs is not the primary motivation for laying out the end-of-life decision quandary addressed in this volume. Other, more important issues are at stake, including the enhancement of patient autonomy, the decrease in suffering for patients at the end of life, and a much needed increase in the degree to which compassion and dignity attend the modern dying process (Emanuel and Emanuel 1994). As such, the cost and resource allocation issues raised here are just one part—potentially important but not preeminent—of the debate about end-of-life decision making. We certainly should not bank on the increased use of advance directives, proliferation of hospice care, and rejection of aggressive life-sustaining therapies at the end of life to solve the more general health care finance problems that face the United States today.

At the same time, the data suggest that some money, perhaps a substantial amount of money, could be saved if patients and their surrogates agreed not to extend life interminably after severe dementia develops. Adopting a less medically aggressive, more natural approach to dying in the United States would be, according to a number of ethicists and clinicians, just as defensible for severely demented patients as it is for PVS patients, for both could easily be covered under the consensus position's umbrella. A review of some notable cases involving life-sustaining treatment decisions for patients suffering from severe dementia helps to illustrate the point.

State Court Cases Involving
Severe Dementia and the Right to Die

There have been approximately eighty appellate-level court cases in the states involving the right to die since 1977, when the parents of Karen Ann Quinlan became the first to stake an explicit, right-to-die claim in the state courts.[12] Eighty percent of those cases have involved patients who were incompetent to make decisions for themselves (Ahronheim and Mulvihill 1991: 1124). And fully one-quarter of all cases heard at the appellate level have involved patients over the age of sixty-five. In all but three of these cases, the patient was determined to be too demented to be involved in making medical treatment decisions. A review of the medical conditions and judicial decisions in some of the more important of these cases will shed further light on the parallels between the PVS and senile dementia, at least in the eyes of the courts.

Shirley Dinnerstein

One of the earliest cases to deal with dementia involved Shirley Dinnerstein, a sixty-seven-year-old Massachusetts woman with advanced Alzheimer's disease. Her adult son and daughter brought this case to the courts in 1978, just two years after the *Quinlan* decision was handed down in New Jersey.

Dinnerstein's children petitioned the court for permission to execute a "do not resuscitate" order on behalf of their mother. The court ruled that the family could decide to put DNR orders in place without court involvement in "hopeless" cases such as the one at hand. Perhaps more important, the court also backed away from an earlier Massachusetts ruling that involved a terminally ill, mentally retarded adult by the name of Joseph Saikewicz. In *Saikewicz*, the court ruled that the judiciary should be involved in *any* decision to forgo treatment. In *Dinnerstein*, the court indicated that judicial approval would be required *only* if the treatment in question would offer the incompetent patient hope of cure or remission (Choice in Dying 1994b, *In re Dinnerstein*: 2).

Claire Conroy

The 1985 case of Claire Conroy in New Jersey is among the most important and most cited cases to date in which surrogate decisionmakers attempted to implement a palliative care treatment plan on behalf of an elderly, demented family member.[13] Miss Conroy was described as having led a simple, even cloistered life that involved only her sisters (with whom she lived) and a few friends. Conroy was admitted to a nursing home at age seventy-nine after her sisters had died and her own physical and mental condition began to decline. She had never been to the doctor and had "scorned medicine" her entire life (Stryker 1989: 228).

After five years in the nursing home, Conroy had deteriorated to the point where she was entirely bedridden and in a semifetal position. She suffered from hypertension, diabetes, and arteriosclerotic heart disease. Conroy had extensive bedsores, and her left leg was gangrenous to the knee. She was entirely incontinent and was fed through a nasogastric tube. Assessments of her mental state varied, depending on the physician, from unaware and confused to severely demented. "Though unable to speak, she occasionally scratched herself, [and] pulled at her bandages, [nasogastric] tube, and [urinary] catheter" (Choice in Dying 1994b, *Conroy:* 1).

The surrogate decisionmaker in this case was Conroy's only surviving blood relative, Thomas Whittemore, a nephew. Whittemore had known Conroy for over fifty years and visited her weekly during the four years prior to her admittance to the nursing home. Eventually, Whittemore asked that his aunt's nasogastric tube be removed so that she could be allowed to die. He was supported in his request by a Roman Catholic priest who testified at a subsequent trial that Catholic moral theology, as laid out in the *Vatican Declaration on Euthanasia*, would consider withdrawal of Conroy's feeding tube a morally acceptable course of action (Stryker 1989: 231–232).

The New Jersey Supreme Court ruled that artificial nutrition and hydration was just another form of invasive medical treatment that might be withheld or withdrawn as long as one of three tests was met. Under the court's "subjective test," surrogates would be allowed to direct that life-sustaining treatment be withdrawn from a patient if the surrogate could demonstrate—through written or oral statements, through reactions the patient had to the treatments of others, or through consistent patterns of conduct—that the patient would reject such treatment if he or she were competent to make the decision. (This standard is roughly equivalent to the substituted judgment standard.)

If the subjective test could not be satisfied, one could move on to the "pure-objective test," which would permit termination of treatment if, on balance, the pain and suffering of the patient's prolonged life were considered to outweigh the benefits the patient was thought to derive from continued life. (This standard is roughly equivalent to the best interests standard.)

The third standard of decision making, the "limited-objective test," is really a mix of the first two, to be used when there is insufficient evidence under either of the first two standards. It allows the withdrawal of treatment if some trustworthy evidence of the patient's desire to have treatment withdrawn (substituted judgment) could be combined with some evidence that continued treatment would only serve to prolong suffering without providing significant benefits beyond continued biological existence (best interests).[14]

Fairly rigorous review standards were also proposed by the court. First, the decision was applied only to elderly nursing home residents who were expected to die within a year. Second, the court indicated its desire to become involved in determining incompetency. The court also wanted to play a role in the designation of a guardian, if one were required. The court ruled that this guardian had to inform the state Office of the Ombudsman, which then had to notify other state agencies and initiate an adversarial investigation of any request to forgo treatment. Finally, the court ruled that life-sustaining medical treatment could be withdrawn only if the guardian, the attending physician, two unaffiliated physicians, the state ombudsman, and (in the case of the pure- or limited-objective tests) the patient's next of kin all concurred on the proposed course of action.

The *Conroy* decision was an important landmark for several reasons. It endorsed a new, hybrid decision rule—the mix of best interests and substituted judgment—for situations in which there was not enough information to support either the best interests standard or the substituted judgment rule alone. *Conroy* also explicitly rejected the use of language that, it was argued, only tended to muddy the waters regarding end-of-life decision making. Drawing heavily on the President's Commission report, the court set aside as unhelpful the ordinary-extraordinary distinction, the distinction between withholding and withdrawing treatment, and the application of the term *euthanasia* in cases involving the forgoing of life-sustaining medical treatment. In essence, it began wiping the slate clean and led courts across the country to start over with a new set of language and concepts that allowed decisionmakers to deal more with "proportionality" and the "benefits and burdens" of life-sustaining medical treatment.[15] These principles have endured and now serve as a central part of the general consensus on end-of-life decision making, as discussed earlier in this volume.

The rigid rules associated with the appointment of a guardian and the determination of incompetence were not adopted by other courts or embraced by the consensus groups, however. In fact, these rules did not even work very well in New Jersey. For example, Joseph Sullivan (1986) reported that families and health care professionals in the state appeared to be avoiding the *Conroy* court's prescribed procedures for withholding and withdrawing life support as too cumbersome. Despite data suggesting that scores of these decisions were being made on a weekly basis in hospitals across the state, the Office of the Ombudsman reported that only a couple of telephone inquiries were made regarding the new procedures in the first year. In all but one case, callers failed to follow up by initiating official proceedings to establish incompetency and assign a surrogate.

Common sense suggests that business is still going on as usual in New Jersey, with caregivers and family members quietly collaborating to make end-of-life decisions for incompetent patients, all without the assistance of the courts. Not surprisingly, no other appellate courts have adopted New Jersey's review standards, and even the New Jersey court has since backed away from its rigid stance (see *In re Peter* 529 A. 2d 404 [1987]).

Mildred Rasmussen

Mildred Rasmussen left behind no evidence of her medical treatment preferences and had no close relatives to help make those decisions for her when, after a series of three strokes, she became severely demented at age sixty-eight. She lay in a fetal position, unable to move, speak, or participate in her own care, and all physicians involved in her case agreed that her lack of awareness was irreversible. An out-of-state relative deferred to the judgment of the primary care physician, who proposed writing two treatment orders—one directing caregivers not to resuscitate the patient should her heart stop (a DNR order) and a second directing that the patient should not be tube fed if she were no longer able to swallow.

The patient died of pneumonia in 1987 before an Arizona court could decide whether the physician's proposed orders could have been authorized under the best interests standard that had been adopted by other states. But the court nonetheless pressed ahead with the case because it believed an important question was at stake, and it wanted to establish a case law precedent to guide decision making in the future (the supreme court in Pennsylvania pressed ahead with the Fiori case after Joey Fiori had died for the same reasons).

Ultimately, the Arizona court determined that none of the state's interests in preserving life outweighed Rasmussen's right to privacy and autonomy. The court cited the AMA's Council on Ethical and Judicial Affairs regarding the propriety of withdrawing life-prolonging medical treatment for those who appear to be irreversibly vegetative: "Even if death is not imminent but a patient's coma is beyond doubt irreversible . . . it is not unethical to discontinue all means of life-prolonging treatment (Choice in Dying 1994b, *Rasmussen* v. *Fleming*: 2). The court also cited the President's Commission report (1983) in formulating the meaning of "best interests" as "the course that will promote the patient's well-being as it would probably be conceived by a reasonable person in the patient's circumstances" (see President's Commission 1983: 136). Finally, the court ruled that, in the future, its role should be limited to dispute resolution. Where no dispute existed, the court would not need to be involved, it said.

Mary O'Connor

The New York case of seventy-seven-year-old Mary O'Connor cut sharply across the grain of decisions handed down by appellate courts almost everywhere else, including the three cited earlier in this chapter. O'Connor had suffered a series of strokes, which led to severe dementia. She was conscious but bedridden, unresponsive, and unable to stand or feed herself when members of her family decided that further life-sustaining treatment was not desirable.

In court proceedings to determine if tube feeding could be withdrawn, O'Connor's two daughters (both practical nurses) testified that their mother had clearly stated she would not want to be a burden to anyone or be maintained by artificial means if unable to care for herself. These statements were made after O'Connor had tended her husband and brothers during long final illnesses and after she had worked as a hospital employee for twenty years. A longtime friend and coworker also testified that O'Connor had said it was "monstrous to keep someone alive by using 'machinery,' things like that when they were not going to get better" (Choice in Dying 1994b, *In re Westchester County Medical Center:* 1). Meanwhile, in court, doctors disagreed over whether the dehydration that would follow the course proposed by the daughters would be painful.[16]

In a 5-to-2 decision, New York's highest court found that Mrs. O'Connor's statements regarding medical treatment were insufficient evidence of her desires under the clear and convincing evidence test adopted previously by that court (see *In re Eichner* and *In re Storar*).[17] The court went on to reject the substituted judgment approach that had been adopted by other courts and a wide variety of professional organizations, stating that it was inconsistent with "the fundamental commitment to the notion that no person or court should substitute its judgment as to what would be an acceptable quality of life for another" (Choice in Dying 1994b, *In re Westchester County Medical Center:* 2). Furthermore, according to the court's decision, "every person has a right to life, and no one should be denied essential medical care unless the evidence clearly and convincingly shows that the patient intended to decline the treatment under particular circumstances" (Choice in Dying 1994b, *In re Westchester County Medical Center:* 2).

The court's opinion also echoed that of the doctors in the case who testified that the death that would ensue if nasogastric feeding was withheld might be painful (Lo, Rouse, and Dornbrand 1990: 1228). They came to this conclusion even though the medical literature on the subject suggests that people in a state of severe dementia have very little sense of pain and that dehydration is not painful and may even be a relatively comfortable way to die (see Chapter 5). In the end, the court ordered that a nasogastric tube be inserted, over the objections of O'Connor's daughters. O'Connor died one year after the decision was rendered, with her nasogastric tube in place.

Life After O'Connor

Nearly all hospitals in New York State interpreted the *O'Connor* ruling to mean that, in the absence of any written statements, families must prove—by presenting clear and convincing evidence—that an incompetent patient would not want to be kept alive by machines before life-sustaining treatment could be withheld or withdrawn. The case of Rosemarie Doherty provides a good illustration of the effect of New York's decision.

Doherty's husband, with the concurrence of their son, attempted to have life support—feeding and endotracheal tubes—removed after Mrs. Doherty lapsed into a persistent coma. But acting in accordance with the *O'Connor* decision, a Brooklyn nursing home declined to honor these requests. "They said I would need five people to swear Rosie had specifically said she never wanted this tube, that tube, this antibiotic, that transfusion. . . . We never talked like that. Who talks like that?" said Mr. Doherty. "But I know she would not want to live like this. No one would. Would you?" Continuing, Mr. Doherty said his wife should have signed a health care proxy. "She should have—she didn't. . . . She didn't sign and she can't sign now," he said. "Does that mean she has to be sentenced to this?" (Belkin 1992).

Subsequently, the New York State Task Force on Life and the Law (1992: 74) argued that the standard for decision making charted by the *O'Connor* court and applied in the case of Rosemarie Doherty has proven untenable: "In practice, the clear and convincing evidence standard is often unworkable and inhumane. It is a legal standard that translates poorly at the bedside where families and health care professionals must confront the hard choices that incurable illness and medical advances present."[18]

Summary

Although the decisions rendered in the *Dinnerstein* (Massachusetts), *Conroy* (New Jersey), and *Rasmussen* (Arizona) cases differed from the *O'Connor* ruling in New York, these cases do have something in common. None involved a patient diagnosed to be in a PVS, and in none of the cases was the clinical diagnosis a determining factor. Rather, it was the permanence of the incompetence that was important; the technical cause of incompetence was irrelevant.

An extensive review of case law on end-of-life decision making reveals that severe dementia and PVS are equivalent in the eyes of many courts, for most decisions have turned on the degree of evidence required to make end-of-life decisions, not on the conditions of the patients themselves. Almost nowhere has the prognosis of dementia given the courts pause.[19] Regardless of the final decision (and the vast majority of such cases have been resolved in favor of the families, in accordance with the consensus position), dementia, like the PVS, has been accepted as just one of any number of diagnoses involving incompetence in which surrogate decisionmakers might be empowered to make end-of-life decisions for patients.

As noted earlier, there are really only four important differences between PVS and advanced dementia. First, it has become relatively easy to identify the PVS through clinical testing and observation, whereas severe dementia can be difficult to accurately diagnose. Second, a few PVS patients have experienced "miraculous" (if far from complete) recoveries, but severely demented patients never recover. Third, PVS patients cannot feel pain, anguish, or agitation at all, whereas severely demented patients may retain some ability to experience these sensations. And fourth, the PVS patient population numbers in the tens of thousands and is remaining relatively stable, while the severely demented population, currently around 2 million, is expected to grow to 4 million in the not too distant future.

The first of these differences suggests that we should use some caution before treating severely demented patients as if they were persistently vegetative. But the other three differences might suggest that patients with advanced dementia have an even greater interest than PVS patients in being treated only with palliative care.

There is a sticking point here, however—a complication tied to the concept of palliative care that has caused a great deal of anxiety, confusion, and dissent in recent years. This complication involves the issue of artificial nutrition and hydration. One of the hallmarks of severe dementia is the gradual loss of the ability to swallow; consequently, whenever the question of moving away from aggressive treatment and toward palliative care arises, the issue of artificial nutrition and hydration inevitably comes up as well.

The consensus position, public opinion polls, religious writings, and court decisions all suggest that ANH is just another medical treatment that can be appropriately withheld or withdrawn from irreversibly incompetent patients, using either a substituted judgment test or a best interests analysis. Nonetheless, it is clear that some physicians and a significant segment of the lay public continue to struggle with this issue. Food and drink have strong symbolic significance in our culture, even when they are provided by artificial means. Can Americans come to terms with the idea of declining ANH for members of their families as death draws near? The answer to this question may well turn on the degree to which decisionmakers are fully informed about the costs and benefits associated with the decision to either accept or refuse tube feeding at the end of life.

Chapter Five

Artificial Nutrition and Hydration

The consensus position of medical, ethical, legal, and religious bodies, together with public opinion, is clear on the subject of tube feeding: Artificially provided nutrition and hydration is a medical procedure that can be withheld or withdrawn like any other. ANH is not categorized as a treatment that must always be provided, and in coming to a decision about forgoing or continuing ANH, the patient's surrogates are allowed to either use their knowledge about the patient's desires and values or weigh the costs and benefits of tube feeding against the costs and benefits of waiving this treatment.

At the same time, Americans still have a good deal of anxiety about the prospect of discontinuing food and fluids, both for themselves and for their loved ones. This is one reason why there are approximately 1.5 million patients being tube fed in the United States today (Council 1992: 2229). Half of this group is over the age of sixty-five, and many if not most of these patients are severely and irreversibly demented (OTA 1987b: 293). The clinical reality is that tube feeding is often provided as a matter of course and that the choice of whether to tube feed or not is never fully explored. This situation contrasts markedly with the situation just a few decades ago.

Prior to the 1960s, when technological advances in artificial feeding made ANH a practical, widely accessible treatment,[1] the severe stage of dementia could also be considered the terminal phase: Patients simply stopped eating and drinking as the disease progressed, and in the end, they died. As Ronald Cranford (1991a: 18) writes, these patients died

> the way my great grand-mother died in 1958 at the age of 83. At that time, when she died at home, there were no CPR, no paramedics, and no intensive care units. The family never even gave a thought to putting her in a nursing home, and certainly no consideration was given to starting artificial nutrition and hydration, even though she was unable to eat or drink naturally as her condition worsened. We did have one thing back then that is unusual today: A family physician coming to the home almost daily to attend to his patient

whom he had known for years, and finally to pronounce her dead, at home in her own bed. Back then, people died of old age. Even though a feeding tube was never started, she was never abandoned by her loving, caring family.

Today, the modus operandi of physicians and families is turned on its head. In past decades and centuries, family members provided around-the-clock palliative care in the home, and physicians occasionally stopped by to do what they could (which was usually little, if anything, given the *lack* of technology). Today, by contrast, caregivers provide various levels of technologically sophisticated care twenty-four hours a day, and family members drop by on occasion to do what they can (which is usually nothing, given the *presence* of technology). In the past, diseases were allowed to run their natural courses, largely because the technology had not been developed to accurately diagnose and treat mortal pathologies. Death was simply accepted as a natural and ultimate phase of living, an essential element of our humanity. Today, death tends to be regarded by many as a conquerable evil that must be resisted at all costs. With the widespread use of ANH and antibiotics, each of which can help to sustain the body in a vegetative or near-vegetative state for months and perhaps even years, dementia no longer has a terminal phase per se (Peck, Cohen, and Mulvihill 1990: 1195).[2]

A number of researchers have suggested that we return to the mind-set of the 1950s, when aggressive medical procedures (being scarce and costly, if available at all) were not blindly applied in the absence of thought about the ultimate goal of the intervention. Walshe and Leonard (1985: 1047) locate themselves squarely in this camp, arguing that "as in patients who develop the [vegetative] syndrome after acute injury, patients with progressive neurological disease should be treated without undue intervention to preserve a mindless life."[3] Mark Wicclair (1993: 60) advances the same position: "The severely demented elderly constitute another category of patients about whom it might be claimed that they will receive no benefit from life-prolonging measures. Although they are not unconscious, it is nevertheless arguable that their quality of life is so low that extended life is of no benefit to them."

If only we knew a bit more about what tube feeding entails and what death after forgoing ANH was like, then ANH might become more than something we *say* we would forgo in response to a public opinion poll. It might instead become something we actually *do* forgo in real life, as Cranford, Walshe and Leonard, Wicclair, and others recommend.

Methods of ANH

Generally speaking, there are two kinds of ANH—enteral and parenteral. *Enteral* feeding (from the Greek term meaning intestines or entrails) delivers a nutritional slurry directly into the gut through a plastic nasogastric tube, inserted through the nose and down through the throat or through a gastrostomy tube, inserted directly into the stomach or upper intestine. *Parenteral* feeding delivers fluid and nutrients through a needle inserted in the patient's vein. This can be accomplished in one of two ways: intravenous feeding, using lines inserted into the veins of a patient's limbs, or total parenteral nutrition (TPN), which uses lines inserted into the central veins in the neck and upper chest area. Enteral and parenteral feeding—like any medical procedures—both have their drawbacks and potential complications.

Gastrostomies

Gastrostomies, first practiced on humans in 1875 (Major 1989: 23), involve the surgical insertion of plastic tubes into the stomach under local anesthesia. Over time, a track forms between the skin and the stomach wall, much like the track that develops in the earlobe a few months after ordinary ear piercing. The tube can be relatively comfortable after the incision heals.

Though gastrostomy tubes are probably the preferred method of artificially feeding and hydrating patients over the long term, there are several possible complications associated with this method of enteral feeding. Some researchers have noted the prevalence of local infections and painful insertion sites (where the tube passes though the skin), inflammation of the stomach lining, hemorrhaging, and splitting open of the incision site in gastrostomy patients (Peck, Cohen, and Mulvihill 1990: 1198). The feeding formula may also be aspirated into the lungs, leading to pneumonia.

Often, demented patients have to be physically restrained to prevent them from inadvertently dislodging or purposefully pulling out their tubes. Patients who are at least partially conscious may be confused and irritated—physically, emotionally, or both—by the stomach tube and its associated apparatus.

Nasogastric Feeding

Nasogastric feeding is the most common mode of delivering enteral formulas to patients who need assistance in the short term.[4] NG tubes can be placed by a trained health care professional without resorting to surgery, and for that reason, they are often considered to be "less invasive" than stomach tubes. Although consent is typically sought for the placement of a gastrostomy tube, NG tubes are often inserted without bothering to solicit approval from the patient or a surrogate decisionmaker; consent is generally thought to be implied when patients or their surrogates complete general "consent to treat" forms on admission to health care facilities.

The insertion of an NG tube involves passing a flexible plastic tube, lubricated with a tasteless jelly, up through the nostril, then down through the back of the throat and into the stomach. The process can be quite uncomfortable and possibly painful, especially if the tube hits the upper nasal cavity and if the individual doing the insertion forces the tube to make the downward turn toward the throat. As the tube moves down past the esophagus, it often causes a gag reflex that can result in vomiting.

For confused patients, tube insertion can be frightening, requiring that they be physically restrained during the procedure. And once the tube is in place, it can be irritating and frightening to the demented patient; caregivers are sometimes forced to put the patient's hands in mittens, which are tied to the sides of the bed or chair. Although there are few empirical data on the frequency of using restraints in demented patients, anecdotal evidence suggests that their use is widespread (OTA 1987b: 283).

If the NG tube becomes dislodged or if the patient continues to vomit, gastric contents can be aspirated into the lungs, leading to the development of aspiration pneumonia. If formula is introduced into the stomach too rapidly, diarrhea, regurgitation, aspiration, or vomiting can result. The average charges for enteral nutrition—delivered either through an NG tube or via a gastrostomy tube—run about $100 a day, or about $36,000 a year.[5]

Intravenous Feeding

The intravenous line is the most common method of delivering parenteral nutrition and hydration to patients over the short term. This method, first employed in the 1890s, can be used to supply a patient with water, saline, glucose solutions, and medications, infused through a needle inserted in the patient's arm or leg.

Intravenous feeding is typically used over the long term only when the gastrointestinal tract is blocked or diseased to the point where absorption of food and fluids is compromised. The method cannot be used too long, however, because of the risk of infection at the site of the IV needle.

Intravenous feeding can become very expensive, running as much as $425 a day (over $155,000 per year, if it were ever employed for that length of time).[6] As with NG tubes, the placement of IV lines is often considered part of routine care that is consented to on admission. Only rarely do hospitals require the specific consent of the patient or surrogate to begin IV feeding and hydration support (Hastings Center 1987). This practice only heightens the concern that may be raised regarding patient and surrogate autonomy (OTA 1987b: 320).

Total Parenteral Nutrition

Total parenteral nutrition, a process that was developed in the late 1960s and widely applied beginning in the 1970s, provides an alternative to the IV line for patients who need to be artificially fed over the long term but cannot tolerate stomach (enteral) feeding. With TPN, formula is fed into the body through a catheter inserted into a large, central vein in the patient's chest or neck.

Although TPN is an improvement over IV feeding, it, too, has its drawbacks. TPN patients run a significant risk of catheter- and formula-related infections. Mechanical problems with insertion and maintenance of the catheter have also been noted (OTA 1987b: 284). As with any form of tube feeding, confused patients may have to be physically or chemically restrained to prevent them from tampering with the TPN line. Anecdotal evidence suggests that TPN is not regularly used for long-term demented and confused patients because of the costs and complications associated with this form of ANH. Total parenteral nutrition runs upwards of $200 a day, or more than $73,000 a year.

General Drawbacks of ANH Summarized

Whatever the method used, artificial feeding (particularly NG feeding) is likely to add to a dying patient's distress rather than alleviate it. This sentiment, expressed over twelve years ago by Dr. Judith Ahronheim, has been echoed among clinicians in more recent years (e.g., Enck 1994: 25; Cundiff 1992: 47–48). Perhaps even more disconcerting than the distress caused by tube feeding is the need to restrain patients who are uncooperative or confused and demented (Peck, Cohen, and Mulvihill 1990: 1197; Ahronheim 1984).

One study found that almost all of the fifty-two tube-fed patients in one skilled nursing facility required some form of continuous physical restraint to prevent self-extubation. Ninety percent of those patients with restraints had to have their hands enclosed in mittens, and 71 percent required some form of additional restraint (Peck, Cohen, and Mulvihill 1990). For patients who retain some level of awareness, restraints might be considered an affront to their dignity, and many patients who are aware of their situation tend to become depressed or angry over being tied down (Major 1989: 25). Restraints can also violate the dignity of demented and vegetative patients, for, legally, these individuals retain an interest in being cared for humanely (as opposed to being treated only as a biological entity) regardless of their mental state.

In addition to whatever indignity might be suffered, restraints can, over time, put the patient at increased risk for developing bedsores and pneumonia. According to one study, tube-fed patients were more than three times as likely to develop aspiration pneumonia (57 percent versus 15 percent in the control group). Restrained patients were also 50 percent more likely to suffer from painful decubitus ulcers (Peck, Cohen, and Mulvihill 1990: 1197; Ahronheim 1984). Tube feeding can also cause edema (swelling) in the abdomen and extremities. Accumulations of fluid in the upper respiratory tract can cause increased secretions, and accumulations in the lower tract can increase coughing and shortness of breath (Ahronheim 1984).

Artificially provided food and fluids may also precipitate psychological problems for friends, family members, and caregivers. The feeding tubes and their associated apparatus may serve as a barrier between relatives and the patient and may divert the attention of caregivers from tending to the patient to maintaining the equipment. Ultimately, the relief of the patient's suffering, which should be the primary goal, can be overwhelmed by the drive to correct nutritional imbalances and restore electrolyte levels (Oliver 1984: 631; Sutcliffe 1994: 62; Peck, Cohen, and Mulvihill 1990: 1197). In addition, artificial feedings provided to hopelessly ill patients may give them (if they are conscious and aware), their friends, and members of the family a false sense of hope (Sutcliffe 1994: 62).

The Dehydration Alternative

There is a time-honored, foolproof alternative to tube feeding for terminally ill patients who are prepared to die: dehydration. The health care community is, of course, aware of this approach, but most members of that community are reluctant to speak openly about it—despite the fact that their professional journals are virtually brimming with evidence about the benefits of dehydration. Just as pneumonia was referred to as "the old person's friend" years ago, before the development of antibiotics, a substantial body of literature indicates that dehydration might well be thought of as "the dying person's friend" today.

When food and fluids are withheld or withdrawn, patients, in fact, die of dehydration, not starvation. The distinction is an important one that must be addressed before anything else about the subject of dehydration is considered.

Pathogenesis of Starvation

The word *starvation* inevitably conjures up gruesome images. Emaciated children in Third World countries come to mind, or one might recall the haggard visages of the ten Irish hunger strikers who fasted to death as part of a political protest in 1981. Whatever the vision, starvation seems to be anything but a satisfactory alternative for elderly demented patients at the end of life—and for good reason.

Death by starvation is a long, arduous process that can easily drag on for a number of weeks. The Irish nationalists who starved themselves to death in 1981 lived an average of sixty-two days after they stopped eating. This corresponds with the findings of Maurice Shils, James Olson, and Moshe Shike (1994: 938), who suggest that the length of survival without food for nonobese adults is sixty to seventy days.[7]

Starvation, involving drastic weight loss and body wasting, begins after feeding stops and the body has burned up all the readily available sugars in the blood. Thereafter, muscles and fatty deposits throughout the body are metabolized as sources of energy. As the muscles are converted to fuel and begin to wither away, the limbs appear to shrink, taking on a sticklike appearance. Without fat to support it, the skin begins to sag and become wrinkled, sometimes giving even the youngest victims of starvation the withered, emaciated look of an old man.[8] Other victims of starvation may suffer from kwashiorkor, a malnutritional deficiency that allows fluid to leak from blood vessels into the body. The primary symptom of kwashiorkor is severe edema, often manifested as a grotesquely swollen belly. Psychological changes such as apathy and irritability are common as well.

As the process of starvation wears on, bodily functions begin to shut down. One of the most critical functions that slows down is the reproduction of white blood cells. This weakens the immune system and leads to a sort of starvation-induced immunodeficiency. This condition is quite similar to AIDS, and it turns relatively common and typically benign infectious diseases into killers. Toward the end of the starvation process, the intestines begin to fail, leading to uncontrollable diarrhea. Finally, if the starvation victim has survived the ravages of infection by twist of fate or through good nursing care, the heart muscle, shrunken like all the other muscles in the body, gives out and the individual dies of cardiac arrest (Lemonick 1992: 36; Shils, Olson, and Shike 1994: 1460–1461).

Medical studies of political hunger strikers add gruesome details to this clinical picture. W. J. Kalk, M. Felix, E. R. Snoey, and Veriawa Yosuf (1993) reported that twenty-two of the thirty-one South African hunger strikers under observation had symptoms so severe (abdominal cramping, headaches, and clinical depression) that hospitalization was required. Dominique Fromme, Elisabeth Questiaux, Marth Gautier, and Leon Schwarzenberg (1984) reported that French hunger strikers opposing the nuclear arms race in 1983 agreed to begin the refeeding process about five and a half weeks into their fasting after severe nausea and abdominal cramps, bleeding gums, tremors, and tinnitus made continued fasting unbearable. Protesters in Ireland who carried their hunger strikes to the end suffered from vomiting so acute and so wrenching they could not even hold down springwater as they neared death (Cranford 1991a: 18–19).

There can be no doubt that starvation, planned or not, is a grim process. Obviously, it is not a death that most would wish for themselves and their loved ones.

Pathogenesis of Dehydration

Dehydration is entirely different from starvation. Whereas death by starvation is a drawn-out and unnatural process, dehydration is much more natural and common, and it leads to death relatively quickly and painlessly. It is for exactly this reason that political hunger strikers continue to take flu-

TABLE 5.1   The Hydration of Political Hunger Strikers

Political Hunger Strikers	Fluid Intake	Source
800 South African political detainees in 1989	A teaspoon of sucrose dissolved in a jug of tap water daily, occasionally with a tablespoon of salt	Kalk et al 1993: 391
French hunger strikers opposing the nuclear arms race in 1983	1.5 liters of water daily	Fromme et al. 1984: 1451
10 Irish hunger strikers in 1981	Normal amounts of water as long as they could hold it down	Cranford 1991a: 18–19

ids during their fasts; if they did not, they would die of dehydration with some dispatch. Death by dehydration is not nearly as politically effective as the death that results from the drawn-out and wrenching process of starvation (see Table 5.1).

Good, clinically based studies of death associated with dehydration are uncommon in the medical literature. This dearth of empirical studies can be explained, in part, by the reluctance of health care providers to intrude on dying patients and their families, for ethical and humanitarian reasons. In addition, many clinicians tend to treat the patient's lack of interest in eating and drinking toward the end of life as a problem requiring active intervention rather than a condition worthy of passive study.

Others, however, view dehydration in the elderly in historical (rather than technological) terms, as a naturally occurring phenomenon. According to Shils, Olson, and Shike (1994: 1460–1461), for example, prior to the development and popularization of tube-feeding techniques in recent years, dehydration tended to be the direct cause of all "natural" deaths (i.e., those not associated with violent trauma or acute infection) (see also Meares 1994: 10; Cranford 1991a: 18). Even today, it is generally accepted that food and fluid intake decreases naturally with age and that elderly people often report a decreased interest in eating and drinking (Justice 1995: 41; Ahronheim and Gasner 1990: 278). Similarly, Christopher Justice (1995: 42) argues that "cultural norms that allow either force-feeding or gentle encouragement of non-hungry, dying persons to eat—and which encourage the dying person, him or herself, to always continue eating—may act to 'unnaturally' extend the dying process."

The research that does exist on dehydration suggests that patients who stop taking in food and fluids slowly sink into unconsciousness and coma over a period of five to eight days and die peacefully several days after that. The transition from a fully hydrated state to unconsciousness is typically made without complaint of pain or discomfort, as long as comfort care measures are continued (Sullivan 1993: 221; Ahronheim and Gasner 1990: 278).[9] In the words of Dr. Robert J. Sullivan, a geriatric researcher and medical specialist, a review of the literature on this subject suggests that

> it is likely that prolonged dehydration and starvation induce no pain and only limited discomfort from dry mouth, which can be controlled.[10] For individuals carrying an intolerable burden of illness and disability, or those who have no hope of ever again enjoying meaningful human interaction, the withdrawal of food and fluid may be considered without concern that it will add to the misery (Sullivan 1993: 222).

A few symptoms are associated with dehydration, but each is easily treated. One symptom, thirst, is experienced in only a small percentage of dehydrating patients at the end of life, and it is never hard to alleviate (Billings 1985: 810; Maillet and King 1993: 46–47; Hastings Center 1987: 59–60). In one study involving ninety-six hospice nurses, 73 percent indicated that dehydrated patients rarely complained of thirst (Andrews and Levine 1989: 31). Whatever thirst or mouth dryness that develops can easily be palliated with lip moisturizer, sips of water, ice chips, and hard candies (Schmitz and O'Brien 1989: 32; Printz 1988: 85; Andrews and Levine 1989: 31; McCann, Hall, and Grath-Junker 1994: 1265). In a small percentage of patients, electrolyte imbalance may lead to neuromuscular irritability and twitching, both of which are easily treated with antispasmodics and sedation (Schmitz and O'Brien 1989: 32; Sutcliffe 1994: 61). Nausea, another symptom of dehydration that emerges on occasion, is easily controlled with antiemetics (Printz 1988: 85). Bedbound patients may also report varying degrees of lethargy, drowsiness, and occasionally fatigue, but these symptoms are rarely a source of much distress (Billings 1985: 810).

Phyllis Schmitz and Merry O'Brien (1989: 36), two hospice nurses, write that "we have not seen evidence that dehydration occurring at the termination of life results in any pain or distressing experiences for the patient."[11] These conclusions are echoed in more general surveys of caregivers who are familiar with dehydration in dying patients: The vast majority of those *experienced* with treating patients at the end of life believe that dehydration is not painful.[12]

There is also substantial evidence to suggest that dehydration carries some significant advantages. Schmitz and O'Brien (1989: 32) found that dehydration reduces nausea, vomiting, and abdominal pain. Sullivan (1993: 222) and Stephen Post (1990: 185) both reported that dehydration reduces the diarrhea that is often suffered by dying patients. Furthermore, the decreased urine output secondary to dehydration means fewer bedpans, precarious trips to the commode, catheterizations, and bed-wetting episodes (Schmitz and O'Brien 1989: 32; Andrews and Levine 1989: 31).

Pulmonary secretions also decrease with dehydration. This reduces coughing, congestion, gagging and choking, and shortness of breath. Often, in fact, the need to suction congesting secretions is completely eliminated (Schmitz and O'Brien 1989: 32; Sullivan 1993: 222; Post 1990: 185; Andrews and Levine 1989: 31).

Last and perhaps most interesting is the reduction of pain that some clinicians have linked to dehydration. Medical researchers report that terminally ill patents who become dehydrated tend to experience less discomfort than those receiving medical hydration, to the point where the dehydrated patients required less analgesia than the hydrated group (Printz 1988: 84, 1992: 698; Sutcliffe 1994: 61; Ahronheim and Gasner 1990: 278). "Indeed," writes Sullivan (1993: 222), "mild euphoria can be anticipated [with dehydration], accompanied by an increased toleration of pain." The slow but steady decrease in consciousness associated with advancing dehydration may serve as part of the protection against discomfort and suffering experienced by patients who are forgoing food and fluids (Post 1990: 185). Dehydration also reduces swelling in the body, improving a patient's overall sense of well-being. Reduced swelling also relieves pressure on any tumors that exist, and that, too, may relieve some discomfort (Andrews and Levine 1989: 31).

Clinical Attitudes About Dehydration

Unfortunately, there is little reliable evidence to indicate how—or how often—decisions are made to withhold artificially provided food and fluids from chronic, irreversibly demented elderly patients. There is, however, a fair amount of data on the attitudes of clinicians in these matters. One recent study by Candace Meares indicated that 95 percent of hospice nurses believe aggressive nutritional support does more harm than good (Meares 1994: 13). In another study conducted in 1994, 326 practicing internists who had personal experience with tube-fed patients were surveyed. Of this group, 84 percent opposed the initiation of tube feeding for a patient with advanced dementia when the patient's wishes were not known (Hodges et al. 1994).[13]

Another study, involving 156 directors of nursing and 124 house physicians, revealed a bit more ambivalence. Respondents were asked to indicate their preferences on the tube feeding of demented patients on a scale of 1 (strongly favor tube feeding) to 8 (strongly oppose tube feeding) in various patient scenarios. An average score of 4.5 would indicate that, in the aggregate, the respondents were neither for nor against hydration. The registered nurses in the study leaned slightly in the dehydration direction; they had an average score of about 5 on the 8-point scale when asked about the tube feeding of old, confused, and seemingly unhappy patients. The physicians in the study, with an average score of about 6, appeared to lean a bit more strongly in the direction of forgoing tube feeding for such patients (Watts, Cassel, and Hickam 1986: 607).

In a larger and more comprehensive study conducted by Daniel Luchins and Patricia Hanrahan (1993: 25–26), 1,408 members of the American Geriatric Society and members of the Alzheimer's Association (essentially, family members of individuals afflicted with DAT) were asked to recommend 1 of 5 levels of care for a patient with end-stage dementia,[14] ranging from level 1 (do everything possible) to level 5 (provide comfort care measures only—no CPR, no respirators, no antibiotics, and no tube feeding). Sixty-one percent of the physicians, 55 percent of the other geriatrics health care professionals, and 71 percent of the family members in the survey indicated that they would opt for treatment level 5 (comfort care only, no tube feeding).

Dr. David Cundiff, a hospice physician and unabashed critic of euthanasia, is another caregiver who finds the tube-feeding option wanting.[15] Cundiff states clearly that, as a rule, he does not recommend tube feeding for his terminally ill patients and that he recommends withdrawal of feeding tubes if they are in place. This sentiment was widely accepted among other clinicians as well, especially when physical restraints are required to keep patients from pulling out their feeding tubes or catheters (OTA 1987b: 315). At least two studies found that the more exposure a caregiver has to dehydration in dying patients, the more acceptable the dehydration option becomes (Andrews and Levine 1989: 31; Luchins and Hanrahan 1993: 25).

Overall, there is very little doubt that those experienced with death and dehydration believe the benefits of dehydration far outweigh the burdens for certain patients, namely, the terminally ill, the irreversibly unconscious, and the severely demented. This is not to say that the hopelessly ill should be forced to undergo dehydration against their expressed wishes. But when the vast majority of Americans say they would not want to be tube fed if irreversibly demented or vegetative (see Tables 3.2 and 4.4), when the consensus position holds that forgoing ANH is an entirely appropriate and ethical medical response to hopeless illness, when clerics formulate positions that sanction the forgoing of food and fluids if the benefits are outweighed by the burdens, and when clinicians explain the considerable drawbacks of tube feeding and the benefits of dehydration and express (through surveys) their solid support for the dehydration alternative, one can only wonder why any rational decisionmaker would choose long-term tube feeding at the end of life.

The dehydration alternative may also prove helpful to competent patients who are suffering from chronic and debilitating conditions and would like to have the option of physician-assisted suicide (PAS). Choosing dehydration overcomes many of the criticisms associated with PAS. More knowledge about the benefits of forgoing hydration might actually take some of the wind out of the sails of those who think physician-assisted suicide is the only or the best way to control one's end-of-life destiny. At the

---

BOX 5.1   Dehydration and Physician-Assisted Suicide

Physician-assisted suicide (PAS) has been the subject of regular news cover-age and has spawned much legal, ethical, and medical debate across the coun-try. Given the interest and controversy that surround this subject, it seems curi-ous that so little attention has been paid to the forgoing of fluids as a practical alternative for the seriously ill who seek to hasten death.

Dehydration, like PAS, provides a comfortable exit from life, and both processes shorten a dying process that might otherwise drag on interminably. Since the time of death is predictable with both dehydration and PAS, family members and friends can rearrange schedules and take the time to travel to the bedside of the loved one at the time of his or her passing. In both cases, the pa-tient need not die alone, cared for only by strangers. Friends and family mem-bers can be there at the end to provide comfort care and give their support.

Dehydration also has some advantages that PAS does not:

- Dehydration provides control. Physician-assisted suicide involves having the patient breathe poison gas, take lethal injections, or swallow lethal amounts of pills, all of which begin processes that, for all practical purposes, are irre-versible. In contrast, individuals who initiate death by dehydration have sev-eral days to change their minds.
- Dehydration requires no help. Patients who decide to use dehydration to hasten death are not forced to beg help from family, friends, or health care professionals, who may have moral qualms about PAS. Even the most debil-itated patient can exercise his or her constitutional right to forgo hydration, allowing nature to take its course.
- Dehydration is natural. Physician-assisted suicide requires wrenching changes in medical ethics and practice that dehydration does not. Prior to the 1960s, dehydration was almost always present in the dying patient as ei-ther a direct or contributing cause of death. Just as pneumonia was once de-scribed as the sick person's friend, dehydration was usually a close, amicable neighbor.

---

very least, dehydration provides another option for seriously ill patients who are intent on hastening death in an amenable way. (See Box 5.1.)

Why Is Tube Feeding So Common?

Empirical studies of tube feeding in clinical practice suggest that the use of artificially provided food and fluids in the severely ill is much more preva-lent than one might expect, given the consensus position, public opinion, and caregiver experience. There is relatively clear and strong support for the legitimacy of forgoing ANH in the medical community (expressed via position statements of professional associations and the attitudes of bedside clinicians), in the lay community (in public opinion poll data), in the legal community (in judicial decisions at the state and federal levels), and in both the secular and religious ethics communities. But when push comes to shove, tube feeding is initiated and continued more often than not.

According to an international study by Thierry Collaud and Charles-Henri Rapin (1991), 28 percent of responding physicians *said* that they would recommend tube feeding, but 44 percent of them actually did recommend tube feeding in practice. Another study indicated that 54 percent of the physicians surveyed were concerned that ANH was used inappropriately in their critically ill and terminally ill patients, and 55 percent of the physicians responded affirmatively to the statement, "Sometimes I feel the treatments I offer my patient are overly burdensome" (Solomon et al. 1993: 14, 16). What is at the root of the dichotomy between clinical, public, and ethical *sentiment*—which accepts the notion of withdrawing tube feeding from seriously ill patients—and clinical *reality*—in which tube feeding is the norm?

The practices in nursing homes, where many elderly and infirm patients receive their care, provide a partial answer. Hand feeding patients is a time-consuming process, and it is regularly alleged that some hospitals and nursing homes use tube feeding because sufficient staff time cannot be allocated to hand feeding every patient who cannot feed him- or herself (OTA 1987b: 279). Some caregivers indicate they know of nursing homes that simply will not accept patients with eating problems unless tubes are in place at the time the patient is admitted to the facility. According to a study published by the New York Sate Task Force on Life and the Law (1992: 11), nursing homes may favor tube feeding because they receive a higher reimbursement for patients who are tube fed versus those who are fed by hand.

Caregiver anxiety about withdrawing food and fluids also comes into play, at least partly because of the important role that food plays in American culture. As R. A. Carson notes: "The simple act of offering to allay hunger and to slake thirst of a dying person is deemed across time and cultures not only right but good. Denying food and water for any reason seems the antithesis of expressing care and compassion" (cited in Sutcliffe 1994: 62). J. Andrew Billings (1985: 810) adds that "the decision to administer fluids to a dehydrated patient is often determined by the symbolic or emotional meaning of such measures to the patient, family, and caretakers." It is not surprising, then, that when faced with a real-life decision, families often ask and physicians advise that tube feeding be provided.

The natural aversion to withholding and withdrawing food and fluids is understandable, especially when that aversion is compounded (mistakenly) by the thought that those who forgo ANH will be left to "starve" to death.[16] In addition, providing food to those we love has always symbolized and expressed the essence of care and compassion. Dr. Joanne Lynn (1989: 47) notes that "there is a link made in the mind between feeding and loving that is difficult to dismiss in the practice of making decisions for those who can no longer make decisions for themselves." Eating and drinking are associated with social interchange and the celebration of life, and providing others with food and drink is a common way of honoring them.

All of our holidays and social occasions, big and small, are marked by the provision of food and drink. All this, combined with the negative personal experiences people have with even relatively low levels of thirst and hunger and the horrific stories in the media about starvation in other parts of the world, often predispose family members to pursue tube feeding. There are also religious admonitions that pervade our culture regarding the duty to feed the hungry and provide drink to the thirsty. As a result, "tube feedings are often initiated to alleviate the anxiety of caregivers and families of patients," and that is a response that cannot help but "cloud the real issues of providing comfort to the patient" (McCann, Hall, and Grath-Junker 1994: 1266).

Physicians also get caught up in the crosscurrents on feeding the hopelessly ill and demented patients in their care, especially when family members (and perhaps nurses) are imploring the physicians to "do something!" This external pressure, when combined with the influence of training that still regards infusions as the hallmark of serious treatment (Collaud and Rapin 1991: 238), may conspire to undermine the abstract clinical indications to forgo feeding tubes. The technological imperative, the sense that one needs to employ every means of technology available regardless of the costs or benefits of treatment, also drives physicians to act in ways that, in the abstract, may make little or no sense.

The preeminence of the technological imperative among clinicians may be rooted in medical schools where, according to James Lindgren, a doctor's "instincts are well trained to intervene to prolong life. Indeed, physicians are rarely challenged for intervening but often criticized for 'going slow.' Physicians do not easily accept the conception that it may be best to do less, not more, for a patient. The decision to pull back is much more difficult to make than the decision to push ahead with aggressive support" (Lindgren 1993: 186). Continuing this line of thought, Ezekiel Emanuel writes that "whether it is positively affirmed, liberally espoused, or instinctively assumed, prolonging life becomes the 'default' response for physicians facing clinical decisions without clear guidelines on terminating care. As a result, aggressive medical treatment, without concern for the 'whole' patient—the physicalization of medicine—is the standard of care" (cited in Lindgren 1993: 186).

Mark Siegler and David Shiedermayer (1987: 34) have commented along these lines as well:

> Many physicians believe the denial of fluids and nutrition would injure the therapeutic relationship and that continuing fluids and nutrition, even in the terminally ill, affirms the physician's role as a caring professional. They con-

sider the provision of food and fluids to be both a form of treatment and a nurturing and symbolic act that avoids any appearance of abandoning the patient.

Of course, abandonment is exactly what physicians accomplish when they fuel false hopes with their symbolism and interpose a medical technology between the patient and the rest of the world. The predisposition on the part of physicians to tube feed is not shared universally, however. Ronald Cranford (1991a: 20) recounts that

> on a recent trip to the Netherlands I spoke with health care professionals in nursing homes. One topic was the use of feeding tubes in profoundly demented patients. I asked some physicians what they do when patients become so profoundly demented they are unable to feed themselves naturally. Some didn't seem to know how to respond to this question. One particular physician in a nursing home near Amsterdam kept repeating, "What do we do?" She didn't seem to understand the question because the answer was so obvious to her. Finally she answered, "Well, we wait." The idea of starting a feeding tube on a profoundly demented patient who has no chance of recovery is a truly "foreign" concept to the common sense and humane approach of many Dutch physicians and health care providers. When I told them of the common practice in the United States, they often stared at me in disbelief. Some asked "Why would you do that?" I didn't have a very convincing answer.

Collaud and Rapin (1991: 238) argue against the American instincts the Dutch find so befuddling and suggest that "the therapeutic choice should be aimed at the patient's well-being [e.g., best interests], and should not be aimed at relieving the anxiety of relatives or nursing staff." Unfortunately, anxiety often overwhelms reason in these situations.

No doubt, some physicians are distracted by the writings of those who have argued that doctors should fight the impulse to accede to patient's wishes when they express an interest in forgoing food and fluids because patients who choose this route are not thinking clearly, by definition. According to geriatrician John Morley (1989: 184), "Half of underweight older patients have abnormal attitudes toward eating." He also reports that geriatricians commonly encounter older patients who, having lost their locus of control, use "food as a weapon in an attempt to manipulate the caregiver."[17]

There is also the physician's fear of legal liability (Hodges et al. 1994: 1019), a fear that may, in part, be grounded in reality. Despite the widespread acceptance of ANH as a medical treatment that can be legitimately withheld at the end of life, some state statutes continue to treat ANH as a separate class of procedure that can only be forgone in very limited circumstances, if at all. In the *Barber* case in California, two physicians, Neil Barber and Robert Nejdl, were charged with murder by state prosecutors after they withdrew artificial nutrition and hydration from the irreversibly vegetative Clarence Herbert, at the behest of his family.[18] Although the *Barber* case, like other similar cases,[19] was ultimately resolved in favor of the physicians involved,[20] the very fact that the doctors were charged in the first place may leave physicians troubled by "the brooding presence of . . . possible liability" (Kapp and Lo, cited in OTA 1987b: 72; also cited on 185, from *Quinlan*) when the issue of suspending ANH arises.

Research conducted by Dr. John Ely and his colleagues certainly brings this point home (Ely et al. 1992). The Ely team surveyed 439 members of the Missouri Academy of Family Physicians regarding a hypothetical case involving an eighty-nine-year-old stroke victim who had indicated a desire not to be tube fed. The researchers found that 66 percent of those physicians who said they would comply with the patient's legitimate wish to forgo tube feeding would reverse that decision and order artificial feeding if "pushed" to do so by members of the patient's family. The researchers explained this result in simple terms: It is the family, not the demented patient, who may initiate legal proceedings if treatment preferences are not honored. The family has the ability to sue, while the patient has none, and even if the physician wins his or her case after acceding to the patient's wishes not to be treated, the emotional and financial costs of legal proceedings may not be viewed as worth the effort.[21]

In addition, there seems to be a fair amount of confusion among physicians about medical-ethical issues associated with ANH. For example, although many physicians apparently feel that tube feeding can be withdrawn from vegetative patients at the request of a surrogate, they are reluctant to do so, thinking that they would be violating professional norms (NYSTFLL 1992: 11) or that withdrawal would increase patient discomfort.[22] A 1993 study by Mildred Solomon and colleagues revealed that 42 percent of 1,446 responding physicians and nurses thought ethical standards required that food and water always be continued (Solomon et al. 1993: 20). Many respondents also reported that they thought permission to withhold or withdraw treatment applied only to so-called heroic measures such as CPR, while "ordinary" measures such as tube feeding had to be continued in the absence of a court order.[23] The same survey revealed that 12 percent of health care professionals in the study thought withholding tube feeding was tantamount to killing.

Follow-up interviews in the Solomon study revealed that one of the primary motivations for not wanting to withdraw ANH was a fear that to do so would cause discomfort in the patient, despite the stream of research on the subject that suggests that continued feeding and hydration can be much more problematic when it comes to pain and discomfort than forgoing this treatment.[24] Other studies have found that most doctors who advocate the use of ANH for dying patients would use this treatment to ensure their patients' comfort (Sutcliffe 1994: 62; Andrews and Levine 1989: 31),[25] even though studies of hospice nurses who have extensive experience with terminal dehydration view dehydration as generally beneficial (Enck 1994: 27).[26] In the end, a number of reasons conspire to yield a simple yet troubling reality, according to a study led by Sidney Wanzer (Wanzer et al. 1984): "Physicians worry too much about withholding treatment."

Dr. Judith Ahronheim (1984) sums up the situation well:

> Although potentially valuable and life saving in many situations, artificial nutrition and hydration do not provide comfort care for dying patients. Experience and available scientific evidence have shown that death without artificial nutrition and hydration is natural and pain free. . . . In contrast, tube feeding prolongs and often worsens the dying process. Terminally ill patients sometimes benefit from artificial feeding. But to assume that it must always be provided fails to consider the patients' needs. Because we ourselves tend to see the provision of food and water as intrinsic to caring, we sometimes feel uncomfortable about withholding artificial nutrition and hydration. When we are entrusted with the decision for the dying, we need to broaden our understanding of caring so that we address the *patient's* comfort, not our own (italics in original).

Antibiotics: Another End-of-Life Dilemma

Infection, like dehydration, is very common in the old and debilitated patient population. In one study of elderly nursing home residents, infections were found to account for 54 percent of all acute medical problems and 63 percent of all deaths (Mott and Barker 1988: 820).

Infections stem primarily from the incontinence and immobility that are so common in elderly patients. Immobility allows fluid to settle in the lungs, leading to the development of pneumonia, the most common of killer infections. Patients who are tube fed face the added risk of aspirating their feeding solutions even if the feeding tubes are properly placed. Meanwhile, incontinence leads to the increased risk of developing urinary tract infections (UTIs), the second most common terminal infection. In addition, incontinence, immobility, and low levels of blood protein in the elderly population lead to the development of another serious problem: bedsores. Sherwin Nuland graphically describes them as "ghastly to look at as they deepen to the point of exposing muscle, tendon, and even bone, coated in layers of dying tissue and pus" (Nuland 1994: 104). In the end, most patients whose dementia progresses to the vegetative point die of some sort of infection, whether treated or not. Consequently, Nuland (and others) suggest that it may be best to forgo the use of antibiotics and "let grim nature have its way" (Nuland 1994: 104).

Burdens of Antibiotics

The medical literature indicates that, like the use of artificial nutrition and hydration, the administration of antibiotics has costs as well as benefits.

There can be no denying that, beginning with the development of sulfon-amide in the 1930s, antibiotics have saved millions of lives and relieved an untold amount of suffering brought on by infections in otherwise potentially healthy individuals. At the same time, antibiotics—again, like artificial nutrition and hydration—should be used judiciously rather than reflexively, for such medical therapy can be excessively burdensome for some, especially those who are severely debilitated and chronically or terminally ill.

Sherwin Nuland is not alone in suggesting that we allow "grim nature to take its course" when infection strikes those who are already mortally ill. According to the Hastings Center's *Guidelines*:

> Although administering these drugs [antibiotics] can constitute a beneficial and welcome form of life-sustaining treatment for many patients, for others it can be disproportionately burdensome. . . . [The] decision about using antibiotics and other life-sustaining medication, like decisions about other forms of life-sustaining treatment, requires patients and their surrogates to balance carefully the potential burdens of the treatment and the life it offers against the benefits. . . . The patient or surrogate should be able to evaluate and forego antibiotics as they can other forms of treatment (Hastings Center 1987: 65–66).

According to William Osler's *Principles and Practice of Medicine,* a medical textbook of 1,600 pages now in its twenty-first edition: "Pneumonia may well be called the friend of old age. Taken off by it in an acute, short, not often painful illness, the old escape those 'cold gradations of decay' that make the last stage of life all so distressing" (cited in Nuland 1994: 60). Dr. P. R. Katz (1993: 173), an internist and geriatric specialist, is another clinician who argues that antibiotics are not always desirable and should not always be used to address infection in nursing home patients. He recommends that physicians and nursing home administrators and staff work in concert to avoid inappropriate use of antibiotics, prescribing them only in situations in which clear benefit has been demonstrated. Beverly Volicer and colleagues (B. Volicer et al. 1993), writing specifically about DAT patients, suggest that increased use of hospice care for patients in this condition would have advantages for both the patient and for society (antibiotics are rarely used in hospices). According to Volicer, "Treatment of infections inflicts a burden on the DAT patient without proven benefit. Therefore, there is a need to compare the benefit and burden of the intervention to determine which are justified for an individual patient" (B. Volicer et al. 1993: 539, citations omitted; also see L. Volicer et al. 1986: 2213; Hurley et al. 1993: 21).

The potential burdens of antibiotic treatment begin with the diagnostic workup, which is required to identify the type of infection so that the appropriate course of antibiotic therapy can be prescribed. This workup can involve the sometimes painful harvesting of material for analysis from the site of the infection (B. Volicer et al. 1993: 539; Hastings Center 1987: 65–66). Transfer to an acute medical unit where clinicians who are unfamiliar to the patient proceed with diagnostic testing and follow-up therapy, if required, can also prove frightening for a patient who may not fully comprehend the situation (B. Volicer et al. 1993: 539). The possibility of adverse drug reactions (B. Volicer et al. 1993: 539) and other complications secondary to the use of the antibiotics (Hastings Center 1987: 65–66) must also be weighed in the balance.[27] The need for repeated injections and the problem of finding suitable injections sites in already compromised skin must also be considered (Nuland 1994: 104; Hastings Center 1987: 65–66).

Another negative factor involves the possible need to use physical or chemical restraints while administering antibiotic treatment (B. Volicer et al. 1993: 539). According to Greg Sachs and his colleagues,

> Even routine measures used to address intercurrent infections cause demented patients who cannot understand the purpose of the procedure to become agitated and combative, necessitating the use of physical restraints which only exacerbate the discomfort and agitation felt by the patient, while stirring feelings of guilt, helplessness, and despair in members of the patient's family (Sachs et al. 1995: 558–559).

In many cases, no cause for the infection is identified, even though the patient has been subjected to burdensome diagnostic tests (B. Volicer et al. 1993: 539; Sachs et al. 1995: 558–559). And even when the proper diagnosis is made and therapy is started, patients who are noncommunicative and immobile often die in spite of the aggressive treatment they receive (Hurley et al. 1993; Sachs et al. 1995). In fact, research suggests that antibiotics do no better than a therapeutic course of analgesics and antipyretics (e.g., aspirin or acetaminophen to reduce fever) when treating infections in the severely demented patient (Hurley et al. 1993). In those whose illness is not as advanced, life may be prolonged, but suffering will be prolonged as well as one (or more likely several) underlying chronic pathologies continue on their course toward the inevitable death (Sachs et al. 1995: 558–559).[28]

Clinical Realities

How has the medical community reacted to the ethical dilemma of treating infections aggressively in cases in which the treatment itself is burdensome? In one landmark study conducted in 1979, physician Norman K. Brown and medical researcher Thompson Donovan (Brown and Donovan 1979) found that antibiotics were regularly withheld from long-term care patients who had developed serious fevers (the primary symptom of infection). In reviewing 1,256 patient records from 9 Seattle-area institutions, Brown and Donovan found that although 190 patients developed serious fevers, only 109 were treated actively with antibiotics, hospitalization, or both. Antibiotics were withheld from 81 patients, of whom 48 (59 percent) died within

48 hours (mostly, the primary cause of death was pneumonia), and 13 more patients died within the next month. Thus, the total 1-month mortality rate in the untreated group was 75 percent.[29]

In summarizing the results of their study, Brown and Donovan stated: "We believe that most of the decisions not to actively treat these [infections] were part of an intentional plan by physicians and nurses. . . . The medical records of 23 untreated patients showed that grave illness would not be treated. Medical personnel undoubtedly took the same approach for [the] other [58] patients" (Brown and Donovan 1979: 1250).

Peter Mott and William Barker (1988) found similar patterns of practice in the late 1980s. These two authors, both physicians, placed each of the 110 nursing home patients in their study into 1 of 4 treatment categories, ranging from category 1 (51 patients for whom all care was to be provided, including hospitalization and intensive care, as necessary) to category 4 (12 patients who were to receive comfort care only and no antibiotics).[30] After seven years of monitoring, Mott and Barker found that antibiotics were withheld in 14 percent of all cases and in 43 percent of the cases involving patients assigned to treatment category 3 (for whom antibiotics could be prescribed but who were not to be hospitalized) and category 4.

Perhaps more significant still, however, is the entire concept of assigning patients to a "comfort care only" category that involves withholding antibiotics. Apparently, given the straightforward way in which the categorization process was reported, withholding antibiotics is relatively routine and not particularly controversial. Although there is a fairly substantial body of literature on the benefits of withholding artificial nutrition and hydration from patients in the advanced stages of a mortal pathology, there is almost nothing written beyond what is cited here on the withholding of antibiotics. The few studies that have been published on the subject clearly indicate that withholding antibiotics is something of an open secret among health care professionals and that physicians who know the patient best are the ones most likely to do the withholding.[31]

Summary

In the 1950s, patients were not typed with the classification DNR because the technology and know-how associated with modern cardiac resuscitation did not exist. Attempts at resuscitating heart attack patients became widespread only after the introduction of CPR and the development of electronic defibrillators in the mid-1960s.[32] In the 1970s, physicians began "coding"[33] patients on their own, realizing that, as important as CPR was, it did not make sense to attempt aggressive resuscitation for everyone who suffered a myocardial infarction (especially if the patient was already seriously or terminally ill). Shortly thereafter, patients gained the ability to sign their own DNR orders. There were four phases in the evolution of CPR technology and the patient's right to control that technology, moving from (1) a lack of technology to (2) the development, proliferation, and universal use of technology to (3) the selective use of technology and finally to (4) patient control. The evolutionary process took about fifteen years to complete (from 1960 to 1975).

Today, approximately 70 percent of patients who die in the hospital have DNR orders in place (Council 1991: 1869). Patients now have the right to execute such orders, and obviously, many of them exercise that right.[34] In fact, a number of jurisdictions have expanded this right even further to include nonhospital DNR orders, allowing patients to carry DNR orders home with them whether they are seriously ill or not (in some cases).[35] The fact that some patients have a relatively good chance to benefit from CPR does not diminish their right to have a DNR order. Likewise, the fact that CPR can be simple to employ (e.g., mouth-to-mouth resuscitation and external chest massage), requiring no invasive or technologically sophisticated equipment whatsoever (Capron 1989), does not impair the right to refuse such treatment. Clearly, patients or their surrogates are now in the driver's seat. Virtually no one questions their right to sign DNR orders today.

We now may be in the throes of an evolution in thinking about tube feeding and antibiotic therapy that parallels—and lags by ten years—the evolution in thinking that has taken place regarding resuscitation. Perhaps "DNI" (do not intubate) orders will be available in the near future, just as DNR orders are today.

Prior to the 1960s, chronically ill patients who became dehydrated simply died. Then and over the history of civilization up to that time, dehydration was among the most common primary or secondary causes of death (Lynn 1989: 47). Only since the 1970s has tube feeding routinely been available to patients requiring long-term assistance with feeding and hydration. Then, in the early 1980s, physicians began to realize something about ANH that they had come to appreciate about CPR in the late 1960s and early 1970s: It simply does not make sense to treat every patient just because the treatment is available. Only then did certain physicians start to become comfortable with the unilateral decision not to offer tube feeding as an alternative to seriously ill patients who otherwise would have been candidates for the treatment.

In the early 1980s, the professional associations began revising their ethical codes to reflect the clinical reality that not all patients are suitable candidates for long-term intubation. Ten years later, around 1990 (the year the Supreme Court decision regarding Nancy Cruzan was handed down), the general public began to appreciate the futility of tube feeding for the mortally ill. If present trends and the parallel with the evolution of DNR orders continue, we should expect to see DNI orders being as commonly discussed, accepted, and employed in the very near future as DNR orders are today.

We might also see the popularization of "DNA" (do not use antibiotics) orders. Indeed, DNA orders may evolve more quickly than DNI orders even though the administration of antibiotics, either orally or intra-venously, is much more straightforward and may involve fewer complica-tions from a medical standpoint than the provision of artificial nutrition and hydration. The more important difference, from a cultural standpoint, is this: The provision of antibiotics is perceived as an entirely medical process and does not hold the same emotional and symbolic significance in our culture as the provision of food and drink does.

The popularization of DNI and DNA orders will result, sooner or later, from the slow but steady increase in the public's understanding of the futil-ity of using ANH and antibiotics in cases in which the costs of treatment so clearly outweigh the benefits. As long as no effective treatments exist to al-ter the course of serious, debilitating, dementing illnesses such as Alzheimer's disease, tube feeding and antibiotics seem only to prolong and increase patient suffering, without providing significant benefits beyond the continuation of biological life.

When it is impossible to affect the pathogenesis of an ultimately—if not imminently—terminal disease such as Alzheimer's, decisionmakers would be well advised to focus on providing comfort care without striving to max-imize survival time (L. Volicer et al. 1986: 2210; Wanzer et al. 1984: 959). To take the opposite position and argue that a patient must be subjected to every possible medical intervention that holds out even the slightest hope of prolonging life reduces the patient to "a biological mechanism" or, as Lynn (1989a: 51) puts it, "an array of measurable variables."

But what about the special place that the provision of food and drink has in our society? The aversion to forgoing ANH, however well fortified by culture and religion, does not constitute a moral imperative to provide tube feeding in every case. The presence of such an aversion simply means it is psychologically uncomfortable to forgo ANH. It does not render the action in question immoral by definition. As Lynn (1989a: 58) suggests, "The symbolic connection between care and nutrition or hydration adds useful caution to the decision making." The symbolic connection—which creates the presumption that ANH should be used—is hardly sufficient to settle the matter, however. The presumption can be rebutted if there is evidence to suggest that the patient would choose to forgo ANH if he or she were able to express an opinion or if the burdens of continued treatment outweigh the benefits.

The fact that one may be maintained for a long time with ANH and an-tibiotics does not weaken the claim that both are morally optional treat-ments. The patient's autonomy interest does *not* depend on the length of life that patient might have if the treatment was forced upon him or her (see Choice in Dying 1994b, *Bouvia* v. *Super. Ct.*). As a matter of fact, according to Norman Cantor (1989: 401), "the long prospective duration of a dying process only enhances the importance of respecting a patient's wishes. . . . Respect for the patient's decision is viewed instead as an affirmation of human dignity as embodied in the patient's exercise of self determination."[36]

The situation parents face when children are about to leave home in their later teens or early twenties presents a useful analogy. The parents may be averse to seeing their children leave, but the existence of this aversion does not mean that allowing them to leave is an immoral choice. Indeed, it may be immoral to force the children to stay (assuming that could be done), even though allowing the children to leave is upsetting to the parents and may run counter to the parents' nurturing and protecting instincts. Parents of grown children understand that there comes a time to let go, even if that means putting their children in harm's way. The same could be said for caregivers, family members, and friends of patients who are at or near the end of life's journey.

Some also worry about the deteriorating state of trust between patients and caregivers in our increasingly skeptical, litigious, and disconnected society. But the participation of health care professionals in forgoing treatment at the end of life does not jeopardize patient trust in those professionals. On the contrary, any failure to make the forgoing of life-sustaining medical treatment a fully appreciated option toward the end of life will only drive the wedge of distrust further between health care providers and family members. The key, it seems, is knowing when to shift the focus from curing to caring. Such a decision can often be made much earlier than it typically is today, when DNR orders are often drawn up only a few hours or days before death.

If we really care for those for whom we must make medical decisions near the end of life, we will think long and hard about whether to impose artificially provided nutrition and hydration. As Stephen Post (1990: 186, 190, citations omitted) suggests:

> What could be less caring than artificially feeding a patient in the terminal stages of a dementing illness? It is far from evident that the provision of nutrition and hydration constitutes caring in all cases. . . . Such patients should not be forced to endure the burden and indignity of permanent artificial nutrition and hydration just to assuage the feelings of the health care professional or family members. To withhold or withdraw nutrition and hydration amounts to proper reverence for the wisdom of the body that knows the limits of restoration.[37]

Chapter Six

Conclusion and Recommendations

Death is not extinguishing the light. It is putting out the lamp because the dawn has come.
—Rabindranath Tagore (cited in Bertman 1991)

If dying patients want to retain some control over their dying process, they must get out of the hospital if they are in, and stay out of the hospital if they are out.
—George Annas (1995)

An eight-year study of death in the United States, involving nearly 5,000 seriously ill patients and published in the *Journal of the American Medical Association* (SUPPORT 1995), found that despite the emergence of the right-to-die movement and the increased sensitivity to end-of-life decision making that was expected to follow implementation of the Patient Self-Determination Act,[1] patients are still reluctant to make their treatment preferences known. Even when patients execute advance directives or discuss preferences about limiting treatments with family members, doctors are often oblivious to those preferences and proceed with aggressive treatments anyway.

"The system," according to Dr. William A. Knaus, one of the study's codirectors, "doesn't know when or how to stop. . . . Physicians are acknowledging that patients are dying, but only at the last minute" (Knaus 1995). He concluded that "we're going to have to develop a better vision for living well while dying."[2]

A number of things can be done to bring that vision into clearer focus, including (1) developing a set of standards within the medical profession that would apply to the care of mortally ill patients, (2) making better use of hospice care, (3) developing a better, more widely shared sense of the concept of "medical futility," (4) providing better education about death and end-of-life decision making for caregivers and the general public alike, (5) modifying the old "slippery slope" theory of ethics to take account of changing, more complicated realities, and (6) making better use of advance directives.

Standards of Care

Developing standards of care is one way to begin resolving some of the troubling and contentious issues regarding end-of-life decision making that now are handled either behind closed doors at the bedside or publicly and confrontationally in the courts. Standards of care are panned by some as nothing more than "cookbook medicine." But standard protocols are really only models or patterns of clinical practice that serve as a baseline from which variations in treatment can be adapted, given the specific clinical circumstances and the stated or implied preferences of the decisionmakers involved.

The federal Agency for Health Care Policy and Research (AHCPR) has already moved decisively in this direction by developing a number of standard care protocols as part of its Medical Treatment Effectiveness Program (MEDTEP). Specific MEDTEP guidelines for seventeen clinical diagnoses have been issued to date (e.g., treatment for backaches, cancer pain management, and the management of breech births). A number of other standards are being developed.

AHCPR does not require or expect that physicians will act strictly according to protocol in every case. The standards do, however, put physicians in touch with the very latest consensus regarding the treatment of illness and may help shield them (to a degree) from legal liability if things go badly after standard protocols were followed. Treatment standards are also becoming popular with third-party payers and managed care systems that require physicians to document—and in many cases, get approval for—deviations from established standard practices. Standards of care are clearly the wave of the future in health care, and there is no reason why they should not encompass life-sustaining medical treatment as well.

Standards of Care at the End of Life

Medical ethicists and clinicians have been formulating and experimenting with end-of-life treatment standards since the mid-1980s. As Table 6.1 reveals, the standards promoted to date are really no more than menus of treatment approaches from which patients or their surrogates can choose, in consultation with their physician(s). "Aggressive treatment"—the application of any and all medically reasonable treatments to save the patient's life—typically lies at one end of a continuum of care. "Comfort care

TABLE 6.1 Proposed "Standards of Care" Grid

Authors of Standard Care Protocols Patient Population	Wanger et al. 1984 "Hopelessly Ill"	Volicer et al. 1986 Advanced Alzheimer's and Dementia	Mott and Barker 1988 Nursing Home Residents	Luchins and Hanrahan 1993 End-Stage Dementia
Aggressive treatment	All treatments provided, including emergency resuscitation	Diagnostic workups, CPR tube feeding, hospitalization	Maximum care, including hospitalization for surgery and intensive care	Do everything; use respirators, CPR, tube feeding, and electric shock for heart attacks
"High-end" level of intermediate care	Intensive care and advanced life support provided but no CPR	Aggressive treatment but no CPR; patient has a DNR order	Hospitalization but avoid surgery and intensive care if possible	Aggressive treatment but avoid electric shock in case of heart attack
Intermediate level of care	General medical care: surgery, chemotherapy, antibiotics, and other drugs, ANH	No CPR, artificial respiration, or hospitalization for intercurrent illnesses	Avoid hospitalization but use antibiotics, as needed, for infection	Aggressive treatment but avoid using respirators and electric shock
"Low-end" level of intermediate care	General nursing (comfort care), no vital sign checks, diagnostics, or antibiotics	No CPR, hospitalization, diagnostic work-ups, or antibiotics	[a]	Avoid using respirators, electric shock, or drugs to treat acute illness
Comfort care only	General nursing care, food and fluids only as needed for comfort	Supportive care, no CPR, no diagnostics, no antibiotics, no tube feeding	Avoid hospitalization; no antibiotics or IV fluids, except for comfort	Avoid using tube feeding; avoid antibiotics, CPR, and respirators

[a]Mott and Barker describe only two intermediate care levels: "high-end" intermediate and intermediate.

only"—an alternative associated with the hospice approach and with the emphasis on treating symptoms (holistically and in their entirety) rather than trying to arrest or reverse the patient's underlying pathology—lies at the other end of the spectrum.

Currently, there are no standard, widely accepted treatment protocols apart from the essentially illegitimate default response: aggressive treatment.[3] Doctors will occasionally act unilaterally or in consultation with the patients or members of the patient's family and move across the treatment continuum in the direction of the comfort care only option. But that decision is usually made only toward the very end of a chronically degenerating illness, long after the patient and family have endured a substantial amount of preventable suffering. "On a day to day basis," writes Ellen Goodman (1995), summarizing the results of the SUPPORT study, "neither doctors nor patients were talking about what the patients wanted. They were both following the cultural script, talking about the next chemotherapy, the next procedure. They were patching, fixing, going from crisis to crisis without ever asking, 'How can I live well while dying?'" A standard of care that required physicians to present patients with an array of treatment approaches might go a long way toward reversing this less than ideal, largely illegitimate status quo.

If some variation of this menu was adopted, a patient or a surrogate could be apprised of the full range of acceptable treatment options available.[4] All decisionmakers need not elect the comfort care only option, but all should be informed that this is a perfectly acceptable treatment level (from both a medical and a legal perspective). And why should it not be? Most people believe the comfort care level is desirable (see Tables 3.1, 3.2, 3.3, and 3.4), and it is an option that many ultimately choose for themselves or for their loved ones, even if they wait (too long) to do so.

Introducing a treatment grid into the bedside decision-making process would remove the often erroneous assumption that all possible medical treatments are desired and should be provided, and it would replace the "aggressive treatment reflex" with a deliberative choice process that emphasizes the autonomy and dignity of the patient. Erring on the side of life has been the standard of care ever since the technology required to prolong life by artificial means was developed. Given the evidence regarding preferences of the public, however, it may be time to question this presumption openly in order to give patients and surrogates the option of doing only what makes sense for them, from their own informed perspective.[5]

The AMA's Council on Ethical and Judicial Affairs has already begun to back away from the aggressive treatment presumption in considering the plight of the permanently unconscious. In its report on forgoing life-sustaining treatment for incompetent patients, this group (Council 1991: 67, 69) notes:

In the situation of a permanently unconscious patient, prolonging life may not be in the best interests of the patient. An existence that is severely degraded and causes constant suffering of loved ones who must stand by to watch the patient linger on the edge of life may not be worth prolonging from the patient's perspective. In addition, there may be a patient interest in the kind of memories left behind.

Some would argue caution here, for there is always the hope for a miraculous recovery. Regarding this notion, Dr. Sherwin Nuland (1994: 233–234) writes that

> in this high-tech biomedical era, when the tantalizing possibility of miraculous new cures is daily dangled before our eyes, the temptation to see therapeutic hope is great, even in those situations when common sense would demand otherwise. To hold out this kind of hope is too frequently a deception, which in the long run proves far more often to be a disservice than the promised victory it seems at first.

Aggressive treatment is the norm, continues Nuland, but "usually, [patients] suffer for it, they lay waste their last months for it, and they die anyway, having magnified the burdens they and those who love them must carry to the final moments." If Nuland's account is accurate, then the default rule, which presumes the desirability of aggressive treatment to the end, deserves to be thoroughly rethought; indeed, perhaps it should be replaced by a treatment protocol that emphasizes patient autonomy and dignity and provides more palliative-oriented treatment options from the earliest days of mortal illness, when selecting them can still do some good.

A Duty to Die?

Does providing treatment options for patients start us on a road that will lead, inevitably, to a belief that the infirm and the elderly have a duty to select comfort care only when they become sick or frail? Does this standards-of-care proposal create a "duty to die" mentality?

Richard D. Lamm, formerly the governor of Colorado, irritated many when he suggested, in a speech delivered in 1984, that elderly, terminally ill persons have "a duty to die and get out of the way. Let the other society, our kids, build a reasonable life" (cited in Worsnop 1992: 149). It may have been a grating sentiment, but it was not an original one. Thomas Jefferson himself penned a very similar thought near the end of his life: "There is a ripeness of time for death, regarding others as well as ourselves, when it is reasonable we should drop off, and make room for another growth. When we have lived our generation out, we should not wish to encroach on another" (cited in Nuland 1994: 73).

Sherwin Nuland (1994: 86–87) is among the authors who made this poignant point most recently:

> Far from being irreplaceable, we *should* be replaced. Fantasies of staying the hand of mortality are incompatible with the best interests of our species and . . . the best interests of our very own children. . . . [To] die and leave this stage is the way of nature—old age is the preparation for departure, the gradual easing out of life that makes its ending more palatable not only for the elderly, but for those also to whom they leave the world in trust. . . . Persistence can only break the hearts of those we love and of ourselves as well, not to mention the purse of society that should be spent for the care of others who have not yet lived their allotted time.

One need not accept the musings of Jefferson, Lamm, or Nuland as determinative, however, for patient self-determination and palliative care that saves money, decreases suffering, and enriches the dying time can be advocated without concluding that anyone has a *duty* to die. One of the larger points of this book is that if patients were fully empowered with the knowledge and autonomy needed to make truly informed treatment decisions for themselves or their loved ones, the vast majority would likely choose comfort care only when illness progresses beyond the point at which life can be consciously enjoyed. This would, in large part, obviate the need to force palliative care on those who would prefer a more aggressive approach, which could and should remain an appropriate, acceptable (and reimbursable) treatment option.

The Hospice Alternative

One major problem with the comfort care only option is that many health care institutions do not consider comfort care a legitimate treatment alternative (e.g., see Tables 3.7 and 3.8). This was certainly the case with the nursing home that forced Rosemarie Sherman into court when she requested that the tube feeding of her son be stopped. Consequently, it may do little good for physicians to offer the comfort care only option if the institutions in which they practice do not recognize this as a legitimate treatment modality. Hospices will have to take up the slack in the interim, until the hospice approach is more widely and generally accepted (and paid for by third-party payers).

The hospice alternative replaces the aggressive "curing-based" approach to extending life at all costs with a "caring-based" approach to living well while dying. Those using the hospice philosophy work in interdisciplinary teams to address the full range of physical symptoms and psychosocial problems that the patient and family endure as a disease runs its course toward death. Simply put, caring and symptom management are emphasized while cure is accepted as beyond reach (Wheeler 1993: 756).

Hospice care, covered by Medicare since 1982, has become more popular over the years; in 1992, 154,000 Medicare decedents (about 10 percent of all recipients who died that year) made use of hospice services. This group of hospice patients consumed less than 1 percent of the Medicare budget in 1992 (approximately $700 million, or about $5,000 per decedent) (Scitovsky 1994: 581). The remaining 90 percent of Medicare recipients who died that year consumed approximately 27 percent of the Medicare budget, with over $19 billion in medical bills, or about $14,000 per decedent—nearly three times as much per capita as the hospice patients. (See Chapter 4 for more on medical costs at the end of life.)

Currently, there are about 1,800 hospice programs in the United States. Most are home care programs in which hospice nurses, social workers, and physicians travel to the homes of dying patients to provide medical and psychosocial support and guidance.

Decreased suffering and increased quality of what life remains are both associated with this palliative-oriented approach. Suffering decreases quantitatively because the dying process is no longer protracted indefinitely. At the same time, the quality of life is increased because efforts are focused on managing the symptoms of the disease (e.g., controlling pain and discomfort) rather than attempting to reverse or arrest the underlying pathology and perhaps exacerbating the symptoms in the process.[6]

Dr. Nuland's observations regarding common practices at the end of life today are hardly reassuring (Nuland 1994: 142–143):

> By and large, dying is a messy business . . . even for those who do achieve a measure of serenity during separation. The period of days or weeks preceding the decline of full awareness is frequently glutted with mental suffering and physical distress. Too often, patients and their families cherish expectations that cannot be met, with the result that death is made all the more difficult by frustration and disappointment with the performance of a medical community [that] continues to fight long after defeat has become inevitable. . . . Treatment decisions are sometimes made near the end of life that propel a dying person willy-nilly into a series of worsening miseries from which there is no extraction.

Palliative care can be emotionally enriching for patient and caregivers alike, especially when family and friends assume (or reassume) roles as primary caregivers in the process. In fact, palliative care is much more conducive to family participation in the dying process (Wanzer et al. 1989: 845–846). Tubes and machinery often serve as barriers to hands-on, personal contact. But when technology is de-emphasized, backrubs, spoon-feeding, and hand-holding become more important and more possible.[7] When the dying time is interminable, those close to the patient may slowly withdraw, visiting less often and providing less in the way of personal care over time. Alternately, when the decision to forgo life-sustaining treatment is made and the dying time is delimited (those using hospice care typically die in a matter of days or weeks at most), those close to the patient can be present and provide support every step of the way.

When hopelessly ill patients are tube fed, for example, they may live on for years, and there is very little that a family member can do to help out with care. But when tube feeding is forgone, relatives can rearrange work and family schedules to devote increased time and attention to the patient's last days, knowing that the end is near. With tubes and feeding apparatus removed, friends and family members can be invited to participate in the terminal care of the patient—moistening the lips of the dying loved one and providing chips of ice on the tongue to slake any sensations of thirst that might develop. This can be a richly emotional and satisfying time for both patient and loved ones, a time when troubles are resolved, peace is made, and final good-byes are shared. How much better it would be to come to terms with the death in this manner, rather than merely receiving an impersonal call from the nursing home: "Your _____ has died."

Survey data suggest that the vast majority of family members and professionals believe that hospice care is particularly appropriate for persons suffering through end-stage dementia. And reports of pilot programs that provide hospice care to patients suffering from advanced dementia indicate that the approach is feasible on a larger scale (Hanrahan and Luchins 1995: 56). Increased use of hospice services for patients in end-stage dementia would save resources, as well. The latest and most comprehensive evaluation of the small number of patients covered for hospice care under Medicare shows that $1.26 is saved for every dollar spent (Kidder 1992, cited by Scitovsky 1994: 582). Another study showed that Alzheimer's patients getting palliative care had annual expenses of $6,000 less than Alzheimer's patients cared for in a traditional, long-term care facility (B. Volicer et al. 1993: 539).

Hospice placements for such patients are not easy to arrange, however. The problem is that Medicare enrollment criteria require the attending physician and the director of the hospice to certify that the patient is within six months of death before the institution can qualify for reimbursement. As Beverly Volicer and her colleagues point out, hospice-like care may be appropriate for patients with advanced dementia, but "the variable rate of deterioration makes an informed judgment about anticipated survival time for individual patients difficult" (B. Volicer et al. 1993: 535). Consequently, even though 90 percent of responding family members in one study indicated that hospice care would be appropriate for a loved one with end-stage dementia,[8] only about 30,000 of the approximately 2 million patients suffering from severe dementia nationwide ever get into a hospice program (Hanrahan and Luchins 1995: 57).[9] So patients and their families are caught in a vicious circle: The patient cannot get into a hospice program unless he or she can be declared terminally ill, and the patient cannot be declared terminally ill unless he or she can get into a hospice program—a classic catch-22 of grave proportions.

This poses an interesting dilemma: Although caregivers advocate the use of hospice, the lay population desires access to hospice, and resources can be saved through greater use of hospice, current federal regulations stand in the way. One way out of this bind, short of changing the Medicare guidelines, would be to create a statistical model that would predict, within acceptable limits, the six-month survival rate of patients with end-stage dementia. Factors such as age, severity of dementia, management strategy (the agreed-upon level of care, chosen from the standard care menu discussed earlier), and time since admission to a long-term care facility might be statistically weighted and combined to determine if the expected mortality will likely occur within the six-month period required by current rules.

A second alternative would involve modifying Medicare's current six-month rule so that those who could not reliably be said to be within six months of death could still be accepted into hospice (where they would in all likelihood die within six months). A third alternative would be to insert the term *mortal illness* in place of the term *terminal illness* as the qualifying prognosis for hospice care reimbursement (Sachs et al. 1995: 553). *Mortally ill* would be used to refer to "dying patients who have a progressive illness that is expected to eventuate in death and for which there is no treatment expected to alter the course substantially" (Sachs et al. 1995: 553).

Even if the six-month prognosis problem could be overcome at some point, however, funding for hospice care is likely to be problematic. Funding for hospice and home health care has been increasing in recent years, but any significant shifts in the direction of palliative care will require government, third-party payers, and health care alliances to pour more resources into these two areas.[10] Although palliative care may be less expensive than aggressive care in the long run, it is not free. And the fact that more hospital beds (some of them in intensive care wards) would be abandoned by those seeking a more palliative approach will not, in itself, save the institutions providing high-tech care any money. Indeed, moving toward palliative care will lead to a net decrease in revenue for high-tech institutions and a net decrease in income for some specialists, even though health care dollars will surely be saved overall.

Medical Futility

It is important to provide patients and their surrogates with a sense that a range of acceptable options might be open to them—from aggressive care to the hospice alternative. However, there are times when offering the full range of options does not make sense from either a medical or an ethical perspective. At one end of the scale, for example, physicians might reasonably decline to offer surrogate decisionmakers the comfort care only option for an incompetent, seriously ill patient if there was some medically sound reason to believe the patient might regain competence and enjoy a conscious and acceptable quality of life. But because aggressive care is the default position adopted by most physicians and family members, there is little danger that the comfort care only option will be inappropriately applied or overused today.

Actually, the need for limiting options at the aggressive care end of the scale has proven to be more problematic. When physicians argue that a patient is so hopelessly ill and irreversibly vegetative that further aggressive medical treatments would be futile and need not be offered, they run the risk of being charged with "giving up too soon" by patients, family members, colleagues, and maybe even the courts.[11] Many caregivers still shrink from making the call to halt treatment on the grounds that to do so violates the "do no harm" tenet of the Hippocratic oath. But some quote another relevant principle in Corpus Hippocratum that implores physicians to "refuse to treat those who are overmastered by their disease, realizing that in such cases medicine is powerless" (cited in President's Commission 1983: 15–16). Recent studies of physician behaviors suggest that this latter principle guides a significant number of caregivers today.

For example, David Asch, John Hansen-Flaschen, and Paul Lanken (1995: 288) found that an overwhelming majority of the 1,050 critical care physicians in their study had unilaterally withheld (83 percent) or withdrawn (82 percent) patients' treatments on grounds of futility.[12] Furthermore, nearly one-quarter of the respondents (23 percent) indicated that they had withdrawn life-sustaining treatment on the basis of medical futility even though they did not have the oral or written consent of the patient or family, and 12 percent of those respondents claimed to have proceeded in this way without the knowledge of the patient or family. Fully one-third of the respondents reported withdrawing life-sustaining treatment from at least one patient who was not capable of making such a decision and was unrepresented by a surrogate decisionmaker. And a small but significant proportion of respondents (3 percent) reported withdrawing treatment *despite* the objections of the patient or family.

At one time in the not-too-distant past, a decision to withhold treatment despite the objections of the family might have been considered an ethical breach of the first order. Today, however, a stream of literature supports such decisions in cases of persistently vegetative patients and others who are irreversibly, terminally ill once the diagnosis has been established with virtual certainty.[13] Lawrence Schneiderman, Nancy Jecker, and Albert Jonsen (1990: 952) leave no doubt on this score, arguing that "the patient has no right to be sustained in a state in which he or she has no purpose other than mere vegetative survival; the physician has no obligation to offer this option or services to achieve it."[14] Jecker and Schneiderman (1993: 151) contend that offering medically futile treatment only raises false hopes, is emotionally damaging, and extends and maybe even adds to the suffering a patient endures.

Although these liberal interpretations of futility are accepted by many clinicians, acceptance is far from universal. Still, two recent court cases brought by physicians and hospital administrators suggest that some caregivers are beginning to feel more comfortable about discussing the issue of futility in public, which is an important and necessary step in the process of building a general consensus position on what is still a very contentious issue.

Helga Wanglie

In 1990, eighty-six-year-old Helga Wanglie suffered a heart attack. Although she was successfully resuscitated, the interruption of the oxygen supply to her brain during the attack left her with extremely severe and irreversible brain damage. After several months of observation and treatment at the Hennepin County Medical Center (HCMC) in Minneapolis, Minnesota, the diagnosis of persistent vegetative state was confirmed. Wanglie was being sustained by artificial respiration, artificially provided food and fluids, and antibiotics for recurrent pneumonia. Given Wanglie's deteriorating condition and poor prognosis, the medical staff at HCMC urged the family to forgo her life-sustaining medical treatments.[15]

Members of the family—Oliver, Mrs. Wanglie's husband of fifty-three years, and two children—disagreed with the withdrawing of treatment on religious and personal grounds. Oliver Wanglie claimed he fully understood the dismal prognosis but was "hoping for a miracle." He also noted that his wife had told him many times what her preferences would be: "If anything happened to her," he relayed, "she didn't want anybody or anything to shorten her life. I intend to keep that promise" ("Doctors Want to Pull Plug" 1990).

After a series of attempts to persuade the Wanglie family of the hospital's position, Dr. Michael Belzer, the HCMC medical director, wrote a letter to Oliver Wanglie: "All medical consultants agree with [the attending physician's] conclusion that continued use of mechanical ventilation and other forms of life-sustaining treatment are no longer serving the patient's personal medical interest. We do not believe that the hospital is obliged to provide inappropriate medical treatment that cannot advance the patient's personal interest" (Cranford 1991b: 23–24).[16]

When this letter had no effect on the family's decision, the medical center, with the concurrence of its ethics committee and its board of directors, went to court to seek the appointment of an independent conservator with the power to recommend that Mrs. Wanglie's life-sustaining medical treatment be withdrawn. It was the first court proceeding in which an institution (in this case, a public entity) sought to end life-sustaining treatment for an incompetent adult patient against the wishes of family members.

After a hearing, Hennepin County Probate Judge Patricia L. Belois ruled in favor of the family and appointed Oliver Wanglie as conservator of his wife, stating: "He [Mr. Wanglie] is in the best position to investigate and act upon Helga Wanglie's conscientious, religious, and moral beliefs" ("Judge Rejects Request" 1991). Three days later, on July 4, 1990, Helga Wanglie died of sepsis (a poisoning of the blood and tissues) with all life-sustaining equipment connected and operating. The family's medical bill for services provided during her last hospitalization approached $1 million.

Subsequently, Dr. Stephen Miles (1991: 513–514), a medical ethicist at HCMC, criticized the judge's ruling in an article published in the *New England Journal of Medicine*:

> A patient's request for a treatment does not necessarily oblige a provider or a health care system. Patients may not demand that physicians injure them (for example, by mutilation), or provide plausible but inappropriate therapies (for example, amphetamines for weight reduction), or therapies that have no value (such as laetrile for cancer). . . . Patients can refuse any prescribed treatment or choose among any medical alternatives that physicians are willing to prescribe. Respect for autonomy does not empower patients to oblige physicians to prescribe treatments in ways that are fruitless or inappropriate. . . . Disputes between physicians and patients about treatment plans are often handled by transferring patients to the care of other providers. In this case, every provider contacted by the hospital or the family refused to treat this patient with a respirator. These refusals occurred both before and after this case became a matter of public controversy and despite the availability of third-party reimbursement. We believe they represent a medical consensus that respirator support is inappropriate in such a case.

Later in the year, the *Minneapolis Star Tribune* published an editorial that came to a similar conclusion ("Helga Wanglie's Life" 1991): "The hospital's plea is born of realism, not hubris. . . . It advances the claim that physicians should not be slaves to technology—any more than patients should be its prisoners. They should be free to deliver, and act on, an honest and time-honored message: 'Sorry, there's nothing more we can do.'"

Catherine Gilgunn

Catherine F. Gilgunn was not in good medical condition in 1989 when, at the age of seventy-one, she was admitted to the hospital for surgery to repair a fractured hip. She suffered from diabetes, heart disease, chronic urinary tract infections, and Parkinson's disease. One breast had been removed because of cancer the year before, and she had also suffered a stroke. One of her hips had been replaced once, the other twice.

Before Gilgunn's surgery could begin, she suffered a series of uncontrollable seizures that left her comatose, with irreversible brain damage. After six years in this condition, physicians at Massachusetts General Hospital decided to enter a DNR order on Mrs. Gilgunn's chart and began trying to wean her off a ventilator. They did this after consulting with the hospital's optimum care committee and Gilgunn's daughter, Joan.

The hospital committee agreed with the decision, as did John J. Paris, a Jesuit priest and ethicist at Boston College who described the hospital's decision as entirely defensible. Doctors were not obliged, explained Paris, to resuscitate a patient who was so ill that such efforts, even if successful, would accomplish no purposeful medical goals (beyond the sustaining of organic life). The daughter disagreed, however, saying her mother had always wanted everything done for her (Kolata 1995). Mrs. Gilgunn subsequently died, and no attempt was made to resuscitate her.

Joan Gilgunn sued the two doctors directly involved with the decision to write the DNR order, and a jury was impaneled to hear evidence and arguments on both sides of the case. After the case had been presented, Suffolk County Superior Court Judge David Roseman instructed the jury on its responsibilities with regard to the state's interests in the case: "The state's interest in pursuing life is high when human life can be saved and where afflictions are curable, but wanes when the afflictions are incurable." After two hours of deliberation, the jury cleared the two physicians of wrongly ignoring the daughter's demands to keep Catherine Gilgunn alive on life support. Members of the jury agreed that Gilgunn would have wanted her life to be sustained, as the daughter claimed, but also found that continued treatment would be futile and of no medical benefit (Ellement 1995).

Informed Consensus

Evidently, the realm of medical futility is an unsettled area of law, ethics, and medicine. As one observer noted: "Our medical inventions have invited our own dilemma . . . sometimes the machines are a blessing. And sometimes they are a curse. But we haven't invented laws or rules yet to tell the difference" ("To Suffer" 1984). In the meantime, physicians will have to find their own way, with occasional help from judges and juries. All indications are that physicians are moving in the direction of unilaterally withholding or withdrawing treatment when the patient is hopelessly ill and nothing more can be done to restore even a minimal quality of life. For the most part, they are doing this quietly (as reported in the Asch, Hansen-Flaschen, and Lanken study [1995]), but occasionally, the process becomes public (as in the cases of Helga Wanglie and Catherine Gilgunn).

Professional organizations have already begun to codify rules that legitimize physician behavior along these lines (especially with regard to the unilateral writing of DNR orders).[17] And with trial court cases beginning to be heard, appellate-level court decisions—the ones that carry weight as case law—will not be too far behind. Increased economic pressures—manifested as managed care, capitated payment plans (e.g., health maintenance organizations and preferred provider organizations), and cuts in reimbursement rates for Medicare and Medicaid—will, rightly or wrongly, encourage the process of building a consensus on medical futility.

The task of developing a concept of medical futility should not be taken lightly, however. Rather, the process must be deliberate, informed, broad-based, and participative (e.g., involving representative cross sections of the lay public). Polling data already suggest that the public is very much opposed to the current presumption in favor of aggressive therapy for the hopelessly ill. But these polls, like all polls, have some basic flaws that affect the weight that can be attributed to them. Most significantly, the scenarios and treatment options posed in public opinion polls often are simplistically worded, and rarely is any effort made to determine how well the respondents understand the questions or how deeply they have thought about their responses.

Some medical researchers have attempted to solve this problem (at least partially) by educating respondents about the conditions and treatments under consideration. Questions are then posed in the context of detailed vignettes rather than in overly simplistic statements of one or two sentences (e.g., see Emanuel et al. 1991: 881; Lo, McLeod, and Saika 1986: 1613).[18] More of these kinds of vignette-based studies would provide a better idea of where informed opinion (as opposed to mass opinion) is on the issue of medical futility.

A few years ago, the state of Oregon launched an initiative that led to a massive restructuring of its Medicaid program. To fashion the new policy, state officials created a consensus-building process that, in addition to mail and telephone surveys and extensive consultation with medical experts, included focus group research and town meetings to explain and discuss various proposals and solicit public input. The consensus that resulted was not universally embraced within the state. But it was more informed and more legitimate than any consensus based on surveys or expert opinion alone. Perhaps a similar effort, oriented toward developing a concept of "medical futility" that could be generally accepted across the nation, would be worth attempting.

The kind of information gleaned would be very useful to family members and caregivers who currently must bury their feelings of fear, guilt, and anxiety over whether life-sustaining medical treatment is medically futile. The participatory development of a shared sense for what medical futility means would go a long way toward relieving some of the concerns people have, while at the same time diminishing patient (and family) suffering, restoring patient dignity, and conserving resources associated with the dying.

There should be room for a plurality of positions when it comes to end-of-life treatment preferences. However, plurality cannot extend to every patient in every condition regarding every treatment. Rather, this plurality should operate within limits, with boundaries set up at the aggressive care end of the spectrum to prevent patients from demanding medically futile treatment, just as there are boundaries set up at the other end of the spectrum today, when surrogates are prevented from giving up too hastily if serious illness is not yet considered irreversible.

In sum, we need a national dialogue on the issue of medical futility. We now have only anecdotal evidence, limited survey data, and a smattering of qualitative research studies to go on. A systematic effort should be made to collect data on the *informed* views of Americans so that an informed consensus can be established. This project should be a high priority, since enormous costs, resource allocation issues, emotional burdens, and patient autonomy and dignity all hang in the balance. As Handler (*In re Jobes* 1987: 460) notes, just as constitutional norms of personal privacy must be shaped "by the traditions and collective conscience of the people, so the common law of handling dying patients will be shaped by shared notions of how 'we' citizens want to be treated at that critical juncture. That is, shared notions of human dignity will ultimately govern decision making on behalf of incompetent moribund patients." These shared notions can govern, however, only to the degree that they are known, and they will govern well only to the degree that they flow from a process that is both informed and broadly participatory.

Education

One of the most straightforward solutions to the end-of-life decision-making dilemmas Americans face today involves education. As pointed out in Chapters 2 and 3, there is a great deal of agreement on many of the most troubling issues that caregivers and decisionmakers face when life hangs in the balance. The problem is that many caregivers are not aware of this consensus. And though there are no data to indicate the public's level of understanding about the consensus position itself, it seems fair to assume that the level of awareness is low here, as well.

Caregivers and the lay public may generally agree with the consensus position, but since their awareness of its existence is highly variable, they tend to fall back on the safe, culturally scripted position that leads to the decision to treat illness aggressively, every step of the way to the very end. All too often, we act the way we think we are supposed to act.

Public Misinformation

The response to a letter in the syndicated Ann Landers column (1995) is symptomatic of just how much education is required. The letter dealt with the plight of a seventy-two-year-old woman, a victim of Parkinson's disease who had been tube fed for eight years because of an inability to swallow. "The poor woman was flat on her back and unable to move for the entire eight years," wrote the patient's daughter-in-law. In the process, the woman had wasted away to a weight of 65 pounds. The daughter-in-law went on to say that even though all family members agreed that continued feeding was "cruel and inhumane," doctors refused to even consider withdrawing ANH from the patient because doing so, they said, would mean the patient "would starve to death." Eventually, the tube came out by accident, and the patient, coherent at the time, chose not to have it reinserted. She died shortly thereafter and "was kept comfortable the entire time," according to the daughter-in-law, who ended her letter with this: "We need to keep our loved ones who are terminally ill comfortable, but they should be permitted to go when their time comes."

In reply, Ann Landers wrote: "The doctors' refusal to remove your mother-in-law's feeding tube was totally appropriate—not only from a medical viewpoint, but also legally. Had they removed the tube, they could have been charged with murder. When the tube accidentally fell out and your mother-in-law chose not to have it reinserted, the physicians on the case were no longer responsible for what happened."

In her brief reply, Ann Landers managed to completely contradict at least three fundamental principles of the consensus position. First, patients (if they are competent) or their surrogates, acting in good faith, *do* have the right to make end-of-life decisions in cases of hopeless illness, and doctors should either accede to those decisions or transfer the patient to a caregiver who will. The preponderance of medical opinions, legal precedent, and, for that matter, ethical principles all point in this direction, Ann Landers's statement notwithstanding. The doctors' refusal to respect the family's wishes may have been predictable and understandable, but it was *not* appropriate.[19]

The fact is that the consensus position deems it appropriate for families to make end-of-life decisions on any number of bases, including the weighing of benefits and burdens a treatment imposes. The invasiveness of ANH or any other treatment is certainly one aspect to consider.[20] Other relevant issues might include helplessness, immobility, incontinence, subjection of bodily processes to public exposure, extent of mental dysfunction, prolonged physical or chemical restraints, disfigurement (e.g., amputation for gangrenous limbs), and so on (Cantor 1989: 420). These are all quality of life factors that both the President's Commission (1983: 134–135) and the Catholic Health Association have accepted as legitimate criteria to consider.[21]

Third-party concerns associated with treatment have also been considered to be entirely legitimate criteria on which to base life-sustaining treatment decisions. How emotionally troubling is a treatment for the patient's loved ones? How long can treatment be prolonged before the emotional and financial drain on family members begins to outweigh whatever marginal benefit accrues to the patient? And what resources devoted to the hopelessly ill might better be diverted to those who have reason to hope for a return to a good quality of life if treatment is provided? Both the President's Commission report[22] and the Vatican's statement on euthanasia[23] agree that these are legitimate issues to assess when making life-sustaining treatment decisions. It also seems perfectly reasonable to assume what a number of courts have suggested: The emotional and financial impact on the patient's family and friends would generally be an important concern of the dying individual.

Second, the doctors' actions and Landers's comments seem to imply that it was perfectly appropriate to withhold feeding once the tube fell out, although withdrawing feeding would surely invite criminal prosecution. Once again, nearly every significant piece of legal, medical, and ethical writing on this subject has rejected the distinction between withholding and withdrawing treatment. Simply put, any treatment that can be withheld can be withdrawn.

It is true that psychological barriers to withdrawing treatment exist. Psychologically, withdrawing treatment is quite different and much more troubling than withholding it (Solomon et al. 1993: 20). There may be no morally important difference between the two, but there is a *huge* difference for clinicians who have to carry out orders by clamping the feeding tubes or switching off the respirators that sustain the patient, especially when death does not occur immediately or in the expected time frame: Withdrawing just does not "feel the same" as withholding (Printz 1988: 85).[24] At the same time, it is clear that whatever disquieting feelings withdrawal of treatment creates, these feelings should not be determinative, even according to the conservative state courts of New York and Missouri.[25]

Third, caregivers who withdraw treatment are not accessories to a "murder." The consensus position clearly states that forgoing treatment, even ANH, at the behest of legitimate surrogates who are acting in good faith does not constitute murder, suicide, assisted suicide, or euthanasia.[26] Today, even though tube feeding of the hopelessly ill is widespread, the decision to forgo feeding and allow hopelessly ill patients to die of dehydration is made regularly by patients and surrogates, in hospices and elsewhere, all around the country.

As Ann Landers's flawed response suggests, those who would hope to educate caregivers and the general public about what is legally, medically, and morally acceptable at the end of life have their work cut out for them, for they will not be writing on a blank slate. Rather, they will have to erase from the slate the misconceptions that exist both in the general public and in the medical community. Only then can they move ahead with the process of educating Americans about the consensus position and the range of options that should be available to the dying patient.

Denial and Unrealistic Expectations

In addition to the proliferation of public misinformation about end-of-life decision making, there is a great deal of private misunderstanding about the indignity and suffering that accompany modern death. Today, the art of dying seems to have been replaced by the science of living. The sophistication of rescue medicine, the wonder of high-tech interventions, and the seemingly miraculous cures that are reported almost daily in the popular media have fueled a sense of cultural scientism—a faith that medicine can ultimately deliver us from any affliction (Hoefler 1994: 32–35). Scientism also reinforces the ever present denial of mortality that makes end-of-life decision making hard to think about prospectively and even harder to deal with in real time (Hoefler 1994: 21–32).

Perhaps part of this denial of mortality stems from the fact that modern Americans do not see death as often or as intimately as they did in eras past, when death within the immediate family struck, on average, every seven years. The typical American can now expect an average of eighteen years—one full generation—between the deaths of close family members. And when death does occur, it more often than not takes place in an institution of high-tech medicine—out of touch, out of sight, and, in may ways, out of mind.

At the beginning of the twentieth century, 80 percent of all deaths occurred in the home, where the body was prepared by family members, waked in the family's parlor, and buried in a grave dug in the family plot out back by relatives and close friends. Today, more than 80 percent of all deaths occur in institutions, after which the body is prepared by a stranger (a licensed mortician) and waked in that stranger's place of business (the funeral home). The grave is dug by another stranger's backhoe, after which the mound of excavated dirt is covered with grass-green carpet lest graveside mourners dwell on the meaning of that pile of earth. Together, these sanitized, third-person experiences with death lead us to think of death as something that only happens to someone else, not to us.

If we move past the denial phase, we enter another phase in which we either believe (or at least hope) that our passing will be marked by little in the way of pain and much in the way of dignity. Nothing could be further from the truth, according to Sherwin Nuland (1994: 265–268).[27] Dr. Nuland explains that death is often marked by indignities of all descriptions, including the inability to care for oneself, the loss of mental faculties (especially with AIDS and Alzheimer's), and a loss of control that is as frightening for the patient as it is for members of the family. Death is made even more difficult by vain attempts to stave off the inevitable decline at the end of life. A dignified death is something that only a few will have but that more could experience if they faced the reality of death squarely and recaptured the spirit of *ars moriendi* (Latin, meaning "the art of dying"), in which peace is made and the humility of one's own life in the big picture is more fully appreciated. Death should be a celebration of the years that have preceded it, not a process consumed with the suffering and indignities that mark most passings. Squarely facing death and making decisions not to prolong it unnecessarily should be the capstones of a worthy life. Futile attempts to rescue life from the jaws of death when the chances of doing so are remote and marked by further suffering only diminish and desanctify life, blowing the importance of the dying time out of all proportion. The sanctity of life is best honored by leading a good life, not in futile or even wasteful attempts to deny nature and, for those who believe, God what will be theirs, regardless of what we do on earth to forestall the inevitable.

The data on death and dying in the United States are as sobering as Nuland's anecdotal reflections:

- Less than one in four Americans will enjoy a quick and unexpected passing from this life (Nuland 1984: 18). The rest of us will be left to cope with a managed death that can drag on for years or even decades.
- Half the population dies of a chronic condition that had been diagnosed, on average, nearly two and a half years earlier (President's Commission 1983: 18).
- Seven percent of the elderly population become severely demented from Alzheimer's or some other chronic degenerative disease before they die, a process that takes, on average, six to seven years to run its fatal course.
- The vast majority of patients and family members will, at some point, decide to withhold or withdraw life-sustaining treatment and allow a terminal pathology to run its course at the end of life. More often than not, however, this decision is made in the last days of life, after long bouts of suffering and emotional trauma have already been endured.
- Half of all patients who die will be in moderate to severe pain in the last few days of life, and a third or more will spend at least ten of their last days in an intensive care unit (Winslow 1995).

In the end, death in the United States is still considered a taboo subject, and it is not discussed in private or in public. As a result, our unrealistic expectations and our denials are never challenged, which is why so many of us have no idea what dying is like or what the consensus position permits. This was one of the clear messages of the massive SUPPORT study: Essentially, all of the efforts at patient education and empowerment on right-to-die issues failed. "What we learned," said Dr. Joanne Lynn (1995), one of the study's codirectors, "was that the conspiracy of silence about death was stronger than we expected and the force of habit was also stronger than we expected."

Family members are not aware of the latest medical and ethical thinking on the subject of dying. The rituals of denial, the distance that has grown between Americans and death, the emergence of scientism, and the rise of unrealistic expectations together have conspired to shape the modern American culture of death, thwarting efforts at education or introspection.

To educate ourselves about death, we would be wise to volunteer in a nursing home, a hospice, or a hospital. We might decide to care for a dying relative at home or at least give a careful reading to Sherwin Nuland's *How We Die*. In the process, we might then begin to frame realistic goals and expectations about how we wish to die and how aggressively we wish to stave off our inevitable passing.

The Slippery Slope

One of the most enduring of all barriers to enlightened decision making about hopelessly ill individuals is erected by ethicists and others who bandy about the phrase *slippery slope*. The *slippery slope* refers to a continuum of ethical actions; one end of the continuum, the high point of a slanted line, is defined by actions that are ethically acceptable. The further one moves down and away from this point, the more ethically suspect an action becomes. And the more steps one takes down the slope and away from the moral high ground, the easier it supposedly becomes to slide uncontrollably until entirely unethical actions at the lower end of the slope are practiced and accepted as the norm. The moral high ground for slippery slope theorists is often defined by the "never give up" ethic of care, in which everything possible is done to save and extend the patient's life without taking any other concerns into consideration. At the bottom of the slope, the infirm are coerced into thinking they have a duty to die. Ultimately, the specter of active, nonvoluntary euthanasia for the mentally and physically disabled in society, à la Nazi Germany, is raised.[28]

The problem here is that, too often, these slippery slope theorists talk in terms of an overly simplistic world in which options are arrayed along a single inclined line; in this world, anyone who deviates from the moral high ground occupied by never give up ethics risks sliding uncontrollably toward dehumanizing atrocities of the first order. This is an unrealistic and, in some cases, a morally inappropriate position to take because the underlying ethic itself is flawed: Doing everything possible is *not* always the best or most morally appropriate course to take.

A better and more realistically grounded view would envision three ethical inclines instead of one, each with its own moral high ground and each with its own potential to become a slippery slope that, if followed too far for too long and with too little thought, could lead to serious ethical wrongs. The proposed slopes are based on three central themes: futility, autonomy, and dignity.

Futility

The first new incline for ethical analysis is based on the notion of medical futility. The moral high ground here is defined by the judicious use of medical resources; at the bottom of the incline, patients or surrogates demand and get treatments that are so "inappropriate" that providing them constitutes a misuse of resources (see the section on medical futility earlier in this chapter).[29] Medical resources (e.g., space, expertise, machinery, organs, and funding) are scarce, and devoting these resources to hopelessly ill patients when the chances of achieving a worthwhile medical goal approach the vanishing point constitutes an ethical transgression, especially when others who stand a much better chance of achieving a good medical result do not receive the care they need as a result.

When a patient's situation is medically futile, only comfort care should be provided. And when we provide more than that, we begin to slide down the slippery slope, moving toward a point where some have access to care that they cannot put to good use while others suffer and die for lack of care they need but cannot get.[30] This is not to suggest that there will be no controversy regarding what constitutes futile medical treatments. As Nuland (1994: 221) notes: "The boundaries of medical futility . . . have never been clear, and it may be too much to expect that they ever will be." The best we can do is depend on a deliberative process and develop an informed consensus on the meaning and consequences of medical futility, understanding that, at the margins, there will always be some degree of error and even abuse—both in overtreating when treatment really is futile and undertreating when it is not. The expectation here is that using medical futility as one criterion will diminish poor decision making, not eliminate it.

Autonomy

The second of the three ethical inclines is based on autonomy. In this scenario, the patient has made clear, either personally or through a legitimate surrogate, what he or she wants done toward the end of life. If there is a reasonable hope that medical intervention will help the patient achieve a worthwhile goal (i.e., if the proposed treatment is not futile) and if the patient or surrogate desires that the treatment be provided, then treatment *should* be provided. By the same token, the patient or surrogate may reject any treatment, regardless of how good or bad the prognosis is, as long as the decision is informed, uncoerced, and (in the case of surrogate decision-makers) made in good faith.

The autonomy incline actually has not one but two slippery slopes. One leads in the direction of rationed care for the patient who wants a potentially helpful treatment but cannot afford it. The other involves aggressively providing care when it is not desired by the patient or surrogate. There is no controversy whatsoever in the courts regarding a person's right to make decisions for him- or herself. And there is no controversy over the right of surrogates to make those same decisions in the name of an incompetent patient. The only controversy involves who will be the surrogate (does he or she know the patient best, and is he or she acting in good faith?) and what level of evidence will be required to make a decision to forgo life-sustaining treatment. Even in states such as New York and Missouri, where clear and convincing evidence is required, a surrogate need not produce anything in writing; specific oral statements are enough to qualify.

The autonomy incline emphasizes the rights of the individual—rights that are protected as a matter of common law, constitutional law, and, in an increasing number of states, by case and statutory law as well. Here, a decision to forgo life-sustaining treatment, on the moral high ground of this incline, is celebrated as a perfectly ethical (and legal) choice rather than as a morally inferior act (as it might well be using the never give up ethics of the traditional, simplistic slippery slope).

Dignity

The third incline in the triad is based on the notion of dignity—that is, the belief that the decision that affords the patient the most dignity controls. This concept comes into play when (1) the proposed treatment has the potential to provide at least some minimal benefit, at a reasonable cost (rendering the futility slope irrelevant), and (2) it is entirely unclear what the patient would have wanted (rendering the autonomy slope irrelevant). In this scenario, the patient might be a lifelong incompetent or a loner without living family members or close friends. The patient might also be just a typical individual who, like most Americans, happened to keep personal views on end-of-life decision making to him- or herself.

Although no one can say with any certainty what these patients would have wanted, it would be a mistake to return to never give up ethics in such cases. The never give up philosophy leaves no room for a balancing of interests, and it penalizes those who did not or could not make their end-of-life medical preferences known by sentencing them to interminable treatment. When a patient's desires cannot reliably be determined, the patient's "dignity interest" should control,[31] where dignified treatment is defined as the treatment most people would choose for themselves under similar circumstances.

Norman Cantor (1989: 415, emphasis in original) has argued persuasively that

> humane and dignified treatment is probably the touchstone of modern medical ethics and the general movement in the direction of patients' rights that has been ongoing since the middle of the 1960s. . . . Perhaps the key to defining humane treatment for the permanently unconscious being is *broad societal consensus.* . . . The patient's humanity is promoted by medical decisions which reflect a course which the vast majority of competent persons would choose for themselves in the same circumstance.[32]

Those who subscribe to never give up ethics would probably agree with the Pennsylvania attorney general's contention that Joey Fiori should have been kept alive because he "was incapable of suffering pain or humiliation. . . . Fiori's continued life could present no increased loss of dignity or intrusion on privacy" (Unger and Knorr 1995: 30). Those who believe the dignity interest should prevail would take issue with this position, however. The passage of time in an undignified state certainly increases the total indignity, even if the individual is unaware of that indignity—indeed, even if the individual is dead. In fact, the bodies of the dead must be treated with dignity as a matter of law. Can we stand to do any less for those who are living?[33]

Some would also argue that when the patient's desires cannot reasonably be determined, then it is best to continue aggressive treatment, based on the (false) assumption that it is preferable to keep alive all those who would rather have died than it is to let die all those who would have wanted to live. These critics would require—as the courts in New York and Missouri have— that surrogates produce clear and convincing evidence of a desire to forgo life-sustaining treatment in a particular case before honoring such a request.

This is yet another manifestation of never give up ethics that, as Lindgren argues (1993: 186), makes no sense: "If most people would not want to be kept alive with high technology, why do we require proof that they want what most people want?"

Annas (1988) makes the same point by suggesting that it makes no sense to require exacting evidence of the patient's desire to refuse treatment while accepting unquestioningly the mere possibility that the patient would want treatment, especially when the overwhelming majority of Americans say they would not want to be kept alive in a hopelessly ill state of irreversible unconsciousness. Further, he argues, forcing an irreversibly ill and demented patient to endure what many agree to be a humiliating existence is at least as troubling as withholding treatment from such a patient when it may have been desired.[34]

The central problem of requiring clear and convincing evidence boils down to the fact that all indications suggest that the vast majority of Americans would not want to be kept alive in a vegetative state. If this is true, then many more will be harmed by acting on the never give up presumption than would be harmed using a patient's dignity interest as a guide. This may be even more true for the severely demented, a class of patients who may retain some residual ability to sense the pain, discomfort, and frustration of continued life in a seriously degraded and hopelessly ill state.

In the end, decisions to give up on life-sustaining treatment and focus on comfort care can legitimately be made on any one of three bases—futility, autonomy, or dignity—depending on the circumstances of the case. Each of these inclines has its own slippery slope. And all three inclines must be considered together in any holistic view of end-of-life decision making (see the flowchart in Table 6.2). By contrast, never give up ethics provide us with an overly simplistic moral framework that does not respect the constitutionally protected autonomy interest, takes little account of resource

TABLE 6.2 Replacing the "Slippery Slope"

The Old Slippery Slope

Slope	Situation	Implementation	Harms avoided
Sanctity of life	All situations	Do everything possible to save the life of the patient.	Allowing death to take place when life could have been extended.

A New Series of Ethical Inclines

Slope	Situation	Implementation	Harms avoided
Medical futility	Does the proposed treatment have a "reasonable chance" of achieving a worthwhile goal?	Treatment may be provided in the short term if the patient or the members of the patient's family need time to become reconciled to the situation. Long-term treatment is morally optional, and may be morally problematic.	Denying treatment to those who may benefit because scarce resources are devoted to the provision of medically futile treatment to patients at the end of life.

YES

NO

Patient
Autonomy

Is patient competent to make decisions?

Has the patient left an advance directive or otherwise made his or her wishes known?

Is there someone close enough to the patient to know what the patient would want?

Any "YES" response →

Any treatment may be accepted or refused by the patient or appropriate surrogate decision maker, in accordance with the patient's liberty interest.

Denying treatments to a patient who wanted them, or providing treatments to a patient who did not.

All "NO" responses →

Patient
Dignity

An indivual, preferably a close friend or family member, is designated to "stand in the patient's shoes" and use knowledge of the patient's values to decide what is reasonable to assume about what the patient would want done

Any treatment may be accepted or refused by a surrogate decision maker based on knowledge of the patient's views and in light of the balance of benefits and burdens of continued life and treatment, as most members of society would weigh them (the "best interests" standard).

Forcing incompetent, mortally ill patients to accept continued life-sustaining treatment when the vast majority of Americans view continued treatment to be undesirable and inhumane, and there is no evidence to suggest that the patient would think otherwise.

scarcity issues, and discounts as ethically suspect the balancing of interests that leads the vast majority of Americans to favor a less aggressive course of care at the end of life. In short, the never give up philosophy sanctifies the state's common law interest in preserving life without full consideration of patient autonomy, medical futility, or the patient's best interests. It is a dated and paternalistic ethic with little to offer us in the way of guidance in the modern debate about end-of-life decision making. And it should be retired as a relic whose utility has long since passed.

Advance Directives

Currently, living wills are completed by very few individuals. Moreover, even when living wills are completed, most clinicians agree that these documents have a minimal effect on the way they practice medicine (Ely et al. 1992: 473). Indeed, William Knaus (1995) found that advance directives had almost no effect at all on end-of-life decision-making scenarios.[35] Many clinicians reject living wills as too vague to be operative; others simply disagree with the sentiments stated and decide to act on the basis of their own hunches and instincts instead.

One reason living wills are vague is that most patients who fill them out do so with little input from their physicians; providing such input takes time that physicians often do not have (and cannot bill for). There are approximately 115,000 general practitioners in the United States to care for 265 million people, or approximately 1 physician for every 2,300 individuals. If each general practitioner spent just five minutes a year discussing advance directives with every patient, it would take twenty-four eight-hour days; put another way, a whole month would be devoted annually to end-of-life treatment consultations. One way to begin addressing this problem may be to make advance directive consults a reimbursable expense under Medicare and Medicaid.[36] Ethically, this is the right thing to do, and it may well save money and limit suffering in the long run. It would certainly enhance the degree to which patient preferences are identified and honored.[37]

Most hospices address the advance directive problem by creating their own statements of philosophy and protocols regarding end-of-life treatment decisions. According to the President's Commission (1983: 113–114), since the palliative ethos of hospice care is very much at variance with the curative ethos of both the hospital and society at large, most hospices take pains to explain their approach to prospective patients and their families. Many have lengthy admission procedures, wherein the prospective patient is informed of the hospice philosophy and consents to it prior to being accepted into the program. This consent serves the same purpose as an advance directive.

Nursing homes might do well to adopt a similar approach (and no doubt, some already do), although the range of treatment options would surely be broader than it is with hospice. Admission is a good time to establish at least a baseline set of values and expectations about the degree of aggressiveness that patients or their surrogates desire as illness progresses. Admission is also an opportune time to discuss the various kinds of scenarios that come up in nursing homes, scenarios that many patients and surrogates have not considered. Then, regular or "as needed" follow-up conferences should be scheduled to ensure that decisionmakers remain abreast of the patient's evolving clinical situation and that the caregivers remain abreast of the decisionmakers' evolving preferences.[38]

A key part of any protocol along these lines would have to involve patient and surrogate education. As noted earlier, education is vital in making informed decisions about life-sustaining medical treatment. When the patient loses the will or the ability to take in food and fluids orally, for example, a discussion about what it means to forgo ANH should be held (see Box 6.1). Some caregivers may answer questions about forgoing food and fluids if asked, and a few may even initiate a discussion on this subject. But rarely do they document having had such a talk, given the sensitive nature of the subject. Ultimately, if these issues are not brought into the light of day, decisionmakers will forever be making judgments based on flawed assumptions.

There is so much misinformation about how one dies when food and fluids are waived and the provision of sustenance plays such a large role in our culture to begin with that in many cases, surrogates and patients may not even think that forgoing ANH is an option. Therefore, caregivers have some responsibility to initiate discussions on this topic if surrogates are to make decisions that are truly and fully informed. All this consulting will require increases in staff, no doubt,[39] but again, from an ethical as well as a financial point of view, moving in this direction would probably be well worth the effort (and well worth reimbursing).

Summary

We have concluded that the cases that involve true ethical difficulties are many fewer than commonly believed and that the perception of difficulties occurs primarily because of misunderstandings about the dictates of law and ethics. Neither criminal nor civil law precludes health care practitioners or their patients and relatives from reaching ethically and medically appropriate decisions about when to engage in or forego efforts to sustain the lives of dying patients (President's Commission 1983: 184).

Today, thanks to a dizzying array of advanced medical technologies and procedures, the day of death can be forestalled for months, years, and even decades in some cases. But these advances have proved to be a mixed blessing. Although the *quantity* of the average life has increased dramatically since the beginning of the twentieth century, the *quality* of those last years

BOX 6.1   Forgoing ANH—A Primer

The following points regarding the forgoing of ANH might be discussed (for more on ANH, see Chapter 5).

- ANH is uncomfortable and irritating at best; it is often physically painful and mentally distressing, almost always requiring continuous restraints when the patient suffers from dementia.
- Starting ANH does not mean it cannot be stopped.
- Forgoing ANH is a perfectly acceptable course of action to take from a medical, legal, and ethical standpoint; it does not constitute abandonment.
- If fluid intake is halted, death comes relatively quickly (almost always within fifteen days, often much sooner)—the way it had for years prior to the popularization of ANH.
- Dehydration leads to a relatively comfortable passing that is usually accompanied by less pain and perhaps even a sense of euphoria. Symptoms are easily managed.
- Terminal dehydration puts the patient (or surrogate) in control; death from dehydration occurs without the need for assistance from others (except for the provision of comfort care and emotional support). No expertise is required; one simply stops taking in fluids, and nature does the rest.

If Americans only knew these things, they might feel sufficiently empowered to choose the dehydration alternative—calmly, confidently, and maybe even proudly—when the prospects of returning to a relatively good quality of life are dim. The old cliché "information is power" could not be more appropriate to this dimension of end-of-life decision making. In the not-too-distant future, perhaps Americans, armed with information about ANH and the dehydration alternative, will begin asking for a DNI (do not intubate) order as often as they ask for the now commonplace DNR order in the twilight of life.

of life—as perceived by the patient or, if he or she is incompetent, by the patient's family—leaves a good deal to be desired. Life can be and has been extended in years, but many people have come to ask if the quality of life that results is worth the cost, both in financial terms and in the coin of false hope and prolonged suffering.

The problem is that increases in our qualitative health expectancy have not kept pace with increases in our biological life expectancy. As David Crippen (1994) notes: "An unintended side effect of modern technological advances has been the plausibility of maintaining moribund patients in a state of suspended animation for prolonged and sometimes indefinite periods." We can attribute this situation, in large part, to the never give up ethic of medical care, a moral frame of reference that dictates (to caregivers and patients alike) that life is sacred and should be preserved at any cost.

It is time we made a conscious effort to revisit this basic and misguided presumption, a point the authors of the President's Commission report made in the early 1980s: "There is a legitimate moral and legal presumption in favor of preserving life and providing beneficial medical care with the patient's informed consent. Clearly, however, avoiding death should not always be the preeminent goal; not all technologically possible means of prolonging life need be or should be used in every case" (President's Commission 1983: IV).

The status quo on end-of-life decision making is largely the product of cultural myth and misunderstanding. The myth is that we should always err on the side of life. Only a small percentage of Americans actually support this myth, but because so few recognize it as myth, most continue to go along with it, thinking that they are acting as the culture expects. Consequently, it becomes incumbent upon those who assist families in decision-making situations to inform themselves and then their patients and their patients' surrogates about the emerging standards and clinical realities of medical care. If caregivers and decisionmakers were fully aware of the modern consensus in this regard, it would lessen the confusion, anxiety, and guilt associated with making the weighty life-and-death decisions that must be made in most cases.

In sum, though perfecting end-of-life decision making is beyond the reach of this or any text, it is hoped that the words laid down here will help move us in the right direction—away from the never give up ethics of the status quo and toward a more reasoned and thoughtful approach to death and dying. That approach would be advanced through (1) establishing medical standards for the care of mortally ill patients, (2) making better use of hospice care, (3) developing a more useful and widely shared concept of medical futility, (4) improving education about death and end-of-life decision making for caregivers and the general public alike, (5) modifying the old slippery slope theory of ethics to encompass changing, more complicated realities, and (6) making better use of advance directives. Then, perhaps, autonomy and dignity will (re)assume their rightful places as the goals of health care in life, in death, and especially in that hazy area that many of us pass through in the twilight of life—when we find ourselves in the moribund limbo Rosemarie Sherman called "between two worlds."

Notes

Chapter One

1. This is one reason why Sherman eventually had her son transferred to the hospice wing of another facility in the area, where the staff and the operating philosophy were much more sympathetic to her predicament.

2. Two superior court judges issued opinions to accompany Judge Beck's majority opinion. An important concurring opinion was issued by Judge Wieand. And Judge Popovich, part of the original two-judge majority that had overturned the trial court ruling in November 1993, issued another opinion, which concurred in part and dissented in part with Beck's majority opinion.

3. According to one of the judges on the majority side of the superior court decision, the majority's ruling did not deny the possibility that abuse could occur in family and surrogate decision-making situations. The question was: Would abuse occur often enough to warrant a restrictive ruling that would require court involvement in every end-of-life decision? Should a ruling be issued to cover these exceptional cases, or should the ruling address the more common situations of families acting in good faith? This dilemma—whether rules should be made to cover the general case or the exceptional case—is faced regularly by appellate court judges specifically and policymakers more generally. The lack of "bad faith" determinations in the courts suggests that the majority ruled appropriately in this case and that the Popovich dissent (which will be reviewed later in this chapter) was overly cautious. See also the discussion of the brief filed by Alan Meisel and Betty Adler regarding the issue of bad faith, later in this chapter.

4. *Parens patriae* is a Latin term meaning "parent of the homeland or fatherland"; it refers to the state's role in protecting incompetents, minor children, and others who may not be able to defend themselves adequately without assistance from the state.

5. Popovich would require that these statements be directly relevant to the patient's current condition and the proposed treatment. For example, if the diagnosis was persistent vegetative state and withdrawing artificially provided nutrition and hydration (ANH) was the proposed course of action, then patients would have to have specifically stated that they would not want ANH if they ever ended up in a PVS. Otherwise, such statements would not carry weight sufficient to meet the clear and convincing evidence test (Popovich 1995: 18).

6. One official in the AG's office indicated that he would like to see the legislature involved in providing statutory solutions to end-of-life decision-making dilemmas such as the ones raised in the Fiori case. But this same official explained that the AG

had little in the way of manpower, political support, or institutional inclination to lobby the legislature on contentious issues of this type.

7. As evidence of this motivation, one might note the appeal of the 2-to-1 panel decision of the superior court that went in the AG's favor. The attorney general's lawyers appealed the decision because they were not satisfied that the reasoning of the decision would stand up as policy over the long run.

8. *Guardians ad litem* are individuals appointed by the court to report on a range of issues in a dispassionate and neutral way. They are not necessarily the advocates of the principal, although it often works out that way because the principal is either without representation or is considered to have "suspect" representation. The guardian ad litem is there to make sure all points of view are represented.

9. The AG's lawyers pointed out that conflicts of interest could just as easily cut the other way. That is, a surrogate decisionmaker might benefit by maintaining the incompetent patient's life in order to continue receiving welfare or pension benefits, even though the incompetent patient had expressed a wish not to be kept alive in such circumstances (Unger and Knorr 1995: 17).

10. Not surprisingly, neither the AG's brief nor the Catholic bishops' brief mentioned the fact that the Pennsylvania Catholic Conference's position on this issue was very much at odds with the more progressive positions of Catholic conferences in other states, such as Texas, Florida, Washington, Oregon, and Rhode Island (Eastburn and Schaeffer 1994: 26; see Paris 1992 and McCormick 1992).

11. Later, Hoffman argued that "there is every reason to believe that concerned families and physicians, working together, will make proper decisions in most if not all instances, and that the courts will be asked to intervene when they do not" (Hoffman 1995: 38).

12. Choice in Dying was created in 1991 by the merger of two separate right-to-die organizations: Concern for Dying and the Society for the Right to Die. The new group, claiming membership of approximately 65,000, serves as a clearinghouse for information on an individual's right to be free of unwanted medical treatment toward the end of life.

13. Of these twenty-six states, only Ohio requires court authorization for discontinuing artificial nutrition and hydration. The only requirement mentioned in the remaining statutes is the stipulation, in some states, that treatment decisions go to the court when irreconcilable differences exist among the interested parties.

14. The case of Jean Elbaum is also illustrative. Elbaum, a sixty-year-old Long Island woman in a persistent vegetative state, had told her husband and children on several occasions that she would not want to be kept alive if she was comatose. After Elbaum was diagnosed in a PVS, the nursing home refused to remove the feeding tube that kept her alive despite anguished requests from the family that treatments be discontinued. Ultimately, nearly three years after the family had first asked that medical treatment be stopped, Jean Elbaum was transferred to a New York hospice, where tube feeding was ended. Four years later, adding insult to injury, the state's highest court upheld a lower court ruling that Mr. Elbaum had to pay for the unwanted medical treatment his wife had received for nearly three years (Choice in Dying 1994b, *Grace Plaza of Great Neck Inc.* v. *Elbaum*, and *Elbaum* v. *Grace Plaza of Great Neck*).

15. The University of Pittsburgh Center for Medical Ethics was established in 1987 "to promote the study and teaching of medical ethics at the University and in the western Pennsylvania region. . . . The Center is staffed by faculty members from a variety of disciplines, including history, law, philosophy, public health, sociology, and medicine" (among them, specialists in family practice, internal medicine, and pediatrics). The Ethics Center of the University of Pennsylvania Medical Center (UPMC) consists of an interdisciplinary group of doctors, nurses, faculty, members of the clergy, lawyers, social workers, and former patients (Meisel and Adler 1995: 1–2).

16. Meisel and Adler cited several other state court decisions on this score: "The list of cases in which courts 'grant' a right of privacy only after the patient has expired, grows longer every day" (*In re Guardianship of Browning*, 543 So. 2d at 269; *In re Browning*, 543 So. 2d 258 [Fla. Dist. Ct. App. 1989], aff'd). "No matter how expedited, judicial intervention in this complex and sensitive area, it may take too long. Thus it could infringe the very rights that we want to protect" (*In re Jobes*, 529 A. 2d at 449). They also cited the Uniform Law Commissioner's Uniform Health Care Decision Act (comment to Section 6): "The delay attendant upon seeking court approval may undermine the effectiveness of the decision ultimately made" (Meisel and Adler 1995: 26–27).

17. Following are some pertinent examples:

In Florida: "The decision to terminate artificial life-sustaining measures is being made over and over in nursing homes, hospitals, and private homes in this nation" (*In re Guardianship of Browning*, 568 So. 2d 4, 15).

In Illinois: "Frequently the courts are not consulted at all. . . . For many years, members of patient's family, together with doctors and clergy, have made decisions to withdraw life sustaining equipment from incompetent, hopelessly ill patients without seeking judicial approval" (*In re Estate of Longway*, 549 N.E. 2d 292, 295).

In Massachusetts: "The importance of the role of the family and the doctor is highlighted by the self-evident fact that the vast majority of treatment decisions relative to persons who are incompetent by reason of senility or retardation are made for them, by their family and the doctor, without court proceedings" (*In re Spring*, 399 N.E. 2d 493, 499 n. 9).

In New York: "There is reliable information that for many years physicians and members of patients' families, often in consultation with religious counselors, have in actuality been making decisions to withhold or to withdraw life support procedures from incurably ill patients incapable of making critical care decisions themselves" (*In re Storar*, 420 N.E. 2d 64, 75).

18. Other court cases that raised the prospect of bad faith decision making include *In re Estate of Longway*, 549 N.E. 2d 292, 300–301 (1989): "We can foresee other cases, however, where the surrogate decision maker stands to profit from the patient's demise and covets ill-gotten wealth to the point of fatal attraction." See also *In re A. C.*, 573 A. 2d 1235 (D.C. 1990): "There may . . . be conflicting interests, or family members may be inclined for their own reasons to disregard what the patient herself would want." See also *In re Guardianship of Browning*, 568 So. 2d 4, 18 (Fla. 1990), and *Cruzan* v. *Director*, 110 S. Ct. 2841, 2855–2856 (1990).

19. As Meisel noted elsewhere (Meisel 1992: 123), the best and perhaps only example of a decisionmaker being openly accused of attempting to withdraw life sup-

port from a family member for purely financial purposes involved the Florida case of *In re Stone* (No. 90-5867 [Cir. Ct. 17th Dist. Broward County, Fla., June 24, 1991]). In that case, the patient's wife attempted to stop the patient's son (the wife's stepson) from terminating life support, arguing that the son was doing so only to inherit the father's estate (thereby depriving the wife of continued support under an antenuptial agreement). The patient's son argued that he was only attempting to carry out the wishes of his father, and the trial court agreed.

20. Eastburn and Schaeffer (1994: 20–21) had also raised this point in their brief before the en banc session of the superior court.

Chapter Two

1. Meisel coauthored the friend-of-the-court brief submitted jointly by the University of Pittsburgh Center for Medical Ethics and the University of Pennsylvania Medical Center, reviewed in Chapter 1.

2. This statement is made in the context of a discussion regarding the execution of do not resuscitate (DNR) orders.

3. This comment is made in the context of a discussion regarding the decision to forgo artificial nutrition and hydration (ANH).

4. The NCSC properly notes that not all courts have embraced the "best interests" standard in life-sustaining treatment decisions.

5. The President's Commission cites many of the reasons already mentioned for favoring members of the family as the most desirable decisionmakers: (1) The family is generally most concerned about the good of the patient; (2) the family will also usually be most knowledgeable about the patient's goals, preferences, and values; (3) the family deserves recognition as an important social unit that ought to be treated, within limits, as a responsible decisionmaker in matters that intimately affect its members; (4) especially in a society in which many other traditional forms of community have been eroded, participation in a family is often an important dimension of personal fulfillment; and (5) since a protected sphere of privacy and autonomy is required for the flourishing of this interpersonal union, institutions and the state should be reluctant to intrude (President's Commission 1983: 127).

6. The "double effect" phenomenon refers to cases in which death is hastened, unintentionally, by pain medication provided for the primary purpose of alleviating suffering.

Chapter Three

1. The ordinary-extraordinary distinction can be traced back to sixteenth-century Roman Catholic moral theology. At that time, the distinction was understood to refer to a medical procedure's potential for providing some benefit to the patient, in accordance with the principle of proportionality. That is, patients were thought to be required to accept all treatments as morally obligatory only if the burden of the treatment did not outweigh the benefits of continued life. As such, the historically rooted use of the ordinary-extraordinary distinction is very much in tune with the best interests analyses proposed by those arguing on Rosemarie Sherman's side in

the Fiori court case discussed in Chapter 1 and adopted by consensus groups (see Chapter 2). See Hoefler (1994: 140–141).

2. This distinction has also been rejected by most courts since the mid-1980s, largely because it is extremely "fact sensitive." That is, the distinction cannot be applied universally. The courts have tended to find that "extraordinary treatment" in one case may be perfectly "ordinary" in another and vice versa. The bottomline finding has been that the right to self-determination is *not* fact sensitive: A competent patient can refuse virtually any treatment, and incompetent patients enjoy the same rights as competent ones do. The only time, then, when the nature of the treatment itself becomes an issue is in cases involving incompetent patients when no one can say with any confidence, under the substituted judgment principle, what treatment choices the patients themselves would make. This situation precipitates the need to make a best interests determination that might well take into account the nature of the treatment in question. Even here, however, the courts have tended to find that the burdens of treatment (e.g., invasiveness, pain, humiliation, and disorienting effects) should be balanced against the possible benefits of treatment. No treatments, then, are ever considered legally obligatory, prima facie, because they fit into an "ordinary" category of treatment.

3. For elaboration on the important role Catholics have played in the right-to-die politics of several states, see Glick (1992: 94–104 re: California; 104–120 re: Florida; 124–128 re: Massachusetts) and Hoefler (1994: 215–217 re: Pennsylvania). More generally, see Glick (1992: 177) and Hoefler (1994: 219–222).

4. The vast majority (over two-thirds) of Americans claiming a religious affiliation identify with some version of Christianity. A small percentage (2 percent) identify the Jewish faith, but there are no formal position statements issued that authoritatively represent Jewish teachings in this area.

5. Paris is a Jesuit priest, a professor of ethics at Boston College, and the author of a number of articles on end-of-life decision making from a Catholic perspective (e.g., see Paris 1992). McCormick, another Jesuit priest who is widely published in this area, is a professor of Christian ethics at the University of Notre Dame (see McCormick 1992).

6. Many Catholic theologians today agree, according to theologian Edward Bayer (1989: 92), that "if a patient is irreversibly unconscious, his or her life need not be prolonged by artificial means, including artificial feeding and hydration . . . even if such artificial means would considerably extend the unconscious person's life span." This is because (1) the individual is unable to engage in an activity that clearly identifies us as human beings (e.g., the ability to give or receive communication), and (2) "the organ responsible for all truly organic life of the body is dying . . . the brain" (Bayer 1989: 92, 93).

7. The Catholic Health Association has been a vociferous proponent of individual autonomy for some time. At the federal level, representatives of the CHA testified in favor of and lobbied for passage of the Patient Self-Determination Act in 1990, a law that requires hospitals and nursing homes to provide patients with information about making advance directives (e.g., living wills and durable powers of attorney for health care). At the clinical level, the CHA has issued its own quite progressive policy statement (for excerpts, see Chapter 2).

8. Both groups were instrumental in delaying passage of basic living will legislation in their respective states. Given the relatively urban, heterogeneous nature of the population in these two states (especially New Jersey), one would have expected that living will legislation would pass relatively early on in both places (see Glick 1992 on the determinants of "policy innovation"). To the contrary, New Jersey was the forty-third state to pass a living will law (which it did in 1991), and Pennsylvania was the forty-sixth (doing so in 1992). Two other generally progressive and innovative states, New York and Massachusetts, still do not have basic living will legislation on the books. It is no coincidence that the Catholic Conferences are relatively strong and conservative in both states.

For their part, the Pennsylvania bishops have distinguished themselves (in stark contrast to the CHA) by issuing statements such as the following: "The patient in a persistent vegetative state is not imminently terminal (provided there is no other pathology present). The feeding—regardless of whether it be considered as treatment or as care—is serving a life-sustaining purpose. Therefore, it remains an ordinary means of sustaining life and should be continued (Catholic Bishops of Pennsylvania 1991: 14). . . . As a general conclusion, in almost every instance there is an obligation to continue supplying nutrition and hydration to the unconscious patient. There are situations in which this is not the case, but those are the exceptions and should not be made into the rule. We can and do offer our sympathy and support to those who must make such hard decisions in those difficult cases" (Catholic Bishops of Pennsylvania 1991: 22).

9. The distinction was critiqued not because it was wrong per se but because it has been misunderstood and misapplied over the years.

10. Nancy Cruzan was left in a permanent vegetative state after a car accident in rural Missouri in 1983. After she had been tube fed for five years, Cruzan's family asked hospital personnel to halt ANH. The hospital refused, and four years of legal proceedings began. The case was ultimately appealed to the U.S. Supreme Court.

11. Blacks also exhibited an unusually high "no opinion" response of 17 percent (overall, only 7 percent of respondents said they had no opinion).

12. Also see Danis et al. (1991: 881) and Lo, McLeod, and Saika (1986: 1613).

13. This last result regarding hospital administrators might give pause to those who tout the benefits of routine involvement of hospital ethics committees in end-of-life decision making (e.g., see the *Quinlan* decision). To the degree that these bodies are viewed as an arm of the hospital's administrative hierarchy, they may not have the trust they need to deliver decisions that would be considered legitimate by the public.

14. Peritonitis is an abdominal infection that can be fatal if left untreated, especially in the frail elderly.

15. Prior to that, physicians had sometimes executed informal DNR orders unilaterally, without consulting the patient or family (Rothman 1991: 253).

16. Deciding not to resuscitate elderly patients has also been rationalized on similar grounds: "Many elderly patients are unnecessarily resuscitated, only to increase their suffering and prolong the dying process, with no benefit to them or their families" (Griffin 1993).

17. Sometimes, the determination of incompetence is made formally, but this determination is more typically made by physicians and communicated to family members on an informal basis (Buchanan and Brock 1989: 1–2).

18. See also Buchanan and Brock (1989: 271) and Maksoud, Jahnigeen, and Skibinski (1993: 1250), who found that less than one in five patients with DNR orders participated in the decision to enter this designation on their medical records and that rarely was a court ever summoned to appoint a surrogate decisionmaker to help make the DNR determination.

19. Saying "Yes, I would want the plug pulled on me if I am ever in an irreversible vegetative state" when being surveyed while healthy is a very different thing than actually requesting that life-sustaining medical treatment be withdrawn from a loved one in a similar situation, even when it is clear that the decisionmaker and the patient agreed, before the illness began taking its toll, that continued existence in a seriously degraded state was undesirable.

20. Another motivation for the reluctance to act on the basis of attitude might include second thoughts on religious grounds. In spite of the religious positions that seem to be very understanding of the acceptability and desirability of withdrawing life-sustaining treatment in some cases, physicians may still wonder whether a particular case at hand would fall within the category of cases covered by the religious position. More important, the physician may not even be aware of the progressive religious consensus on these issues.

21. There are, indeed, limits to institutional autonomy. For instance, in the case of *In re Requena* (517 A. 2d 870), the court found that although "St. Claire's [hospital] policy, embodied in its resolution of September 1986, is that it will not participate in withholding or withdrawing artificial feeding or fluids. . . . That policy is valid and enforceable only if it does not conflict with a patient's right to die decision and other protected interests." Regarding the question of a "prolife" versus an "antilife" ideology, the court went on to argue that "this poor woman [Beverly Requena] is not anti-life and her decision is not anti-life. She would dearly like to be well and to have a decent life. Unfortunately, a decent life is not hers to have. She has suffered much. It simply is not wrong in any sense for this good woman to want relief from her suffering" (*In re Requena*, p. 981).

22. Combined objection rates are calculated by summing the individual rejection rates for hospitals (Table 3.7) and nursing homes (Table 3.8) and dividing by 2.

23. In each case, the "objection to forgoing treatment" percentage was calculated by averaging the "objection to withholding" and the "objection to withdrawing" percentages, then rounding off.

Chapter Four

1. The Multi-Society Task Force on PVS estimated the cost to be between $1 billion and $7 billion in its 1994 report (1994b: 1572). Joey Fiori's annual health care bill was running in excess of $150,000 in his last year of life. If we adopt 25,000 as a reasonable, mid-range estimate of the number of PVS patients in the United States today, the total annual cost of caring for PVS patients would be approximately $4 billion (using Fiori's cost of care as a baseline).

If a particular patient's care is funded publicly, we all help to underwrite that patient's treatments through taxes. If private insurance pays the bill, we are ultimately affected by some combination of increases in our own premiums, increases in deductibles, increases in copayments, and decreases in coverage.

2. *Sui generis* is a legal term derived from Latin, meaning "of its own particular kind, in a class by itself."

3. For a detailed account of the progression of a typical patient's disease, see Nuland's (1994: chap. 5) discussion of the subject in *How We Die*.

4. Cranford, a neurologist at the Hennepin County Medical Center in Minnesota, has served as a member of the Multi-Society Task Force on PVS (1994a, 1994b) and served on the Greenwall Coordinating Council, the body that directed the development of *Resolving Disputes Over Life-Sustaining Treatment: A Health Care Provider's Guide*, published by the National Center for State Courts (Hafemeister and Hannaford 1996).

5. Cranford (1991a: 17) notes that "prior to the proliferation of CPR, ventilators, antibiotics, dialysis, artificial feeding, ICUs and other medical technologies, individuals died long before they ever had a chance to enter these states."

6. Those who do end up in a PVS get there quickly even though it may take weeks or months before a reliable diagnosis of PVS can be rendered.

7. There have been reports in the popular media of cases in which patients were purported to have made "miraculous" recoveries from vegetative states. In fact, however, the only patients who have made documented recoveries after the PVS was reliably diagnosed remained permanently and severely paralyzed. Other cases of "miraculous recovery" either were anecdotal and not well documented or involved patients in comas, not in a PVS. For the difference between coma and PVS, see Table 1.1.

8. Morphine and other narcotic agents commonly used to control pain also tend to depress respiration and heart rates; if the dosage is high enough, they can actually cause death indirectly. This phenomenon—in which death is hastened unintentionally by pain medication provided to alleviate suffering—is often referred to as the "double effect." See the section "Forgoing Treatment Versus Suicide" in Chapter 2.

9. Tresch also found that only about half the vegetative patients had a resuscitation status designation in their medical charts. Presumably, all attempts would be made to resuscitate these vegetative patients without DNR orders.

10. It should come as no surprise that spending on those who die is higher than spending on those who survive. Survivors may need only minor medical attention in any given year, but those who died obviously had serious medical problems. However, although some skewing in health care spending is to be expected, the data do raise important questions about the degree of disparity in spending within the Medicare population.

11. This upsurge in spending is a major factor in predictions of insolvency for the Medicare program (Fuchs 1984: 151).

12. The 1976 case of Karen Ann Quinlan in New Jersey is often thought of as marking the beginning of the national debate on right-to-die issues in the United States. The seventeen-year-old Quinlan was left in a persistent vegetative state in 1975 after imbibing a combination of prescription medicine and alcohol. After several months, Quinlan's parents asked that their daughter be taken off her respirator, but hospital personnel refused to do so. The Quinlans took legal action and ultimately prevailed when the New Jersey Supreme Court granted them the right to have artificial respiration withdrawn from their daughter. Karen Quinlan was successfully weaned from her respirator and, to everyone's surprise, began breathing

on her own. She continued to receive artificial nutrition and hydration and survived for another eight years. Karen Quinlan died in 1985 from acute pneumonia. Antibiotics that might have fought off the infection were not administered.

13. Palliative care implies that the only measures employed will be directed at managing the symptoms of the disease. Beyond that, nothing will be provided to artificially extend the life of the individual.

14. The court found the evidence in this case was insufficient to satisfy any of its three proposed standards.

15. Many state courts regularly look to the New Jersey court as a beacon of jurisprudence regarding cutting-edge issues, such as the right to die, for which there is no well-developed body of case law to reference in their own state. See Hoefler (1994: 183–185).

16. One doctor testified that a death following extubation would be painful, but another indicated that any discomfort could probably be managed with pain medication.

17. The discussions Mary O'Connor had with her daughters when a family friend underwent a long and painful course of chemotherapy for cancer were characterized by the court of appeals as "general reactions to the unsettling experience" that did not apply to her particular treatment (Choice in Dying 1994b, *In re Westchester*: 3).

18. Decisions about withholding CPR are covered by New York's DNR statute and are the only statutory exceptions to the clear and convincing evidence requirement.

19. This is not to say that the cause or extent of the incompetence has been considered entirely irrelevant. In New Jersey, for example, the state supreme court was more lenient in its *Jobes* decision, which involved a woman in a PVS, than it was in its *Conroy* decision, which involved a woman in the advanced stages of dementia. Illinois's *Longway* decision can be read as covering only those individuals in a PVS, and the *Fiori* decision was written to apply specifically to patients in a PVS. Still, plenty of evidence around the country supports the notion that courts have been sympathetic to requests that life support, including ANH, be withdrawn from patients who are suffering from severe and irreversible brain damage, whether PVS is part of the diagnosis or not.

Chapter Five

1. Important advances include the development of flexible, small-bore plastic nasogastric tubes, well-balanced nutritional products, controlled-drip apparatus, and total parenteral nutrition, discussed later in this chapter.

2. Even with these technologies (or perhaps in spite of them), severe dementia can still be considered the fourth leading cause of death in the United States today, after heart disease (38 percent), cancer (21 percent), and stroke (8 percent) but ahead of accidents (5 percent) (OTA 1987b: 14, 479). Dementia does not often show up in death statistics for one simple reason: Coroners and medical examiners are not in the habit of citing dementia as a cause of death.

3. In a caveat to readers, Walshe and Leonard (1985: 1047) note that "severely demented patients may appear vegetative when overtreated with sedative and neurological drugs or when ill from infection, heart failure, or other systemic illness.

Clinical and laboratory signs of underlying illness will prevent the premature identification of a persistent vegetative state."

4. Researchers from the Office of Technology Assessment cited one New Jersey hospital in particular, where 89 percent of all tube-fed patients were using this method of delivery (OTA 1987b: 283).

5. This figure is derived using the OTA (1987b: 13) estimate of $46 a day in 1987 dollars, adjusted to 1997 dollars using an 8 percent medical inflation rate.

6. According to the OTA, the average charge associated with provision of IV parenteral nutrition was $196 per day in 1987. The charge in 1997 dollars is calculated assuming an 8 percent rate of medical inflation (OTA 1987b: 13).

7. Obesity can add substantially to the length of survival under conditions of starvation. One obese individual survived a fast for 310 days (Shils, Olson, and Shike 1994: 938).

8. The condition is called *marasmus* and is sometimes referred to as "old-man syndrome" for just this reason.

9. Of course, patients who are completely vegetative to begin with will be unaware of any symptoms associated with the onset of this dying process.

10. Starvation is not a problem here because the individual dies of dehydration long before the ill effects of starvation are manifested.

11. Dr. S. S. Cox, having observed over 4,000 patients while practicing as a geriatric specialist in an Arizona hospice, came to the same conclusion (OTA 1987b: 315–316).

12. For example, in one survey of 96 hospice nurses, 82 percent of the respondents indicated that they did not think hydration was painful (Andrews and Levine 1989: 31).

13. This percentage was even higher than the 80 percent of the respondents who said they favored the withdrawal of tube feeding from a patient in a persistent vegetative state when the patient's wishes were not known. In both cases (severe dementia and PVS), a majority of those who provided a rationale for their response indicated the irreversibility of the condition and the unlikelihood of recovering significant function as the primary reasons for their decision not to favor feeding (Hodges et al. 1994: 1017). Eighty-four percent of the survey's respondents considered tube feeding to be a medical therapy, and only 16 percent thought of it as basic humane care (Hodges et al. 1994: 1017; see also Watts, Cassel, and Hickam 1986: 607). The authors of this study concluded that "when patients' wishes are not known, physicians' decisions regarding tube feeding are strongly influenced by prognosis" and that "state legislation that categorizes tube feedings differently from other medical treatments conflicts with the judgment of the majority of internist respondents" (Hodges et al. 1994: 1013).

14. End-stage dementia is described in the study as a condition in which the patient (1) needs complete assistance with eating and toileting, (2) can no longer recognize loved ones, (3) cannot do any of the things that make him or her happy, (4) cannot talk, and (5) suffers complications (urinary incontinence, falls, pneumonia) (Luchins and Hanrahan 1993: 25–26).

15. The title of Cundiff's book—*Euthanasia Is Not the Answer*—leaves no doubt regarding his position on this subject.

16. As Ahronheim and Gasner (1990: 279) point out, "The cruelty and abandonment implied by the word 'starvation' are not relevant to the dying patient." And as

a New Jersey court observed (cited in Cantor 1989: 389–390, 401), "'Denial' of food connotes a refusal of food to someone who wants it. Honoring [the patient's] request not to be fed artificially is not denying her anything. . . . On the contrary, it is recognizing her dignity and worth as a human being" (*In re Requena* 1986: 981).

17. And what physician wants to be manipulated? Morley goes on to advise that weight loss in the elderly is associated with depression. He recommends that "depressed patients with severe weight loss who are nonresponsive to antidepressants should receive a course of electroconvulsive therapy" (1989: 184).

18. A serious heart attack had caused Herbert to lapse into a vegetative state with severe brain damage, and the family had requested that all life-sustaining medical treatments be discontinued.

19. Physicians, acting in good faith and in accordance with the wishes of a patient or legitimate surrogate, have always been held harmless for withdrawing treatment (Weir and Gostin 1990: 1852), either by statute, by case law, or as a matter of common law.

20. In fact, the judge's opinion in that case was completely in harmony with the consensus position regarding ANH and completely in harmony with the sentiments of experienced researchers and clinicians expressed here: "The prosecution of the attending physicians [on charges of murder] would have us draw a distinction between the use of mechanical breathing devices such as respirators and mechanical feeding devices such as intravenous tubes. The distinction urged seems to be based more on the emotional symbolism of providing food and water . . . than on any rational difference in cases such as the one at bench. . . . Medical procedures to provide nutrition and hydration are more similar to other medical procedures than to typical ways of providing nutrition and hydration. Their benefits and burdens ought to be evaluated in the same manner as any other medical procedure" (*Barber* v. *Super. Ct.,* 195 Cal. Rptr. 484, 147 Cal. App. 3d 1006 [1983]).

21. It should be noted that the legal risks associated with not honoring the wishes of patients may be increasing. Although there is no groundswell of cases that center on the concept of "wrongful life," there is a growing set of cases in which judges chastise health care providers for not acting in accordance with the legally binding wishes of patients. In Ohio, an opinion in *Leach* v. *Shapiro* determined that unconsented, unwanted, nonemergency treatment (ventilator and nasogastric tube) provided for several months could constitute a battery for which the hospital and its physicians could be liable. In the *Strachan* decision in New Jersey, the court found that a hospital could be sued for refusing to take a brain-dead patient off life support. See also the *Bayer* case in North Dakota (Weir and Gostin 1990: 1852).

22. A judge dissenting from the majority opinion in *Brophy,* a case like Joey Fiori's that involved the withdrawal of ANH, wrote that we should not sanction the withdrawal of ANH from dying patients because such withdrawal would lead to "a particularly difficult, painful, and gruesome death" (cited in Berger 1995: 27). Other state statutes and court decisions flatly decree that ANH cannot be withheld or withdrawn because ANH was required to provide comfort care for the patient (Berger 1995: 36). Also see Choice in Dying (1994b, *O'Connor:* 1). Clearly, these positions are not grounded in medical fact.

23. A court order to withdraw tube feeding is specifically required in only a few jurisdictions. In most states, ANH can be withdrawn like any other medical procedure, in accordance with the consensus position.

24. Even those who were aware that forgoing ANH was ethically permissible reported a reluctance to withdraw treatment because of the psychological discomfort and the public nature of withdrawal. Many who were obviously unaware of the consensus standards of care that have emerged also worried about being sanctioned by professional review boards for withdrawing treatment (Solomon et al. 1993: 19).

25. One study indicated that 42 percent of physicians thought dying patients suffered significantly when allowed to become dehydrated, as opposed to only 11 percent of nurses who said they would either "probably agree" or "definitely agree" that dehydration is painful (Andrews and Levine 1989: 33).

26. Physician demographics may also play a role in a doctor's unwillingness to act. In a study of 485 Pennsylvania internists, Christakis and Asch (1995: 367) found that older physicians and Catholic physicians were significantly more likely than others to insist on tube feeding comatose or critically ill patients, even when the family was requesting that feeding be waived.

27. For example, patients who have been "successfully treated" for infection run the risk of developing increasingly serious and painful reinfections (Hastings Center 1987: 65–66).

28. According to Hurley and colleagues (Hurley et al. 1993: 21), those patients treated aggressively for infection had higher discomfort scores (and incurred higher costs) than those who received palliative management in a special care unit.

29. Physicians who had attended to patients in the study seemed to be willing to treat patients in certain conditions less actively. For example, cancer patients were twice as likely to be placed in the nontreatment category. Confused and comatose patients were also more likely to be placed in the nontreatment category, as were patients who were bedridden and suffering from pain. Physicians' and nurses' assessments regarding a patient's deterioration before the onset of fever also were closely correlated with the decision not to provide antibiotic therapy for infection.

30. Treatment category assignments were made after consulting with patients (to the degree possible), caregivers, and members of each patient's family (Mott and Barker 1988: 820).

31. According to Mott and Barker, "It is well known that when the patient's personal physician is off duty and covered by another doctor who does not know the patient, the second physician is more apt to treat or hospitalize" (Mott and Barker 1988: 823, citing the 1979 Brown and Thompson study).

32. Electronic defibrillators are paddles, placed on the chest of a heart attack victim, that deliver a shock to the body in hopes of stimulating a regulated heartbeat.

33. "Coding" refers to the informal process of indicating, on the patient's chart or elsewhere, the degree to which aggressive emergency therapy would be administered in the event the patient has a heart attack. A patient with a "no code" status would not receive any resuscitation attempts. A patient with a "slow code" would receive resuscitation attempts, but there would be no rush to administer said therapy.

34. Some feel that CPR is still used too freely. Only about a third of CPR patients survive the resuscitation effort, and only about one in ten survive to leave the hospital (Council 1991: 1868).

35. Twenty-four states had passed nonhospital DNR statutes by the mid-1990s (Choice in Dying 1994b).

36. Also see Cantor (1989: 393): "If artificial nutrition preserves a dying patient in a state which the clear majority of people would consider demeaning or degrading, then its normal symbolic message has been distorted."

37. Lo and Dornbrand (1984: 404) sum up their presentation in much the same way: "If the patient repeatedly pulls out a nasogastric tube, the goal of care needs to be reconsidered. . . . Tying the patient down to allow tube feedings is difficult to reconcile with the goal of humane care. Although food and water should still be offered by hand, caring may be better expressed by providing attention and affection than by forcing calories."

Chapter Six

1. The Patient Self-Determination Act (PSDA) went into effect in December 1991 and is the only federal law that deals with the right to die. The PSDA requires personnel in hospitals and nursing homes to inform patients, on admission or shortly thereafter, what rights they have to make health care decisions for themselves, under state law, through the completion of advance directives (e.g., living wills and durable powers of attorney for health care). If a patient has an advance directive, he or she will be asked to produce a copy that will be placed in the medical record. Patients who do not have advance directives will be asked if they would like to complete one, and if so, if they would like assistance, which hospital personnel will typically provide.

2. Knaus's (1995) comments were made in reference to an article he coauthored with seven other principal SUPPORT investigators, published in the *Journal of the American Medical Association* (SUPPORT 1995).

3. Justice William Brennan said as much in his dissent to the *Cruzan* decision, where he argued that the status quo—in which "life" is the default rule—is illegitimate because it is "to a large extent a predictable, yet accidental confluence of technology, psyche, and inertia. The general citizenry . . . never said that it favored the creation of coma wards where permanently unconscious patients would be tended to for years and years. Nor did the populace as a whole authorize the preeminence of doctors over families in making treatment decisions for incompetent patients" (cited in Lindgren 1993: 224).

4. Sachs and colleagues (Sachs et al. 1995: 558–559) reports that such a system is already in place in one institution, the E. N. Rogers Memorial Veterans Hospital.

5. As Lindgren (1993: 190) points out, though it is perfectly reasonable to presume that an individual would consent to treatment in an emergency situation, it is *not* reasonable (or necessary) to assume consent would be given in cases where the patient is essentially and irreversibly vegetative. In fact, it is perfectly *unreasonable* to assume that patients in a severely and irreversibly degraded condition would want treatment, if public opinion polls and other more qualitative studies of patient preferences are any guide.

6. For example, the last days of those who are dying of cancer are often made more uncomfortable by the continued use of chemotherapy or radiation treatments; such treatments are often continued long after the point where they would do any measurable good.

7. This is why those who advocate the hospice approach argue that hospice-oriented care does not constitute abandonment. To the contrary, though medical interventions (e.g., respirators, ANH, and antibiotics) are waived with the comfort care approach, the symptom management and personal attention required of this treatment option more than make up for anything lost in the way of technological attention.

8. In another study, 90 percent of family members and 91 percent of health care professionals in the American Geriatric Society reported feeling that hospice care would be appropriate for patients with end-stage dementia (Luchins and Hanrahan 1993: 25–26).

9. Approximately 80 percent of hospice patients suffer from cancer because cancer is one of the few diseases in which life expectancy can be fairly accurately predicted (at least toward the end of life, when a cure is no longer realistic).

10. Home health care spending by Medicaid, only $2 billion in 1990, is expected to grow fivefold to about $10 billion in the year 2000. This will still only amount to about 7.6 percent of what is spent on long-term care and less than 1 percent of overall health care spending. This amount will not begin to cover the services that will be needed as the baby boomers edge closer to retirement and, ultimately, closer to the decision about how they want to die (Sonnefeld et al. 1991: 12; U.S. GAO 1995a).

11. Part of the problem here stems from the fact that there is no consensus on an acceptable definition of *medical futility*. Schneiderman, Jecker, and Jonsen have pushed for a liberal reading of the construct, arguing that "in judging futility, physicians must distinguish between an effect, which is limited to some part of the patient's body, and a benefit, which appreciably improves the person as a whole. Treatment that fails to provide the latter, whether or not it achieves the former, is 'futile'" (Schneiderman, Jecker, and Jonsen 1990: 949).

Some would prefer to define *medical futility* in much more narrow terms. J. D. Lantos and his colleagues are among them: "[Physicians] may acknowledge that therapy is effective, in a limited sense, but believe that the goals that can be achieved are not desirable, as when considering prolonged nutritional support for patients in a persistent vegetative state. Physicians should acknowledge that, in such situations, potentially achievable goals exist. Therapy is not, strictly speaking, futile" (Lantos et al. 1989). Also see Hafemeister and Hannaford (1996: 65–66).

12. About a third of the respondents indicated that they had unilaterally withheld or withdrawn treatment they deemed to be medically futile once or twice in the preceding year, about a third indicated that they had done so three to five times in the preceding year, and about a third indicated that they had done so more than five times in the previous twelve months.

13. For example, see Jecker and Schneiderman (1993: 157); Beauchamp and Childress (1994: 213); and Schneiderman, Jecker, and Jonsen (1990: 949).

14. This strong sentiment is buffered just a bit later in the text when the authors suggest that even though physicians may be entitled to withdraw treatment in futile cases, they "should do so in a manner sensitive to the emotional investments and concerns of caretakers" (Schneiderman, Jecker, and Jonsen 1990: 953). Presumably, the authors would implore physicians to be sensitive to the emotional investments and concerns of family members—and the patient—as well.

15. Specifically, the family was asked for permission to withdraw the respirator. This is a common practice when the respirator can no longer benefit the patient, according to Stephen Miles (1991: 513), a medical ethicist at HCMC.

16. Costs were not an issue for the county facility, since Medicare and a private third-party insurance carrier were underwriting Wanglie's medical bills, $800,000 to that point.

17. The AMA Council on Ethical and Judicial Affairs (Council 1991: 1870) has spoken to this issue explicitly: "In the unusual circumstance when efforts to resuscitate a patient are judged by the treating physician to be futile, even if previously requested by the patient, CPR may be withheld. In such circumstances, when there is adequate time to do so, the physician should inform the patient, or the incompetent patient's surrogate, of the content of the DNR order as well as the basis for its implementation." The American College of Physicians (1992: 954) also sanctions, reluctantly, the writing of DNR orders for patients who are seriously and irreversibly ill: "It is more controversial whether it is appropriate for physicians to write a unilateral DNR order in situations where discharge alive after resuscitation would be unprecedented. . . . If physicians write a unilateral order, they must inform the patient or surrogate."

18. There is a trade-off here, however, because with this level of detailed polling, one must deal with much smaller sample sizes, and that affects the statistical generalizability of the findings.

19. For an extended discussion of the consensus position on surrogate decision making, see Chapter 2.

20. According to the New Jersey State Supreme Court's decision in the first right-to-die case in the United States, that of Karen Ann Quinlan, "The state's interest . . . weakens and the individual's right to privacy grows as the degree of bodily invasion increases and the prognosis dims" (*In re Quinlan*, 70 N.J. 10, 355 A. 2d 647 [1976]).

21. Using the quality of life criterion in end-of-life decision making often raises red flags in the minds of those who equate making decisions on this basis with involuntary euthanasia, wherein those not deemed productive from society's perspective are either allowed to die or even helped to die. The term is used here to denote quality of life from the patient's perspective. In reality, every medical decision can be viewed as a judgment on the patient's quality of life. If doctors decide to treat a patient aggressively, they are making the determination that the life they are saving is, qualitatively, worth saving. If they always react by treating aggressively, then they are saying that all life is of sufficient quality to be preserved. Clearly, this attitude is at odds with what most Americans believe. And just as clearly, this attitude is in conflict with clinical realities, where the vast majority of deaths in U.S. hospitals are managed so that they occur more quickly than they might otherwise, even when the patient is incompetent and has left no advance directive. Apparently, all lives are not worth saving, pronouncements to the contrary notwithstanding.

22. "The impact of a decision on an incapacitated patient's loved ones may be taken into account in determining someone's best interests, for most people do have an important interest in the well-being of their families or close associates" (President's Commission 1983: 28–29).

23. "One cannot impose on anyone the obligation to have recourse to a technique which is already in use but which carries a risk or is burdensome. Such a re-

fusal is not the equivalent of suicide; on the contrary, it should be considered an acceptance of the human condition, or the wish to avoid the application of a medical procedure disproportionate to the results that can be expected, or a desire not to impose excessive expense on the family or the community (Sacred Congregation 1980, cited in Gibbs 1990: 67).

24. Many caregivers may view the withholding of treatment as benign neglect. In contrast, withdrawing treatment requires that clinicians take a positive action that could be perceived as ultimately precipitating death. Withholding treatment seems to implicate no one directly and everyone indirectly. Withdrawing treatment seems to implicate the individual carrying out the decision quite directly.

25. Part of any education effort geared toward overcoming the psychological barrier associated with the withholding-withdrawing distinction should deal with the fact that patient care, after life-sustaining treatment has been withdrawn, often involves more personal attention and responsibility on the part of caregivers and family members than continued treatment does. As such, withdrawing care hardly constitutes abandonment. Rather, good palliative care in the hospice tradition may require more attention, more flexibility, and more involvement of caregivers and family members alike, albeit for a delimited amount of time.

26. For an extended discussion of this point, see Chapter 2.

27. Also see the SUPPORT study of 4,800 seriously ill patients, over half of whom were in moderate to severe pain during their last days of life (SUPPORT 1995).

28. Both may be legitimate concerns. The coerced "duty to die" fear is most troubling because it is most realistic given the U.S. health care system, in which there is no guaranteed right to medical care and in which families need to impoverish themselves before qualifying for long-term health care assistance under Medicaid. Managed care pressures are also a potential factor here, causing providers to be increasingly stingy with medical treatments when it is unclear what long-term benefits, if any, might accrue to the patient.

29. The requested treatment may be deemed "inappropriate" on any one of several grounds. First and most obviously, there may be no sound medical reason for providing the requested treatment. For example, a physician may decline to administer laetrile to a cancer patient who requests it since there is no sound medical evidence to suggest that laetrile is effective in treating the disease. More to the point, a physician may decline to provide a treatment when the resources required are relatively significant and the chances of a good outcome are relatively small. For example, physicians may decline to perform major surgery on a frail, elderly individual, even though there may be a small chance for a reasonably positive outcome. Declining to perform surgery is especially defensible when the requested procedure would require use of a scarce and finite resource, such as a transplantable organ. See the recent revision of priority policy for organ transplants as an example of this ethic in practice (Hauptman and O'Connor 1997).

30. For example, was it ethical to provide Mickey Mantle with a liver transplant just weeks before he died of cancer that had metastasized throughout his body when half a dozen patients die every day in the United States for lack of transplantable organs? The answer to that question might be "Yes, it was ethical" ac-

cording to never give up ethics. On the slippery slope of futility, however, providing the transplant in this case would probably constitute a step down the incline.

31. The "dignity interest" has played an important role in a number of judicial decisions involving the withdrawal of life-sustaining treatment (Cantor 1989: 414), though the concept is not typically or formally referred to as such (e.g., see *In re Gardner*, p. 953, and *In re Jobes*, p. 459).

32. The state's interest in preserving life would be allowed to trump the dignity interest when there was no clear consensus about what most people would want. For more on this argument, see Cantor's more recent article (1996: 1737), where he discusses his concept of "constructive preference" and argues that default preferences can be constructed and applied based on "objectively measurable data about the level of mental and physical debilitation that most people consider intolerably undignified and therefore unacceptable. . . . When a large majority of people would prefer withdrawal of life support, a surrogate should implement the popular preference and withdraw life support, unless significant indicia in the particular patient's history indicate that the patient would prefer otherwise." Cantor adds the important caveat that such default rules would have to receive wide publicity before being used so that those whose preferences differed from the default rule could have the opportunity to make their alternative wishes known.

33. If this were not true, we would have to believe that a dead body that has been sexually abused in a morgue suffers no indignity because there is no understanding on the part of the "victim." More to the point, suppose Mr. Fiori had been the brunt of cruel treatment in an uncaring, unsanitary facility. Would the fact that he had been unaware of his surroundings and the quality of his care mean that continued existence in that state would pose no further indignities to him? Or if Mr. Fiori were regularly left unclothed, would he retain no privacy rights because he would be unaware of his nakedness? Would five minutes in this condition be equally as undignifying as five hours, five days, five months, or five years? (See Wicclair 1993: 60.)

34. The New York State Task Force on Life and the Law, a moderate-to-conservative organization in the spectrum of right-to-die thinking and a group that has come out squarely against physician-assisted suicide, has also categorically objected to the clear and convincing evidence standard (NYSTFLL 1992: 74): "In practice, the clear and convincing evidence standard is often unworkable and inhumane. It is a legal standard that translates poorly at the bedside where families and health care professionals must confront the hard choices that incurable illness and medical advances present. The standard requires that patients forecast in advance what their medical condition will be at some future time and the treatments that will be available. In an age of rapid medical advances, this is a difficult task even for medical experts. It is simply unrealistic and unfair for the vast majority of the public."

35. It seems that, at least to this point, physicians have been able to ignore living wills with impunity. Still, although no tradition of "wrongful life" suits has yet been developed, "there are any number of successful battery cases brought by patients claiming that they were treated without their consent" (Meisel 1989: 48, citations omitted). Physicians would do well to tread carefully when considering whether to honor an advance directive in the future, for it is just a matter of time before more

lawyers start bringing wrongful life suits to court and having more successes with judges and juries.

36. In the long run, it is also clear that the ratio of general practitioners to specialists in the United States could stand to be readjusted. Less than 25 percent of U.S. physicians are general practitioners today, whereas the general practitioner rate is much closer to 50 percent in most other Western democracies.

37. See Peter Ditto's (1995) study of 100 elderly outpatients who discussed advanced directives with physicians. Patients were reported to have responded well to physician-initiated discussions, particularly when they were in good physical and emotional health. Also, though physicians tended to be poor predictors of patient wishes, their predictions improved with experience in discussing advance directives.

38. These conferences are critical in providing a good, patient-oriented service as well as limiting liability exposure down the road. When patients and their family members are made integral to the decision-making process each step of the way, these individuals become coauthors of treatment plans, making it much less likely that they will feel so left out of the decision-making process that they will sue caregivers or the institution at some later date. See Hafemeister and Hannaford (1996: 48–50).

39. Clinical social workers often deal with these issues now, so they may be best suited to the task, but physicians have some responsibility here as well, according to the President's Commission report: "[Physicians are] obliged to mention all alternative treatments . . . so long as they are supported by respectable medical opinion" (cited in Fried and Gillick 1994: 303).

References

The following abbreviations and acronyms are used in the References and in related citations in the text:

ACP	American College of Physicians
AHCPR	Agency for Health Care Policy and Research
ANA	American Nurses Association
ATS	American Thoracic Society
CHA	Catholic Health Association of the United States
Council	Council on Ethical and Judicial Affairs
NCCB	National Conference of Catholic Bishops
NLCMDD	National Legal Center for the Medically Dependent and Disabled
NCSC	National Center for State Courts
NYSTFLL	New York State Task Force on Life and the Law
OTA	Office of Technology Assessment
President's Commission	President's Commission for the Study of Ethical Problems in Medicine and Biomedical and Behavioral Research
PRRC	Princeton Religion and Research Center
Sacred Congregation	Sacred Congregation for the Doctrine of the Faith
ULC	National Conference of Commissioners on Uniform State Laws (Uniform Law Commissioners)
U.S. GAO	U.S. General Accounting Office
U.S. Senate	U.S. Senate Special Committee on Aging

Books and Articles

Agency for Health Care Policy and Research. 1995. "Physician Characteristics Influence Decision to Withdraw Patient Life Support." *Research Activities.* Vol. 185, p. 2.

Ahronheim, Judith C. 1984. "Artificial Feeding: What's Involved?" *Choice in Dying Newsletter.* Summer.

Ahronheim, Judith C., and Gasner, M. R. 1990. "The Sloganism of Starvation." *The Lancet.* Vol. 335, pp. 278–279.

Ahronheim, Judith C., and Mulvihill, Michael. 1991. "Refusal of Tube Feeding as Seen from a Patient Advocacy Organization: A Comparison with Landmark Court Cases." *Journal of the American Geriatric Association.* Vol. 39, pp. 1124–1127.

Ainslie, Nina, and Beisecker, Annalee E. 1994. "Changes in Decisions by Elderly Persons Based on Treatment Description." *Archives of Internal Medicine*. Vol. 154, pp. 2225–2233.

American Academy of Neurology. 1989. "Position of the American Academy of Neurology on Certain Aspects of the Care and Management of the Persistent Vegetative State Patient," adopted by the executive board of the American Academy of Neurology, April 21, 1988, Cincinnati, Ohio. *Neurology*. Vol. 39, pp. 125–126.

American College of Physicians. 1989. "American College of Physicians Ethics Manual II." *Annals of Internal Medicine*. Vol. 111, pp. 327–335.

_____. 1992. "American College of Physicians Ethics Manual." 3d ed. *Annals of Internal Medicine*. Vol. 117, pp. 947–960.

American Nurses Association. 1989. "Guidelines on Withdrawing or Withholding Food and Fluid." In *Biolaw*. Vol. 2. Bethesda, Md.: University Publications of America, pp. 12–16.

_____. 1992. *Compendium of Position Statements on the Nurse's Role in End-of-Life Decisions*. Washington, D.C.: American Nurses Publishing.

_____. 1994a. *Position Statement on Active Euthanasia*. Washington, D.C.: American Nurses Publishing.

_____. 1994b. *Position Statement on Assisted Suicide*. Washington, D.C.: American Nurses Publishing.

American Thoracic Society. 1991. "Withholding and Withdrawing Life-Sustaining Therapy." *Annals of Internal Medicine*. Vol. 115, pp. 478–485.

Anderson, Kenneth N., ed. 1994. *Mosby's Medical, Nursing, and Allied Health Dictionary*. 4th ed. St. Louis: Mosby.

Andrews, Maria R., and Levine, Alan M. 1989. "Dehydration in the Terminal Patient: Perception of Hospice Nurses." *American Journal of Hospice Care*. January–February, pp. 31–34.

Andrews, Maria, Bell, Eric R., Smith, Shirley A., Tischler, James F., and Veglia, Jeanne M. 1993. "Dehydration in Terminally Ill Patients: Is It Appropriate Palliative Care?" *Postgraduate Medicine*. Vol. 93, pp. 201–208.

Angell, Marcia. 1985. "Cost Control and the Physician." *Journal of the American Medical Association*. Vol. 254, p. 1204.

_____. 1994. "After Quinlan: The Dilemma of the Persistent Vegetative State." *New England Journal of Medicine*. Vol. 330, pp. 1524–1525.

Annas, George J. 1988. "Precatory Prediction and Mindless Mimicry: The Case of Mary O'Connor." *Hastings Center Report*. Vol. 18. December, pp. 31–33.

_____. 1995. Cited in Ellen Goodman. "Hospitals No Place of Humane Death." *Carlisle (Pa.) Sentinel*. December 1.

Asch, David A., Hansen-Flaschen, John, and Lanken, Paul N. 1995. "Decisions to Limit or Continue Life-Sustaining Treatment by Critical Care Physicians in the United States: Conflict Between Physicians' Practices and Patients' Wishes." *American Journal of Respiratory Critical Care Medicine*. Vol. 151, pp. 288–292.

Bayer, Edward J. 1989. "Perspectives from Catholic Theology." In Joanne Lynn, ed., *By No Extraordinary Means: The Choice to Forgo Life-Sustaining Food and Water*. Bloomington: Indiana University Press, pp. 89–98.

Beauchamp, Tom L., and Childress, James F. 1994. *Principles of Biomedical Ethics*. 4th ed. New York: Oxford University Press.

Belkin, Lisa. 1992. "New York Rule Compounds Dilemma over Life Support." *New York Times.* May 12.

Berger, Arthur S. 1995. *When Life Ends: Legal Overviews, Medicolegal Forms, and Hospital Policies.* Westport, Conn.: Praeger.

Bertman, Sandra L. 1991. *Facing Death: Images, Insights, and Interventions—A Handbook for Educators, Healthcare Professionals, and Counselors.* New York: Hemisphere.

Besdine, Richard W. 1983. "Decision to Withhold Treatment from Nursing Home Residents." *Journal of the American Geriatric Association.* Vol. 31, pp. 602–605.

Billings, J. Andrew. 1985. "Comfort Measures for the Terminally Ill: Is Dehydration Painful?" *Journal of the American Geriatric Society.* Vol. 33, pp. 808–810.

Blank, Robert H. 1988. *Life, Death, and Public Policy.* DeKalb: Northern Illinois University Press.

Bole, Thomas J. III. 1992. "Why Almost Any Cost to Others to Preserve the Life of the Irreversibly Comatose Constitutes an Extraordinary Burden." In Kevin W. Wildes, Frances Abel, and John C. Harvey, eds., *Birth, Suffering, and Death: Catholic Perspectives at the Edges of Life.* Boston: Kluwer Academic Publishers, pp. 171–188.

Brody, Baruch. 1992. "Special Ethical Issues in the Management of PVS Patients." *Law, Medicine, and Health Care.* Vol. 20, pp. 104–114.

Brody, Jane E. 1993. "Standing Up for a Dying Patient's Rights." *New York Times.* January 27.

Brown, Norman K., and Donovan, J. Thompson. 1979. "Nontreatment of Fever in Extended-Care Facilities." *New England Journal of Medicine.* Vol. 300, pp. 1246–1250.

Buchanan, Allen E., and Brock, Dan W. 1989. *Deciding for Others: The Ethics of Surrogate Decision Making.* New York: Cambridge University Press.

Bulkin, Wilma, and Lukashok, Herbert. 1988. "Rx for Dying: The Case for Hospice." *New England Journal of Medicine.* Vol. 318, pp. 376–378.

Busalacchi, Pete. 1990. "How Can They?" *Hastings Center Report.* September–October, Vol. 20, pp. 6–7.

Callahan, Daniel. 1983. "On Feeding the Dying." *Hastings Center Report.* October, Vol. 13, p. 22.

_____. 1987. *Setting Limits: Medical Goals in an Aging Society.* New York: Simon and Schuster.

_____. 1989. "Public Policy and the Cessation of Nutrition." In Joanne Lynn, ed., *By No Extraordinary Means: The Choice to Forgo Life-Sustaining Food and Water.* Bloomington: Indiana University Press, pp. 61–66.

_____. 1990. *What Kind of Life: The Limits of Medical Progress.* New York: Simon and Schuster.

_____. 1991. "Medical Futility, Medical Necessity: The-Problem-Without-A-Name." *Hastings Center Report.* July–August, Vol. 21, pp. 30–35.

Cantor, Norman L. 1987. *Legal Frontiers of Death and Dying.* Bloomington: Indiana University Press.

_____. 1989. "The Permanently Unconscious Patient, Non-Feeding, and Euthanasia." *American Journal of Law and Medicine.* Vol. 15, pp. 381–437.

_____. 1996. "The Real Ethic of Death and Dying." *Michigan Law Review*. Vol. 94, pp. 1718–1738.

Capron, Alexander M. 1989. "Historical Overview: Law and Public Perceptions." In Joanne Lynn, ed., *By No Extraordinary Means: The Choice to Forgo Life-Sustaining Food and Water*. Bloomington: Indiana University Press, pp. 11–20.

Catholic Bishops of Pennsylvania. 1991. *Nutrition and Hydration: Moral Considerations*. Harrisburg: Pennsylvania Catholic Conference.

Catholic Health Association of the United States. 1993. *Care of the Dying: A Catholic Perspective*. St. Louis: Catholic Health Association of the United States.

Celesia, C. G. 1993. "Persistent Vegetative State." *Annals of Neurology*. Vol. 33, p. 391.

Chambers, Christopher V. 1994. "Living Wills Chop Final Medical Costs, Study Finds." *Archives of Internal Medicine*. Vol. 154, pp. 541–547.

Choice in Dying. 1994a. "State Statutes Governing Nonhospital DNR Orders," map released in December. New York: Choice in Dying.

_____. 1994b. "Fact Sheets." In *Right to Die Law Digest*. New York: Choice in Dying.

Christakis, Nicholas A. 1995. "Physician Characteristics Influence Decision to Withdraw Patient Life Support." In AHCPR, *Research Activities*. Vol. 185, p. 2.

Christakis, Nicholas A., and Asch, David A. 1995. "Physician Characteristics Associated with Decisions to Withdraw Life Support." *American Journal of Public Health*. Vol. 85, pp. 367–372.

Clark, Nicola. 1992. "The High Costs of Dying." *Wall Street Journal*. February 26.

Cogen, Raymond, Patterson, Beth, Chavin, Stephen, Cogen, Jan, Landsberg, Lisa, and Posner, Joel. 1992. "Surrogate Decision-Maker Preferences for Medical Care of Severely Demented Nursing Home Patients." *Archives of Internal Medicine*. Vol. 152, pp. 1885–1888.

Cohen-Mansfield, Jiska, Rabinovich, Beth A., Lipson, Steven, Fein, Adele, Gerber, Barbara, Weisman, Shulamith, and Pawlson, Gregory. 1991. "The Decision to Execute a Durable Power of Attorney for Health Care and Preferences Regarding the Utilization of Life-Sustaining Treatments in Nursing Homes." *Archives of Internal Medicine*. Vol. 151, pp. 289–294.

Coleman, Brenda C. 1995. "Study Doctors Ignore Wishes of the Dying." *Harrisburg (Pa.) Patriot*. November 11.

Collaud, Thierry, and Rapin, Charles-Henri. 1991. "Dehydration in Dying Patients: Study with Physicians in French-Speaking Switzerland." *Journal of Pain and Symptom Management*. Vol. 6, pp. 230–240.

Council on Ethical and Judicial Affairs. 1982. "Quality of Life." In *Code of Medical Ethics: Current Opinions with Annotations*. Chicago: American Medical Association, Sect. 2.10, pp. 9–10.

_____. 1990. "Persistent Vegetative State and the Decision to Withdraw or Withhold Life Support." *Journal of the American Medical Association*. Vol. 263, pp. 426–430.

_____. 1991. "Report 34: Decisions to Forgo Life-Sustaining Treatment for Incompetent Patient." In *Code of Medical Ethics: Current Opinions with Annotations*. Chicago: American Medical Association, pp. 65–76.

_____. 1992. "Decisions Near the End of Life." *Journal of the American Medical Association.* Vol. 267, pp. 2229–2233.

_____. 1994a. "Physician Assisted Suicide." *Issues in Law and Medicine.* Vol. 10, pp. 91–97.

_____. 1994b. "Withholding or Withdrawing Life-Sustaining Treatment." In *Code of Medical Ethics: Current Opinions with Annotations.* Chicago: American Medical Association, Sect. 2.20, pp. 36–38.

Coyle, Marcia. 1990. "How Americans View High Court." *National Law Journal.* Vol. 13.

Cranford, Ronald E. 1991a. "Neurological Syndromes and Prolonged Survival: When Can Artificial Nutrition and Hydration Be Foregone?" *Law, Medicine, and Health Care.* Vol. 19, pp. 13–22.

_____. 1991b. "Helga Wanglie's Ventilator." *Hastings Center Report.* July–August, Vol. 21, pp. 23–24.

Crippen, David. 1994. "The Cost of the Living Dead." *Pittsburgh Post.* October 30.

Cummings, Milton C., Jr., and Wise, David. 1989. *Democracy Under Pressure.* 6th ed. San Diego: Harcourt Brace Jovanovich.

Cundiff, David. 1992. *Euthanasia Is Not the Answer: A Hospice Physician's View.* Totowa, N.J.: Humana Press.

Danis, Marion, Southerland, L. I., Garrett, J. M., Smith, J. L., Hielema, F., Pickard, C. G., Egner, D. M., and Patrick, D. L. 1991. "A Prospective Study of Advance Directives for Life-Sustaining Care." *New England Journal of Medicine.* Vol. 324, pp. 882–888.

Ditto, Peter H. 1995. "Advance Directive Discussions with Elderly Outpatients." In AHCPR, *Research Activities.* Vol. 187, p. 17.

"Doctors Want to Pull Plug; Husband Says No." 1990. *Carlisle (Pa.) Sentinel.* January 10.

Doukas, David J., Waterhouse, David, Gorenflo, Daniel W., and Seid, Jerome. 1995. "Attitudes and Behaviors on Physician-Assisted Death: A Study of Michigan Oncologists." *Journal of Clinical Oncology.* Vol. 13, pp. 1055–1061.

Dyck, Arthur J. 1984. "Ethical Aspect of Care of the Dying Incompetent." *Journal of the American Geriatric Society.* Vol. 32, pp. 661–664.

Eckholm, Eric. 1990. "Haunting Issue for U.S.: Caring for the Elderly Ill." *New York Times.* March 27.

Ellement, John. 1995. "Jury Sides with Doctors on Ending Woman's Life Support." *Boston Globe.* April 22.

Ely, John W., Peters, Philip G., Zweig, Steven, Elder, Nancy, and Schneider, F. David. 1992. "The Physicians' Decisions to Use Tube Feedings: The Role of the Family, the Living Will, and the *Cruzan* Decision." *Journal of the American Geriatric Association.* Vol. 40, pp. 471–475.

Emanuel, Ezekiel J., and Emanuel, Linda. L. 1994. "The Economics of Dying: The Illusion of Cost Savings at the End of Life." *New England Journal of Medicine.* Vol. 330, pp. 540–544.

Emanuel, Linda L., Barry, Michael J., Stoeckle, John D., Ettelson, Lucy M., and Emanuel, Ezekiel J. 1991. "Advance Directives for Medical Care: A Case for Greater Use." *New England Journal of Medicine.* Vol. 324, pp. 889–895.

Enck, Robert E., ed. 1994. *The Medical Care of Terminally Ill Patients*. Baltimore: Johns Hopkins University Press.

English, David M. 1993. "Comment: Defining the Right to Die." *Law and Contemporary Problems*. Vol. 56, pp. 255–259.

Episcopal Church. 1991. "Life-Sustaining Treatment." Proceedings of the 70th General Convention, Resolution A-093a, pp. 52–53.

_____. 1994. "Life-Sustaining Treatment." Proceedings of the 71st General Convention, Resolution A-056, p. 26.

Evangelical Lutheran Church. 1992. *A Message on End-of-Life Decisions*. Chicago: Evangelical Lutheran Church in America.

Faber-Langendoen, Kathy, and Bartels, Dianne M. 1992. "Process of Forgoing Life-Sustaining Treatment in a University Hospital: An Empirical Study." *Critical Care Medicine*. Vol. 20, pp. 570–577.

Foote, Jennifer. 1995. "Inadequate Care All Too Common." *Harrisburg (Pa.) Patriot*. May 16.

Fried, Terri, and Gillick, Muriel R. 1994. "Medical Decision-Making in the Last Six Months of Life: Choices About Limitations of Care." *Journal of the American Medical Association*. Vol. 271, pp. 303–307.

Fromme, Dominique, Questiaux, Elisabeth, Gautier, Marth, and Schwarzenberg, Leon. 1984. "Voluntary Total Fasting: A Challenge of the Medical Community." *The Lancet*. Vol. 324, pp. 1451–1452.

Fuchs, Victor R. 1984. "'Though Much Is Taken': Reflections on Aging, Health, and Medical Care." *Milbank Memorial Fund Quarterly*. Vol. 62, pp. 142–166.

Fulton, Gere B. 1993. "The 'Non-Declarant' in a PVS: Adventures in Ohio's Legal Wonderland." *Ohio Northern University Law Review*. Vol. 20, pp. 571–595.

Galewitz, Phil. 1995. "Court to Rule on Life: Patient's Rights Under Debate?" *Harrisburg (Pa.) Patriot*. May 1.

Gamble, Elizabeth R., McDonald, Penelope J., and Lichstein, Peter R. 1991. "Knowledge, Attitudes, and Behavior of Elderly Persons Regarding Living Wills." *Archives of Internal Medicine*. Vol. 151, pp. 277.

Gelman, David, and Hager, Mary. 1989. "The Brain Killer." *Newsweek*. December 18.

General Synod of the United Church of Christ. 1991. Minutes of the annual meeting, Norfolk, Va., July 27, pp. 46–47.

Gibbs, Nancy. 1990. "Love and Let Die." *Time*. March 19.

Glick, Henry J. 1992. *The Right to Die: Policy Innovation and Its Consequences*. New York: Columbia University Press.

Goodman, Ellen. 1995. "Hospitals No Place of Humane Death." *Carlisle (Pa.) Sentinel*. December 1.

Griffin, Rawson E. III. 1993. "Medical Futility of CPR." *Journal of the American Geriatric Association*. Vol. 41, p. 687.

Grubb, Andrew, Walsh, Pat, Lambe, Neil, Murrells, Trevor, and Robinson, Sarah. 1996. "Survey of British Clinicians' Views on Management of Patients in Persistent Vegetative State." *The Lancet*. Vol. 348, pp. 35–40.

Hafemeister, Thomas L., and Hannaford, Paula L. 1996. *Resolving Disputes Over Life-Sustaining Treatment: A Health Care Provider's Guide*. Williamsburg, Va.: National Center for State Courts.

Hanrahan, Patricia, and Luchins, Daniel J. 1995. "Access to Hospice Programs in End-Stage Dementia: A National Survey of Hospice Programs." *Journal of the American Geriatric Association.* Vol. 43, pp. 56–59.

Hare, Jan, and Nelson, C. 1991. "Will Patients Complete Living Wills?" *Journal of General Internal Medicine.* Vol. 6, pp. 42–46.

Hare, Jan, Pratt, Clara, and Nelson, Carrie. 1992. "Agreement Between Patients and Their Self-Selected Surrogates on Difficult Medical Decisions." *Archives of Internal Medicine.* Vol. 152, pp. 1049–1054.

Harvey, John C. 1992. "The Frail Elderly Person and Those Suffering from Dementia." In Kevin W. Wildes, Frances Abel, and John C. Harvey, eds., *Birth, Suffering, and Death: Catholic Perspectives at the Edges of Life.* Boston: Kluwer Academic Publishers, pp. 33–44.

Hastings Center. 1987. *Guidelines on the Termination of Life-Sustaining Treatment and Care of the Dying.* Briarcliff Manor, N.Y.: Hastings Center.

Hauptman, P. J., and O'Connor, K. J. 1997. "Medical Progress: Procurement and Allocation of Solid Organs for Transplantation." *New England Journal of Medicine.* Vol. 336, p. 422.

"Helga Wanglie's Life." 1991. *Minneapolis Star Tribune.* May 26.

Hilfiker, David. 1984. "Allowing the Debilitated to Die." *New England Journal of Medicine.* Vol. 308, pp. 716–719.

Hinds, Michael deCourcy. 1994. "Uncharted Law for a Man Between Life and Death." *New York Times.* June 6.

Hodges, Marian O., Tolle, Susan W., Stocking, Carol, and Cassel, Christine K. 1994. "Tube Feeding: Internists' Attitudes Regarding Ethical Obligations." *Archives of Internal Medicine.* Vol. 154, pp. 1013–1020.

Hoefler, James M., with Kamoie, Brian E. 1994. *Deathright: Culture, Medicine, Politics, and the Right to Die.* Boulder: Westview Press.

Hurley, A. C., Volicer, Beverly, Mahoney, M. A., and Volicer, Ladislav. 1993. "Palliative Fever Management in Alzheimer Patients: Quality Plus Fiscal Responsibility." *Advanced Nursing Science.* Vol. 16, pp. 21–32.

Institute of Medical Ethics Working Party on the Ethics of Prolonging Life and Assisting Death. 1991. "Withdrawal of Life-Support from Patients in a Persistent Vegetative State." *The Lancet.* Vol. 337, pp. 96–98.

Jecker, Nancy S., and Schneiderman, Lawrence J. 1993. "Medical Futility: The Duty Not to Treat." *Cambridge Quarterly of Health Ethics.* Vol. 2, pp. 151–159.

Jennet, Bryan. 1992. "Letting Vegetative Patients Die." *British Medical Journal.* Vol. 305, pp. 1305–1306.

Jennet, Bryan, and Dyer, Clare. 1991. "Persistent Vegetative State and the Right to Die: The United States and Britain." *British Medical Journal.* Vol. 302, pp. 1256–1258.

Jonsen, Albert R., Siegler, Mark, and Winslade, William J. 1992. *Clinical Ethics: A Practical Approach to Ethical Decisions in Clinical Medicine.* 3d ed. New York: McGraw-Hill.

"Judge Rejects Request by Doctors to Remove a Patient's Respirator." 1991. *New York Times.* July 2.

Justice, Christopher. 1995. "The 'Natural' Death While Not Eating: A Type of Palliative Care in Banaras, India." *Journal of Palliative Care.* Vol. 11, pp. 38–42.

Kalk, W. J., and Veriawa, Yosuf. 1991. "Hospital Management of Voluntary Total Fasting Among Political Prisoners." *The Lancet.* Vol. 337, pp. 660–662.

Kalk, W. J., Felix, M., Snoey, E. R., and Veriawa, Yosuf. 1993. "Voluntary Total Fasting in Political Prisoners: Clinical and Biochemical Observations." *South African Medical Journal.* Vol. 83, pp. 391–394.

Kass, Leon R. 1993. "Is There a Right to Die?" *Hastings Center Report.* January–February, Vol. 23, pp. 34–43.

Kastenbaum, Robert. 1989. "Brain Death." In Robert Kastenbaum and Beatrice Kastenbaum, eds., *The Encyclopedia of Death.* Phoenix: Oryx Press, pp. 32–36.

Katz, Paul R. 1993. "Antibiotics for Nursing Home Residents: When Are They Appropriate?" *Postgraduate Medicine.* Vol. 8, pp. 173–180.

Kelly, David F. 1979. *The Emergence of Roman Catholic Medical Ethics in North America: An Historical, Methodological, Bibliographical Study.* New York: Mellen Press.

Kidder, D. 1992. "The Effects of Hospice Coverage on Medicare Expenditures." *Health Services Research.* Vol. 27, pp. 195–217.

Knaus, William A. 1995. Cited in Brenda C. Coleman. "Study: Doctors Ignore Wishes of the Dying." *Harrisburg (Pa.) Patriot.* November 11.

Kolata, Gina. 1995. "Withholding Care from Patients: Boston Case Asks Who Decides." *New York Times.* April 3.

Landers, Ann. 1995. "Doctors Can't Remove Feeding Tube." *Harrisburg (Pa.) Patriot.* November 11.

Lantos, J. D., Singer, P. A., Walker, R. M., Gramelspacher, G. P., Shapiro, G. R., Sanchez-Gonzales, M. A., Stocking, C. B., Miles, S. H., and Siegler, M. 1989. "The Illusion of Futility in Clinical Practice." *American Journal of Medicine.* Vol. 87, pp. 81–84.

Lee, David K. P., Swinburne, Andrew J., Fedullo, Anthony J., and Wahl, Gary W. 1994. "Withdrawing Care: Experience in a Medical Intensive Care Unit." *Journal of the American Medical Association.* Vol. 271, pp. 1358–1361.

Lemonick, Michael D. 1992. "The Biology of Malnutrition Makes Rehabilitation Difficult." *Time.* December 21.

Lewin, Tamar. 1993. "Man Is Allowed to Let Daughter Die." *New York Times.* January 27.

Lindgren, James. 1993. "Death by Default." *Law and Contemporary Problems.* Vol. 56, pp. 186–254.

Lipton, Helen Levens. 1986. "Do-Not-Resuscitate Decision in a Community Hospital: Incidence, Implications, and Outcomes." *Journal of the American Medical Association.* Vol. 256, pp. 1164–1169.

Lo, Bernard, and Dornbrand, Laurie. 1984. "Sounding Board: Guiding the Hand That Feeds: Caring for the Demented Elderly." *New England Journal of Medicine.* Vol. 311, pp. 402–404.

Lo, Bernard, McLeod, Gary A., and Saika, Glenn. 1986. "Patient Attitudes to Discussing Life-Sustaining Treatment." *Archive of Internal Medicine.* Vol. 146, pp. 1613–1615.

Lo, Bernard, Rouse, Fenella, and Dornbrand, Laurie. 1990. "Family Decision Making on Trial: Who Decides for Incompetent Patients?" *New England Journal of Medicine.* Vol. 322, pp. 1228–1231.

Luchins, Daniel J., and Hanrahan, Patricia. 1993. "What Is Appropriate Health Care for End-Stage Dementia?" *Journal of the American Geriatric Association.* Vol. 41, pp. 25–30.

Lynn, Joanne. 1989a. "Must Patients Always Be Given Food and Water?" In Joanne Lynn, ed., *By No Extraordinary Means: The Choice to Forgo Life-Sustaining Food and Water.* Bloomington: Indiana University Press, pp. 47–60.

_____. 1989b. "Elderly Residents of Long-Term Care Facilities." In Joanne Lynn, ed., *By No Extraordinary Means: The Choice to Forgo Life-Sustaining Food and Water.* Bloomington: Indiana University Press, pp. 163–179.

_____. 1995. Cited in Ellen Goodman. "Hospitals No Place of Humane Death." *Carlisle (Pa.) Sentinel.* December 1.

Lynn, Joanne, ed. 1989. *By No Extraordinary Means: The Choice to Forgo Life-Sustaining Food and Water.* Bloomington: Indiana University Press.

Lynn, Joanne, and Childress, James F. 1983. "Must Patients Always Be Given Food and Water?" *Hastings Center Report.* October, Vol. 13, pp. 17–21.

Maillet, Julie O'Sullivan, and King, Dorothy. 1993. "Nutritional Care of the Terminally Ill Adult." *Hospice Journal.* Vol. 9, pp. 37–54.

Major, David. 1989. "The Medical Procedures for Providing Food and Water: Indications and Effects." In Joanne Lynn, ed., *By No Extraordinary Means: The Choice to Forgo Life-Sustaining Food and Water.* Bloomington: Indiana University Press, pp. 21–28.

Maksoud, Alfred, Jahnigeen, Dennis W., and Skibinski, Christine I. 1993. "Do Not Resuscitate Orders and the Cost of Death." *Archives of Internal Medicine.* Vol. 153, pp. 1249–1253.

Malcolm, Andrew H. 1984. "To Suffer a Prolonged Illness or Elect to Die: A Case Study." *New York Times.* December 16.

Matthews, Elmer M. N.d. "RE: S-1211: Advance Directives for Health Care." Memo on behalf of the New Jersey Catholic Conference.

McCann, Robert M., Hall, William J., and Grath-Junker, Annmarie. 1994. "Comfort Care for Terminally Ill Patients: The Appropriate Use of Nutrition and Hydration." *Journal of the American Medical Association.* Vol. 272, pp. 1263–1266.

McCormick, Richard A. 1992. "'Moral Considerations' Ill Considered." *America.* Vol. 166, pp. 210–214.

Meares, Candace Jans. 1994. "Terminal Dehydration: A Review." *American Journal of Hospice and Palliative Care.* Vol. 11, pp. 10–14.

Meier, Peg. 1994. "Choosing Death." *Minneapolis Star Tribune.* February 13.

Meisel, Alan. 1989. *The Right to Die.* New York: John Wiley & Sons.

_____. 1991. "Legal Myths About Terminating Life Support." *Archives of Internal Medicine.* Vol. 151, pp. 1497–1502.

_____. 1992. *The Right to Die: Cumulative Supplement.* No. 2. New York: John Wiley & Sons.

Meyers, Roberta M., and Grodin, Michael A. 1991. "Decisionmaking Regarding the Initiation of Tube Feedings in the Severely Demented Elderly: A Review." *Journal of the American Geriatrics Society.* Vol. 39, pp. 526–531.

Miles, Stephen H. 1991. "Informed Demand of 'Non-Beneficial' Medical Treatment." *New England Journal of Medicine.* Vol. 325, pp. 512–515.

Miller, Tracy, and Cugliari, Maria. 1990. "Withdrawing and Withholding Treatment: Polices in Long-Term Care Facilities." *The Gerontologist*. Vol. 30, pp. 462–468.

"Missouri Court Rejects Moving Comatose Woman." 1991. *New York Times*. March 6.

Mitchell, John J. 1991. "From Ethical Dilemma to Hospital Policy: The Withholding or Withdrawing of Artificially Provided Nutrition and Hydration." *Health Progress*. Vol. 72, pp. 22–30.

"Mom Fights for Right to Die Law." 1994. *Carlisle (Pa.) Sentinel*. January 29.

Montague, Jim. 1994. "A Futile-Care Formula May Ease End-of-Life Issues." *Hospitals and Health Networks*. Vol. 68, p. 176.

Morley, John E. 1989. "Death by Starvation: A Modern American Problem?" *Journal of the American Geriatric Association*. Vol. 37, pp. 184–185.

Morris, Anne Fahy. 1994. "Mother Hopes to Make a New Law, Let Son Die." *Harrisburg (Pa.) Sunday Patriot-News*. January 30.

Mott, Peter D., and Barker, William H. 1988. "Treatment Decision for Infections Occurring in Nursing Homes Residents." *Journal of the American Geriatric Society*. Vol. 36, pp. 820–824.

Multi-Society Task Force on PVS. 1994a. "Medical Aspects of the Persistent Vegetative State (First of Two Parts)." *New England Journal of Medicine*. Vol. 330, pp. 1499–1508.

———. 1994b. "Medical Aspects of the Persistent Vegetative State (Second of Two Parts)." *New England Journal of Medicine*. Vol. 330, pp. 1572–1579.

Munley, Anne. 1983. *The Hospice Alternative: A New Context for Death and Dying*. New York: Basic Books.

National Center for State Courts. 1992. *Guidelines for State Court Decision Making in Life-Sustaining Medical Treatment Cases*. 2d ed. Williamsburg, Va.: NCSC.

National Conference of Catholic Bishops, Committee for Pro-Life Activities. 1984. *Guidelines for Legislation on Life-Sustaining Treatment*. Washington, D.C.: NCCB.

National Conference of Commissioners on Uniform State Laws. 1993. "Uniform Health-Care Decisions Act." Approved and recommended for enactment in all the states at the Uniform Law Commissioners Annual Conference, Charleston, S.C., July 30–August 6.

National Legal Center for the Medically Dependent and Disabled. 1991. "Medical Treatment for Older Persons and Persons with Disabilities." *Clearinghouse Review*. Vol. 24, pp. 980–990.

New York State Task Force on Life and the Law. N.d. *NYSTFLL: A State Model of Public Policy on Bioethics*. New York: NYSTFLL.

———. 1992. *When Others Must Choose: Deciding for Patients Without Capacity*. New York: NYSTFLL.

———. 1993. *When Others Must Choose: Deciding for Patients Without Capacity, Supplement to Report and Proposed Legislation*. New York: NYSTFLL.

———. 1994. *When Death Is Sought: Assisted Suicide and Euthanasia in the Medical Context*. New York: NYSTFLL.

Nuland, Sherwin B. 1994. *How We Die: Reflections on Life's Final Chapter*. New York: Alfred A. Knopf.

O'Brien, Linda A., Grisso, J. A., Maislin, G., La Pann, K., Krotki, K. P., Greco, P. J., Siegert, E. A., and Evans, L. K. 1995. "Nursing Home Residents' Preference for Life-Sustaining Treatments." *Journal of the American Medical Association.* Vol. 274, pp. 1175–1779.

Office of Technology Assessment. 1987a. *Life-Sustaining Technologies and the Elderly.* OTA-BA–306. Washington, D.C.: U.S. Government Printing Office.

_____. 1987b. *Losing a Million Minds: Confronting the Tragedy of Alzheimer's Disease and Other Dementias.* Washington, D.C.: U.S. Government Printing Office.

_____. 1988. *Confronting Alzheimer's Disease and Other Dementias.* Philadelphia: J. B. Lippincott.

Oliver, David. 1984. "Terminal Dehydration." *The Lancet.* Vol. 323, p. 631.

Ouslander, Joseph G., Tymchuk, Alexander J., and Krynski, Michele D. 1993. "Decision About Enteral Tube Feeding Among the Elderly." *Journal of the American Geriatric Society.* Vol. 41, pp. 70–77.

Paris, John. 1992. "The Catholic Tradition on the Use of Nutrition and Fluids." In Kevin W. Wildes, Frances Abel, and John C. Harvey, eds., *Birth, Suffering, and Death: Catholic Perspectives at the Edges of Life.* Boston: Kluwer Academic Publishers, pp. 189–208.

Payne, Kirk, Taylor, Robert M., Stocking, Carol, and Sachs, Greg A. 1996. "Physicians' Attitudes About the Care of Patients in the Persistent Vegetative State: A National Survey." *Annals of Internal Medicine.* Vol. 125, pp. 104–110.

Pearlman, Robert A., Cain, K. C., Patrick, D. L., Appelbaum-Maizel, M., Starks, H. E., Jecker, N. S., and Uhlmann, R. F. 1993. "Insights Pertaining to Patient Assessment of States Worse Than Death." *Journal of Clinical Ethics.* Vol. 4, pp. 33–40.

Peck, Arthur, Cohen, Camille E., and Mulvihill, Michael N. 1990. "Long-Term Enteral Feeding of Aged Demented Nursing Home Patients." *Journal of the American Geriatrics Society.* Vol. 38, pp. 1195–1198.

Pope Pius XII. 1958. "The Prolongation of Life," in *The Pope Speaks,* Vol. 4. In Kevin W. Wildes, Frances Abel, and John C. Harvey, eds., *Birth, Suffering, and Death: Catholic Perspectives at the Edges of Life.* Boston: Kluwer Academic Publishers, pp. 209–215.

Post, Stephen G. 1990. "Nutrition, Hydration, and the Demented Elderly." *Journal of Medical Humanities.* Vol. 11, pp. 185–192.

President's Commission for the Study of Ethical Problems in Medicine and Biomedical and Behavioral Research. 1983. *Deciding to Forego Life-Sustaining Treatment: A Report on Ethical, Medical, and Legal Issues in Treatment Decisions.* Washington, D.C.: U.S. Government Printing Office.

Princeton Religion and Research Center. 1990. *Religion in America: Approaching the Year 2000.* Princeton: PRRC.

Printz, Louise A. 1988. "Is Withholding Hydration a Valid Comfort Measure in the Terminally Ill?" *Geriatrics.* Vol. 43, pp. 84–88.

_____. 1992. "Terminal Hydration: A Compassionate Treatment." *Archives of Internal Medicine.* Vol. 152, pp. 697–700.

Reiser, Stanley Joel. 1977. "Therapeutic Choice and Moral Doubt in a Technological Age." In John H. Knowles, ed., *Doing Better and Feeling Worse.* New York: W. W. Norton, p. 51.

Rothman, David J. 1991. *Strangers at the Bedside: A History of How Law and Bioethics Transformed Medical Decision Making.* New York: Basic Books.

Sachs, Greg A., Ahronheim, Judith C., Rhymes, Jill A., Volicer, Ladislav, and Lynn, Joanne. 1995. "Good Care of Dying Patients: The Alternative to Physician-Assisted Suicide and Euthanasia." *Journal of the American Geriatric Association.* Vol. 43, pp. 553–562.

Sacred Congregation for the Doctrine of the Faith. 1980. "Declaration on Euthanasia." In Kevin W. Wildes, Frances Abel, and John C. Harvey, eds., *Birth, Suffering, and Death: Catholic Perspectives at the Edges of Life.* Boston: Kluwer Academic Publishers, pp. 217–224.

Schmitz, Phyllis, and O'Brien, Merry. 1989. "Observations on Nutrition and Hydration in Dying Cancer Patients." In Joanne Lynn, ed., *By No Extraordinary Means: The Choice to Forgo Life-Sustaining Food and Water.* Bloomington: Indiana University Press, pp. 29–38.

Schneiderman, Lawrence J., Jecker, Nancy S., and Jonsen, Albert R. 1990. "Medical Futility: Its Meaning and Ethical Implications." *Annals of Internal Medicine.* Vol. 112, pp. 949–954.

Schotsmans, Paul. 1992. "When the Dying Person Looks Me in the Face: An Ethics of Responsibility for Dealing with the Problem of the Patient in a Persistently Vegetative State." In Kevin W. Wildes, Frances Abel, and John C. Harvey, eds., *Birth, Suffering, and Death: Catholic Perspectives at the Edges of Life.* Boston: Kluwer Academic Publishers, pp. 127–144.

Scitovsky, Anne A. 1994. "'The High Cost of Dying' Revisited." *Milbank Quarterly.* Vol. 72, pp. 561–591.

Shapiro, Andrew L. 1992. *We're Number One! Where America Stands—and Falls—in the New World Order.* New York: Vintage Books.

Shils, Maurice E., Olson, James A., and Shike, Moshe, eds. 1994. *Modern Nutrition in Health and Disease.* 8th ed. Philadelphia: Lea and Febiger.

Short, P., Feinleib, S., and Cunningham, P. 1994. "Expenditures and Sources of Payment for Persons in Nursing and Personal Care Homes," National Medical Expenditure Survey, Research Findings 19. AHCPR Publication No. 94-0032.

Sibbison, J. B. 1991. "USA: Right to Live or Right to Die?" *The Lancet.* Vol. 337, pp. 102–103.

Siegler, Mark, and Shiedermayer, David L. 1987. "Should Fluid and Nutritional Support Be Withheld from Terminally Ill Patients?: Tube Feeding in Hospice Settings." *American Journal of Hospice Care.* Vol. 4, pp. 32–35.

Smedira, N. G., Evans, B. H., Grais, L. S., Cohen, N. H., Lo, B., Cooke, M., Schecter, W. P., Fink, C., Epstein-Jaffe, E., May, C., and Luce, J. M. 1990. "Withholding and Withdrawing of Life Support from the Critically Ill." *New England Journal of Medicine.* Vol. 322, pp. 309–315.

Snyder, Lois. 1990. "Life, Death, and the American College of Physicians: The Cruzan Case." *Annals of Internal Medicine.* Vol. 112, pp. 802–804.

Society for Critical Care Medicine Ethics Task Force. 1992. "Attitudes of Critical Care Medicine Professionals Concerning Forgoing Life-Sustaining Treatments." *Critical Care Medicine.* Vol. 20, pp. 320–326.

Solomon, Andrew. 1995. "A Death of One's Own." *The New Yorker.* May 22.

Solomon, Mildred Z., O'Donnell, Lydia, Jennings, Bruce, Guilfoy, Vivian, Wolf, Susan M., Nolan, Kathleen, Jackson, Rebecca, Koch-Weser, Dieter, and Donnelley, Strachan. 1993. "Decisions Near the End of Life: Professional Views on Life-Sustaining Treatments." *American Journal of Public Health.* Vol. 83, pp. 14–25.

Sonnefeld, Sally T., Waldo, Daniel R., Lemieux, Jeffrey, and McKusick, David R. 1991. "Projections of National Health Expenditures Through the Year 2000." *Health Care Financing Review.* Vol. 13, pp. 1–27.

Sprung, Charles L. 1990. "Changing Attitudes and Practices in Foregoing Life-Sustaining Treatments." *Journal of the American Medical Association.* Vol. 263, pp. 2211–2215.

Story, Porter. 1992. "Artificial Feeding and Hydration in Advanced Illness." In Kevin W. Wildes, Frances Abel, and John C. Harvey, eds., *Birth, Suffering, and Death: Catholic Perspectives at the Edges of Life.* Boston: Kluwer Academic Publishers, pp. 67–75.

Stout, Hilary. 1993. "Clinton's Health Plan Must Face Huge Costs of a Person's Last Days." *Wall Street Journal.* March 22.

Stryker, Jeff. 1989. "In Re Claire C. Conroy: History and Setting of the Case." In Joanne Lynn, ed., *By No Extraordinary Means: The Choice to Forgo Life-Sustaining Food and Water.* Bloomington: Indiana University Press, pp. 227–235.

"Study Backs Terminally Ill Refusing Food." 1994. *New York Times.* October 26.

Sullivan, Joseph F. 1986. "Curbs on Ending Life Supports Are Ignored." *New York Times.* November 28.

Sullivan, Robert J. 1993. "Accepting Death Without Artificial Nutrition and Hydration." *Journal of General Internal Medicine.* Vol. 8, pp. 220–224.

SUPPORT. 1995. "A Controlled Trial to Improve Care for Seriously Ill Hospitalized Patients: The Study to Understand Prognosis and Preferences for Outcomes and Risks of Treatment (SUPPORT)." *Journal of the American Medical Association.* Vol. 274, pp. 1591–1598.

Sutcliffe, Jayne. 1994. "Palliative Care: Terminal Dehydration." *Nursing Times.* Vol. 90, pp. 60–63.

"To Suffer a Prolonged Illness or Elect to Die: A Case Study." 1984. *New York Times.* December 16.

Tresch, D. D., Sims, F. H., Duthie, E. H., Goldstein, M. D., and Lane, P. S. 1991. "Clinical Characteristics of Patients in the Persistent Vegetative State." *Archives of Internal Medicine.* Vol. 151, pp. 930–932.

United Church of Christ. 1991. "Resolution: Rights and Responsibilities of Christians Regarding Death." Proceedings of the 18th General Synod, Norfolk, Va., pp. 46–47.

United Methodist Church. 1992. "Understanding Living and Dying as Faithful Christians." In United Methodist Church, *The Book of Resolutions of the United Methodist Church: 1992.* Nashville, Tenn.: United Methodist Publishing House, Abingdon Press, pp. 14–15.

Urofsky, Melvin I. 1994. *Letting Go: Death, Dying, and the Law.* Norman: University of Oklahoma Press.

U.S. Bishops' Pro-Life Committee. 1992. "Nutrition and Hydration: Moral and Pastoral Reflections." *The Ledger.* Vol. 21, April 9, pp. 705–712.

U.S. Department of Commerce. 1990. *Statistical Abstract of the United States.* Washington, D.C.: U.S. Government Printing Office.

U.S. General Accounting Office. 1991. *Long-Term Care: Projected Needs of the Baby Boom Generation* (GAO/HEHS-91-86). Washington, D.C.: GAO.

_____. 1995a. *Long-Term Care: Current Issues and Future Directions* (GAO/HEHS-95-109). Washington, D.C.: GAO.

_____. 1995b. *Patient Self-Determination Act: Providers Offer Information on Advance Directives but Effectiveness Uncertain* (GAO/HEHS-95-135). Washington, D.C.: GAO.

_____. 1995c. *Spending Pressures Drive States Toward Program Reinvention.* (GAO/HEHS-95-122). Washington, D.C.: GAO.

U.S. Senate Special Committee on Aging. 1991. *Aging Americans: Trends and Projections.* Washington, D.C.: U.S. Government Printing Office.

Volicer, Beverly J., Hurley, Ann, Fabiszewski, Kathy J., Montgomery, Paul, and Volicer, Ladislav. 1993. "Predicting Short-Term Survival for Patients with Advanced Alzheimer's Disease." *Journal of the American Geriatric Association.* Vol. 41, pp. 535–540.

Volicer, Ladislav, Rheaume, Yvette, Brown, June, Fabiszewski, Kathy, and Brady, Roger. 1986. "Hospice Approach to the Treatment of Patients with Advanced Dementia of the Alzheimer's Type." *Journal of the American Medical Association.* Vol. 256, pp. 2210–2213.

Walshe, Thomas M., and Leonard, Cheri. 1985. "PVS: Extension of the Syndrome to Include Chronic Disorders." *Archives of Neurology.* Vol. 42, pp. 1045–1047.

Wanzer, Sidney H., Adelstein, James, Cranford, Ronald E., Federman, Daniel D., Hook, Edward D., Moertel, Charles G., Safar, Peter, Stone, Alan, Taussig, Helen B., and van Eys, Jan. 1984. "The Physician's Responsibility Toward Hopelessly Ill Patients." *New England Journal of Medicine.* Vol. 310, pp. 955–959.

Wanzer, Sidney H., Federman, Daniel D., Adelstein, James S., Cassel, Christine K., Cassem, Edwin H., Cranford, Ronald E., Hook, Edward D., Lo, Bernard, Moertel, Charles G., Safar, Peter, Stone, Alan, and van Eys, Jan. 1989. "The Physician's Responsibility Toward Hopelessly Ill Patients, A Second Look." *New England Journal of Medicine.* Vol. 320, pp. 844–849.

Watts, David T., Cassel, Christine K., and Hickam, David H. 1986. "Nurses' and Physicians' Attitudes Toward Tube-Feeding Decisions in Long-Term Care." *Journal of the American Geriatric Society.* Vol. 34, pp. 607–611.

Weiner, J. D. 1990. "Legal Issues Regarding Patients in Coma or in Persistent Vegetative State." *Physical Medical Rehabilitation.* Vol. 4, pp. 569–578.

Weir, Robert F., and Gostin, Larry. 1990. "Decisions to Abate Life-Sustaining Treatment for Nonautonomous Patients: Ethical Standards and Legal Liability for Physicians After *Cruzan*." *Journal of the American Medical Association.* Vol. 264, pp. 1846–1853.

Wheeler, Warren L. 1993. "Hospice Philosophy: An Alternative to Assisted Suicide." *Ohio Northern Law Review.* Vol. 20, pp. 756–760.

Wicclair, Mark R. 1993. *Ethics and the Elderly.* New York: Oxford University Press.

Wildes, Kevin W. 1992. "Life as a Good and Our Obligation to Persistently Vegetative Patients." In Kevin W. Wildes, Frances Abel, and John C. Harvey, eds., *Birth,*

Suffering, and Death: Catholic Perspectives at the Edges of Life. Boston: Kluwer Academic Publishers, pp. 145–154.

Wildes, Kevin W., Abel, Frances, and Harvey, John C., eds. 1992. *Birth, Suffering, and Death: Catholic Perspectives at the Edges of Life.* Boston: Kluwer Academic Publishers.

Winslow, Ron. 1995. "Plan to Ease Pain, Cost of Dying Proves Futile, Study Says." *Wall Street Journal.* November 22.

Worsnop, Richard. 1992. "Assisted Suicide." *Congressional Quarterly Reporter.* February 21, pp. 147–167.

Legal Materials: *In re Fiori*

Beck, Phyllis W. 1995. *In re Daniel Joseph Fiori,* Superior Court of Pennsylvania, No. 00737, Philadelphia, 1993. En banc decision of the superior court, January 17.

Cappy, Ralph J. 1996. *In re Daniel Joseph Fiori,* Supreme Court of Pennsylvania, Eastern District, 652 A. 2d 1350 (1995).

Connell, Richard E., and Quinlan, Maura K. 1995. *In re Daniel Joseph Fiori,* Supreme Court of Pennsylvania, No. 6 E.D. Appeal Docket, 1995. Attorneys for Amicus Curiae, Pennsylvania Catholic Conference, in support of Petitioner, March 16.

Eastburn, William H. III, and Schaeffer, John M. 1994. *In re Daniel Joseph Fiori,* Superior Court of Pennsylvania, No. 00737 Philadelphia, 1993, Brief of Appellee Rosemarie Sherman, Guardian of the Person Daniel Joseph Fiori (on reargument), February 14.

Hoffman, Robert. 1995. *In re Daniel Joseph Fiori,* Supreme Court of Pennsylvania, No. 0006 E.D. Appeal Docket, 1995. Brief of Appellee Rosemarie Sherman, Guardian of the Person Daniel Joseph Fiori and the Pennsylvania Medical Society, March 15.

Kavolius, Anna Moretti, and Fade, Ann E. 1995. *In re Daniel Joseph Fiori,* Supreme Court of Pennsylvania, No. 6 E.D. Appeal Docket, 1995. Attorneys for Amicus Curiae, Choice in Dying, in support of Appellee, March 16.

McEwen, Stephen J., Jr. 1995. *In re Daniel Joseph Fiori,* Superior Court of Pennsylvania, No. 00737 Philadelphia, 1993. Concurring opinion to the en banc decision of the superior court, January 17.

Meisel, Alan, and Adler, Betty S. 1995. *In re Daniel Joseph Fiori,* Supreme Court of Pennsylvania, No. 6 E.D. Appeal Docket, 1995. Attorneys for Amicus Curiae, University of Pittsburgh Center for Medical Ethics and University of Pennsylvania Medical Center, in support of Appellee, March 16.

Popovich, Zoran. 1995. *In re Daniel Joseph Fiori,* Superior Court of Pennsylvania, No. 00737 Philadelphia, 1993. Dissent to the en banc decision of the superior court, January 17.

Sokolove, Leonard B. 1993. *In re Daniel Joseph Fiori,* Court of Common Pleas of Bucks County, Orphans' Court Division, No. 49355, February 3.

Unger, Sue Ann, and Knorr, John G. III. 1995. *In re Daniel Joseph Fiori,* Supreme Court of Pennsylvania, No. 0006 E.D. Appeal Docket, 1995. Appeal of Attorney General, Commonwealth of Pennsylvania, January 25, 1995.

Unger, Sue Ann, Koons, Calvin R., and Knorr, John G. III. 1995. *In re Daniel Joseph Fiori*, Supreme Court of Pennsylvania, No. 416 E.D. Allocatur Docket, 1995. Petition for Allowance of Appeal of Attorney General, Commonwealth of Pennsylvania, March 15.

Wieand, Donald E. 1995. *In re Daniel Joseph Fiori*, Superior Court of Pennsylvania, No. 00737 Philadelphia, 1993. Concurring opinion to the en banc decision of the superior court, January 17.

Other Cases Cited

Barber v. *Super. Ct. of Los Angeles County*, 147 Cal. App. 3d 273, 193 Cal. Rptr. 288 (Ct. App. 1983).

Bouvia v. *Super. Ct.,* 179 Cal. App. 3d 1127, 225 Cal. Rptr. 297 (Ct. App. 1986), review denied (Cal. June 5, 1986).

Brophy v. *New England Mt. Sinai Hospital, Inc.*, 398 Mass. 417, 497 N.E. 2d 626 (1986).

Cruzan v. *Director, Missouri Department of Health*, 110 S. Ct. 2841 (1990).

Estate of Leach v. *Shapiro* (Leach II), 12 Ohio App. 3d 393, 469 N.E. 2d 1047 (1984).

In re A. C., 573 A. 2d 1235 (D.C. 1990).

In re Bayer, No. 4131 (N.D. Burleigh Co. Ct., Feb. 5, 11 and Dec. 11, 1987) (Riskedahl, J.).

In re Dinnerstein, 6 Mass. App. Ct. 466, 380 N.E. 2d 134 (1978).

In re Eichner, 73 A.D. 2d 431, 426 N.Y.S. 2d 517 (1980).

In re Estate of Longway, 133 Ill. 2d 33, 549 N.E. 2d 292 (1989).

In re Gardner, 534 A. 2d 947 (Me. 1987).

In re Guardianship of Browning, 568 So. 2d 4 (Fla. 1990); *In re Browning*, 543 So. 2d 258 (Fla. Dist. Ct. App. 1989), aff'd.

In re Jobes, 108 N.J. 394, 529 A. 2d 434 (1987).

In re O'Connor, 72 N.Y. 2d 517, 531 N.E. 2d 607, 534 N.Y.S. 2d 886 (Ct. App. 1988, amended 1989).

In re Peter, 108 N.J. 365, 529 A. 2d 404 (1987).

In re Quinlan, 70 N.J. 10, 355 A. 2d 647 (1976), cert. denied sub nom., *Garger* v. *New Jersey*, 429 U.S. 922, 97 S. Ct. 319, 50 L. Ed. 2d 289 (1976).

In re Requena, 213 N.J. Super. 475, 517 A. 2d 886 (Super. Ct. Ch. Div. 1986), aff'd, 213 N.J. Super. 443, 517 A. 2d 869 (Super. Ct. App. Div. 1986).

In re Spring, 8 Mass. App. 831, 399 N.E. 2d 493 (1980).

In re Stone, No. 90-5867 (Cir. Ct. 17th Dist. Broward County, Fla., June 24, 1991).

In re Storar, 52 N.Y. 2d 363, 420 N.E. 2d 64, 438 N.Y.S. 2d 266, cert. denied, 454 U.S. 858, 102 S. Ct. 309, 70 L. Ed. 2d 153 (1981).

In re Welfare of Cloyer, 99 Wash. 2d 114, 660 P. 2d 738 (1983).

Ragona, Incompetent v. *Attorney General Preate*, 6 Pa. D & C 4th 202, 11 Fed. Rep. 2d 1 (1990).

Strachan v. *John F. Kennedy Memorial Hosp.*, 209 N.J. Super. 300, 507 A. 2d 718 (Super. Ct. App. Div. 1986).

About the Book and Author

Many Americans, before they die, will go through a stage where they are unable to make competent decisions about their own life-sustaining medical treatment. More and more, family members and care givers are facing these difficult decisions in their stead, becoming engulfed in questions about personal wishes, medical ethics, state and federal law, and quality of life.

Drawing on provocative case studies, personal interviews, and detailed research, James Hoefler examines the medical, legal, ethical, and clinical aspects of such right-to-die issues. Beginning with the legal struggle of a woman whose son existed in a persistent vegetative state (PVS) for seventeen years, the author moves into a broader look at consensus among professional organizations, from the AMA to the President's Commission to the National Center for State Courts; beliefs of mainstream religious groups; public opinion; issues surrounding end-stage Alzheimer's and other organic brain disorders that can slowly lead to PVS; and the role of artificial nutrition and hydration in these cases.

Hoefler concludes with recommendations on how to improve the quality of right-to-die decision making. An absorbing read with a minimum of technical jargon, this book is a valuable guide to care givers, public policy students, medical ethicists, family members, and anyone facing questions about an individual's right to die.

James M. Hoefler, Ph.D., is associate professor of political science and coordinator of the policy studies program at Dickinson College, Carlisle, Pennsylvania. He is coauthor with Brian Kamoie of *Deathright: Culture, Medicine, Politics, and the Right to Die* (Westview Press, 1994) and is coauthor with A. Lee Fritschler of *Smoking and Politics: Policy Making and the Federal Bureaucracy* (1996).

Index

Abortion Control Act, 18
Adler, Betty, 25–28, 165(n3),
    167(n16)
Advance directives, 41, 55, 82–83, 101,
    160–161
  examples of, 169(n7), 177(n1)
  executing, 73, 135
Agency for Health Care Policy and
    Research (AHCPR), 136
AHA. *See* American Hospital
    Association
Ahronheim, Dr. Judith
  on ANH, 128
  on end-stage dementia, 93
Alzheimer, Alois, 90
Alzheimer's disease, 90–91, 93, 95,
    133, 142, 152–153
AMA. *See* American Medical
    Association
American Academy of Neurology, 8
American Academy of Pediatrics, 8
American Association of Neurological
    Surgeons, 8
American Baptist Church
  end-of-life decision making, 67
American College of Physicians (ACP),
    2, 35, 40, 53, 56
  on withdrawing treatment, 47, 50
American Hospital Association (AHA),
    2, 79
American Medical Association, The
    (AMA), 35, 41, 46, 50, 53, 56
  Council of Ethical and Judicial
    Affairs, 39, 138, 179(n17)
American Neurological Association, 8
American Nurses Association (ANA), 2,
    34, 35, 40, 42, 51, 53, 56
  refusal of treatments, 47

American Thoracic Society (ATS), 35,
    40, 42, 53, 56
  on patient autonomy, 47, 50
Amicus curiae brief, 12, 21, 24, 37
Amyotrophic-lateral sclerosis (Lou
    Gehrig's disease), 9
Artificial nutrition and hydration
    (ANH), 3–4, 29, 31, 40, 65, 81,
    111–113, 124, 127, 132, 134,
    137, 160, 162, 165(n5), 166(n13),
    168(n3)
  enteral, 113–114
  forgoing, 86, 113, 176(n24)
  gastrostomies, 114
  intravenous feeding, 115
  invasive medical treatment, 106
  living wills, 87
  medical intervention, 55
  nasogastric feeding (NG), 114–115
  parenteral, 113, 114
  a primer, 162
  surrogate decision making, 151
  total parenteral nutrition (TPN), 115
  withdrawing of, 10, 13–14,
      170(n10), 173(n19), 175(n22), 23
Assisted suicide, 46–49, 151

Barber v. *Superior Court* (1983),
    175(n20)
Bayer, Edward, 169(n6), 175(n21)
Beck, Judge Phyllis W., 12, 15–16, 20,
    60, 165(n2)
"Best interests" standard, 43–47, 55, 82
Brain damage, 7
Brain death, 9
Brennan, Justice William, 177(n3)
Brophy (1986), case of, 96, 175(n22)
Busalacchi (1991), case of, 96

Callahan, Daniel, 97
Cantor, Norman, 156, 181(n32)
Cappy, Justice Ralph J., 29–30, 60
Cardiopulminary resusitation (CPR),
    112, 122, 131–132, 137,
    173(n18), 176(n34)
Catholic Church
    influence of, 63
    right-to-die and, 66
    role of, 62, 169(n3)
Catholic Health Association, The
    (CHA), 39, 40, 50, 52, 53, 59,
    63–64, 150
    on patient self-determination, 46
    Vatican Declaration on Euthanasia,
        59, 63, 106, 150
Child Neurological Society, 8
Choice in Dying (CID), 13, 24, 25, 30,
    166(n12)
Clear and convincing evidence
    standard, 21–22, 24–25, 30, 110,
    157,173(n18), 181(n34)
Clinical Ethics: A Practical Approach to
    Ethical Decision in Clinical
    Medicine, 39, 49, 52, 53, 58
Collaud, Thierry, on tube feeding,
    124
Coma, 7, 9, 110
Comfort care. *See* Palliative care
Connell, Richard, 21–22
Conroy, Claire (1985), case of, 28, 96,
    105, 107, 110, 173(n19)
Consensus building process, 80
Consensus groups, 33–34, 76, 169
    ethics, 38
    legal, 36
    medical, 35
    positions, 40, 50, 520, 60, 62, 112,
        122
Consensus position, xii, 175(n20)
    forgoing treatment, 151
    surrogate decision making, 80, 85,
        88, 110–111, 150
    withdrawing treatment, 151
    withholding treatment, 151
Cooney, Dr. Leo, 77
Corpus Hippocratum, 144

Courts
    "limited-objective test," 106
    "pure-objective test," 106
    role in end-of-life decisions, 24, 28,
        36, 105
    "subjective test," 106
Cranford, Dr. Ronald, 93, 94, 112,
    126, 172(nn4, 5)
Cruzan, Nancy (1990), case of, 24, 68,
    70, 96, 132, 170(n10), 177(n3)
Cundiff, Dr. David, on euthanasia, 122

Death
    final stage, 65
    hastening of, 172(n8)
    indignities of, 152
    managing, 1, 2, 22, 26, 78–79
    reflections on, 153
    by starvation, 117–120
    taboo subject, 153
Decisionmakers
    designated, 45
    identifying, 74, 75
    family members, 168(n5)
    role of, 3, 15–16, 19, 23
    surrogate, 23, 29, 43, 80, 106
Decision making, 26, 29, 40
    consensus principles, xi, xii, 42
    policy, 4
    surrogate, 2, 17, 24, 40, 165(n3),
        166(n9)
Declaration on Euthanasia, 64
DeGrella (1993), case of, 24
Dehydration, 118, 122, 176(n25)
    absence of pain, 119–121, 174(n12)
    benefits of, 117, 123
    symptoms associated with, 120,
        174(n9)
Delio (1987), case of, 96
Dementia, 90, 94, 105, 108
    cause of death, 173(n2)
    degree of, 93, 95, 97–99, 109, 111
    diagnosis, 96
    differences between PVS and, 111
    end-stage, 174(n14), 178(n8)
    equivalent to PVS, 110
    evidence of, 91

level of awareness, 97
treatment, 99
Doerflinger, Richard, 66
Do not intubate (DNI) orders,
132–133
Do not resuscitate (DNR) orders, 79,
101, 105, 130, 132, 134, 137,
147, 168(n2), 171(n1), 172(n98),
176(n35)
Do not use antibiotics (DNA) orders,
133
Durable power of attorney, 82

Eastburn, William, 14–15, 168(n20)
Education
end-of-life decision making,
149–150, 163
general public on death, xii, 151
patient, 153
self, 154
Elbaum (1989), case of, 166(n14)
Emanuel, Ezekiel and Linda, on health
care for elderly, 100, 104, 125
End-of-life
decision making, 1–3, 13–14, 26–27,
34, 38, 60, 107–108, 151–152,
157, 160, 163, 165
suffering, xi
treatment decisions, xi 24, 25, 29
use of antibiotics, 128–129
Episcopal Church
life-sustaining treatment, 69
Ethics
decision making and, 154
on treatment, 77
Euthanasia, 70
morality of, 154
opposition to, 67

Family
as decisionmakers, 127
role of, 16, 17, 167(n17)
Finley, Dr. David, on end-stage care,
100
Fiori, Joey, case of, 2, 3, 7, 9–17,
19–23, 27, 29, 30, 37, 40, 60, 63,
89–90, 96, 108, 156–157, 169,

165(n6), 169(n1), 171(n1),
173(n19), 175(n22), 181(n33)
Foody (1984), case of, 14
Fourteenth Amendment, guarantees of,
19
Fuchs, Victor, on health care spending,
102

Gasner, M. R., on end-stage dementia,
93
Guardians
ad litem, 20, 166(n8)
appointment of, 18
rights of, 14, 20

Handler, Judge Alan B., 31
Hanrahan, Patricia, on dementia, 90,
122, 142
Harvard School of Public Health
survey, 24
Hastings Center, The, 38, 40, 52–53,
58
on substituted judgment, 45
Health care
costs, 8, 24–25, 102–104, 171(n1),
179(n16)
spending, 100–101, 172(n10),
178(n10)
Health Care Finance Administration
(HCFA)
on Medicare spending, 102
Hippocratic Oath, 78, 144
Hoffman, Robert, 22–24
Home health care, 8
Hospices, 160, 163, 165, 178(nn7, 8)
as alternatives, 140
costs, 141, 142
funding for, 143

Incompetent patients, 4, 89
decision making for, 17, 24, 26, 41,
79
determination of, 170(n17)
protecting, 165(n4), 166(n9)
rights of, 28
treatments for, 169(n2)
In re A.C. (1990), 167(n18)

In re Browning (1989), 167(n16)
In re Cloyer (1983), 26, 28
In re Dinnerstein (1978), 96, 105, 110
In re Eichner (1980), 109
In re Estate of Longway (1989),
　　167(n17)
In re Farrell (1987), 27
In re Gardner (1987), 191(n31)
In re Jobes (1987), 30–32, 96, 149,
　　167(n16), 173(n19), 181(n31)
In re O'Connor (1989), 24, 109, 110,
　　173(n17), 175(n22)
In re Peter (1987), 108
In re Requena (1986), 171(n21),
　　175(n16)
In re Spring (1980), 167(n17)
In re Stone (1991), 168(n19)
In re Storar (1981), 109, 167(n17)

Katz, Dr. P. R., on antibiotics, 129
Knorr, John, 19–20, 22

Leach v. *Shapiro* (1984), 175(n21)
Leonard, Cheri, 93, 113
"Liberty interest," 19
Life support
　termination of, 48
Lindgren, James, on technological
　　imperatives, 125
Living wills, 160, 170(n8)
　purpose of, 19
Lowery, F. H., on cost of caring for
　　dying patients, 100
Luchins, Daniel, on dementia, 90, 122,
　　142
Lutheran Church
　end-of-life decision making, 68
Lynn, Dr. Joanne, 124, 133, 153

McCormick, Richard A., 63–64,
　　169(n5)
Medical futility, 144, 147–148,
　　154–155, 158, 160, 163,
　　178(nn11, 12, 14)
Medical Treatment Effectiveness
　　Program (MEDTEP), 126
Meeres, Candace, on aggressive
　　nutritional support, 121

Meisel, Alan, 25–28, 37, 40, 44, 48,
　　51, 53, 57, 84, 165(n3), 167(n19)
Multi-Society Task Force on PVS, 8, 22,
　　97, 171(n1), 172(n4)

National Center for State Courts
　　(NCSC), 26, 28, 36, 40, 43, 48,
　　51, 53, 57, 168(n4)
National Conference of Commissioners
　　on Uniform State Laws.
　　See ULC
New York State Task Force on Life &
　　the Law (NYSTFLL), 36, 40,
　　43–44, 48, 51, 53, 57, 84, 110,
　　124, 181(n34)
Nuland, Sherwin, 78, 129, 139–141,
　　152–154, 172(n3)

O'Brien, Merry, on dehydration, 120
Ordinary-extraordinary distinction, 40,
　　85, 107, 168(n1)

Palliative care, 140, 143, 155, 173(n13)
　discontinuing treatment, 111
　involvement of family in, 113, 141
Parens patriae role, 17, 28, 165(n4)
Paris, John, 63–64, 169(n5)
Patient self-determination, 84, 87
Patient Self-Determination Act (PSDA)
　　(1990), 135, 169(n7), 177(n1)
Patients
　autonomy of, xi, 27, 41, 47,
　　155–156, 158, 160, 169(n7)
　coding, 176(n33)
　competency, 4
　dignity of, 156–157, 159–160,
　　181(n31)
　rationed care, 155
　restraining of, 116
　self-determination, 41, 46, 140
　welfare of, 45–46, 154
Pennsylvania Catholic-Conference, 1,
　　12, 22–23, 65, 166(n10)
　Bishop's statement, 21, 170(n8)
Pennsylvania Medical Society (PMS),
　　12, 22, 29
Pennsylvania's Advance Directive for
　　Health Care Act, 21

Persistent vegetative state (PVS)
  patients, 3, 7, 9, 11, 16, 20–21,
    30, 89–90, 93–94, 98, 165(n5),
    172(nn6, 7)
  caring for, 8, 14
  diagnosis of, 174(n3)
  differences between advanced
    dementia and, 111
  equivalent to dementia, 110
  level of awareness, 97
  right-to-die, 22
  treatment of, 99
Physicians
  assisted suicide, 123
  decision making and, 124–125
  ethics and, 127
  European, 126
Pius XII, Pope, 64
Popovich, Judge Zoran, 17–18, 23, 28,
    165(n2)
Preate, Attorney General Ernest D., 18,
    23, 27–28, 30
"Preservation of life"
  role of state, 13, 30
President's Commission for the Study of
    Ethical Problems in Medicine and
    Biomedical and Behavioral
    Research (1983), 14, 38, 40, 49,
    51, 53, 57, 78, 150, 160, 163,
    168, 179(n22), 182(n39)
  costs of care, 104
  on decision making, 45
  on end-of-life decision making, 24,
    27, 34
  formulate meaning of "best
    interests," 108
PVS. *See* Persistent vegetative state
  patients

"Quality of life," 1, 41
Quinlan, Karen Ann (1976), 28, 96,
    105, 170(n13), 172(n12),
    179(n20)
Quinlan, Maura, 21–22

Ragona (1990), case of, 13, 21
Rapin, Charles Henry, on tube feeding,
    124

Rasmussen (1987), case of, 96, 108,
    110
Religious teachings
  on end-of-life decisions, 62
Rights of Terminally Ill Act, 36
Right-to-die debate, 172(n12),
    173(n15)
Right-to-die litigation, 26, 27
Rovelli, Executive Deputy Attorney
    General Louis J., 11

Saikewicz (1977), case of, 28, 105
Sanctity of human life, 18, 158
Schaeffer, John, 14–15, 168(n20)
Schmitz, Phyllis, on dehydration, 120
Scientism, 152–153
Scitovsky, Anne, on end-of-life care,
    104
Self-determination
  right to, 169(n2)
  state interests and, 30
Sherman, Rosemarie, 2, 3, 7, 9–12,
    14–16, 19–20, 22–25, 29–30, 32,
    81, 140, 163, 165(n1), 168(n1)
Singer, P. S., on cost of caring for dying
    patients, 100
"Slippery slope," 154, 158
Sokolove, Judge Leonard B., 11–13, 18,
    22, 24, 29, 60
Sprung, Dr. Charles, on goal of
    medicine, 76
Standards of care, 137
  comfort care, 138, 140, 144
  developing, 136
  with end-of-life treatment, 136
Substituted judgment standard, 19–20,
    40–41, 43–47, 55, 82
SUPPORT Study (The Study to
    Understand Prognosis and
    Preferences for Outcomes and
    Risks of Treatment), 135, 138,
    153, 177(n2), 180(n27)
Surrogates. *See* Decisionmakers

Technological imperative, 125
Technology, medical, 1, 161
Terminally ill
  right-to-die and, 40

Treatment
  aggressive, 136, 138
  forgoing, 40, 46, 80, 100, 138–139,
    142
  humane, 156
  life sustaining, 23, 26, 29, 73,
    150–151, 157
  refusing, 72
  rejection of, 155
  religious positions on, 70
  rules regarding, 22
  standards of, 48
  termination of, 49, 70
  withdrawing of, 3, 16, 19, 22,
    40–41, 86, 144
  withholding, 12, 40, 70, 71, 81, 84,
    85, 180(n24)
Tube feeding. *See* ANH

Unger, Sue Ann, 19–20, 22
U.S. Bishop's Conference Pro-Life
  Committee (PLC), 64
U.S. Conference of Catholic Bishops, 64
  on forgoing artificial feeding, 66
U.S. Office of Technology Assessment
  (OTA), 91
Uniform Health-Care Decisions Act,
  36, 43

Uniform Law Commissioners
  (ULC), 28, 36, 40, 43, 48,
    51, 53, 57
Uniform Law Commissioner's Uniform
  Health Care Decision Act,
    167(n16)
Uniform Rights of the Terminally Ill
  Act, 1989, 36
United Church of Christ
  end-of-life decisions, 69
United Methodist Church
  end-of-life decisions, 67
University of Pittsburgh Center for
  Medical Ethics, 13, 25, 37,
    167(n15), 168(n1)
University of Pennsylvania Medical
  Center, 13, 25, 37, 167(n15),
    168(n1)

Veterans Administration
  health care cost, 7
Volicer, Beverly, 129–130, 142
Volicer, Ladislav, 94

Walshe, Thomas, on PVS 93, 113
Wicclair, Mark, 113
Wieand, Judge Donald, 16–17, 20,
    165(n2)